VIKRAM-VAMPIRE AND INDIAN FAIRY TALES

VIKRAM-VAMPIRE AND INDIAN FAIRY TALES

Editor-in-Chief

Swami Chidatman Jee Maharaj

ANMOL PUBLICATIONS PVT. LTD.

NEW DELHI - 110 002 (INDIA)

ANMOL PUBLICATIONS PVT. LTD.
H.O.: 4374/4B, Ansari Road, Daryaganj,
New Delhi-110 002 (India)
Ph.: 23278000, 23261597
B.O.: No. 1015, Ist Main Road, BSK IIIrd Stage
IIIrd Phase, IIIrd Block,
Bangalore - 560 085 (India)
Visit us at: www.anmolpublications.com

Vikram-Vampire and Indian Fairy Tales

First Published, 2009
ISBN 978-81-261-3636-0

PRINTED IN INDIA

Printed at Mehra Offset Press, Delhi.

Contents

Preface

India colourful and vibrant, a land as diverse as its people. A mosaic of faiths, cultures, customs and languages that blend harmoniously to form a composite whole. One of the world's oldest living civilizations—which gave to the world—the concept of zero, the primordial sound Aum..., Yoga and Buddhism.

She is old. She is young. The two diametrically opposite, different yet unique and dynamic faces of India coexist even at this turn of the millennium. With a history of heritage, learning and civilisation dating back to almost 5000 years or perhaps even more, the modern India presents itself as an ideal country. From snow clad mountains to breezy sparkling blue sea side. From arid deserts with shifting sand dunes to lush green country sides. From ancient relics and architectural ruins dating back into antiquity to modern cities, India has it all.

To the north it is bordered by the world's highest mountain chain, where foothill valleys cover the northernmost of the country's maximum states. Further south, plateaus, tropical rain forests and sandy deserts are bordered by palm fringed beaches. Its southernmost tip is the meeting point of three Oceans.

India is a land of staggering contrast with a mingling of the tradition and modernity that is an unique experience to be in India. One will forever remember the stay in this wonderful Homeland-a land truly of mystery and enchantment. Only India can offer such an astonishing variety of contrasts.

She has given birth to numerous spiritual leaders and founders of some of the popular religions of the present day world. India probably has the most religious diversity in any country. It's the birthplace of Hinduism, Buddhism, Sikhism and Jainism and is among the few places to have a resident

Zoroastrian population. India with her veritable treasure trove of culture, mysticism, philosophy, art, music and architecture to name a few. Much of India's classical music is devotional and the North Indian Hindustani and South Indian Carnatic streams are distinct and both have a complex 'raga' framework. The legacy of dance in India is tremendous. The classical dances of India are numerous such as Kathakali of Kerala, Bharatnatyam of Tamil Nadu, Kuchipudi of Andhra Pradesh, Manipuri and Odissi from Orissa are the prominent dance forms in this country that sways to an altogether novel beat. The Yakshagana, nautanki and puppetry are ancient folk forms that live on till date. The earliest specimens of Indian painting are the ones on the walls of the Ajanta Caves dating back to 2nd century BC. The Mughals had a huge impact on Indian art. The influence of Persian art brought placid garden scenes, illustrations from myths, legends and history into Indian art. Word craft, handicrafts, architecture and sculpture all contribute to this rich and varied domain. Indian literature, both in English and in the vernacular, is ever more popular around the world.

The book aims at presenting perspectives of different aspects of Indian culture. It has topics on Indian classical music and dance, painting, ayurveda and yoga which are traditional and indigenous system of physical and mental wellbeing, language, philosophy and excellence achievements by Indian in the different branches of science and social sciences. It also includes our ancient religious and classic literature.

It is hoped that this book will be welcomed by the general readers as also scholars who are interested in the Indian heritage.

—*Editors*

1

Vikram and the Vampire

The sage Bhavabhuti—Eastern teller of these tales—after making his initiatory and propitiatory conge to Ganesha, Lord of Incepts, informs the reader that this book is a string of fine pearls to be hung round the neck of human intelligence; a fragrant flower to be borne on the turband of mental wisdom; a jewel of pure gold, which becomes the brow of all supreme minds; and a handful of powdered rubies, whose tonic effects will appear palpably upon the mental digestion of every patient. Finally, that by aid of the lessons inculcated in the following pages, man will pass happily through this world into the state of absorption, where fables will be no longer required.

He then teaches us how Vikramaditya the Brave became King of Ujjayani.

Some nineteen centuries ago, the renowned city of Ujjayani witnessed the birth of a prince to whom was given the gigantic name Vikramaditya. Even the Sanskrit-speaking people, who are not usually pressed for time, shortened it to "Vikram"; and a little further West it would infallibly have been docked down to "Vik".

Vikram was the second son of an old king Gandharba-Sena, concerning whom little favourable has reached posterity, except that he became an ass, married four queens, and had by them six sons, each of whom was more learned and powerful than the other. It so happened that in course of time the father died. Thereupon his eldest heir, who was known as Shank, succeeded to the carpet of Rajaship, and was instantly murdered by Vikram, his "scorpion", the hero of the following pages.

By this act of vigour and manly decision, which all younger-brother princes should devoutly imitate, Vikram having obtained the title of Bir, or the Brave, made himself Raja. He began to rule well, and the gods so favoured him that day by day his dominions increased.

At length he became lord of all India, and having firmly established his government, he instituted an era—an uncommon feat for a mere monarch, especially when hereditary.

The steps, says the historian, which he took to arrive at that pinnacle of grandeur, were these:

> *The old King calling his two grandsons Bhartarihari and Vikramaditya, gave them good counsel respecting their future learning. They were told to master everything, a certain way not to succeed in anything. They were diligently to learn grammar, the Scriptures, and all the religious sciences.*
>
> *They were to become familiar with military tactics, international law, and music, the riding of horses and elephants—especially the latter—the driving of chariots, and the use of the broadsword, the bow, and the mogdars or Indian clubs.*

They were ordered to be skilful in all kinds of games, in leaping and running, in besieging forts, in forming and breaking bodies of troops; they were to endeavour to excel in every princely quality, to be cunning in ascertaining the power of an enemy, how to make war, to perform journeys, to sit in the presence of the nobles, to separate the different sides of a question, to form alliances, to distinguish between the innocent and the guilty, to assign proper punishments to the wicked, to exercise authority with perfect justice, and to be liberal.

The boys were then sent to school, and were placed under the care of excellent teachers, where they became truly famous. Whilst under pupilage, the eldest was allowed all the power necessary to obtain a knowledge of royal affairs, and he was not invested with the regal office till in these preparatory steps he had given full satisfaction to his subjects, who expressed high approval of his conduct.

The two brothers often conversed on the duties of kings, when the great Vikramaditya gave the great Bhartarihari the following valuable advice:

"As Indra, during the four rainy months, fills the earth with water, so a king should replenish his treasury with money. As Surya the sun, in warming the earth eight months, does not scorch it, so a king, in drawing revenues from his people, ought not to oppress them. As Vayu, the wind, surrounds and fills everything, so the king by his officers and spies should become acquainted with the affairs and circumstances of his whole people. As Yama judges men without partiality or prejudice, and punishes the guilty, so should a king chastise, without favour, all offenders. As Varuna, the regent of water, binds with his pasha or divine noose his enemies, so let a king bind every malefactor safely in prison. As Chandra, the moon, by his cheering light gives pleasure to all, thus should a king, by gifts and generosity, make his people happy. And as Prithwi, the earth, sustains all alike, so should a king feel an equal affection and forbearance towards every one."

Become a monarch, Vikram meditated deeply upon what is said of monarchs:—"A king is fire and air; he is both sun and moon; he is the god of criminal justice; he is the genius of wealth; he is the regent of water; he is the lord of the firmament; he is a powerful divinity who appears in human shape." He reflected with some satisfaction that the scriptures had made him absolute, had left the lives and properties of all his subjects to his arbitrary will, had pronounced him to be an incarnate deity, and had threatened to punish with death even ideas derogatory to his honour.

He punctually observed all the ordinances laid down by the author of the Niti, or institutes of government. His night and day were divided into sixteen pahars or portions, each one hour and a half, and they were disposed of as follows:

Before dawn Vikram was awakened by a servant appointed to this special duty. He swallowed—a thing allowed only to a khshatriya or warrior—Mithridatic every morning on the saliva, and he made the cooks taste every dish before he ate of it. As soon as he had risen, the pages in waiting repeated his splendid qualities, and as he left his sleeping-room in full dress, several Brahmans rehearsed the praises of the gods. Presently he bathed, worshipped his guardian deity, again heard hymns, drank a little water, and saw alms distributed to the poor. He ended this watch by auditing his accounts.

Next entering his court, he placed himself amidst the assembly. He was always armed when he received strangers, and he caused even women to be searched for concealed weapons. He was surrounded by so many spies and so artful, that of a thousand, no two ever told the same tale. At the levee, on his right sat his relations, the Brahmans, and men of distinguished birth. The other castes were on the left, and close to him stood the ministers and those whom he delighted to consult. Afar in front gathered the bards chanting the praises of the gods and of the king; also the charioteers, elephanteers, horsemen, and soldiers of valour.

Amongst the learned men in those assemblies there were ever some who were well instructed in all the scriptures, and others who had studied in one particular school of philosophy, and were acquainted only with the works on divine wisdom, or with those on justice, civil and criminal, on the arts, mineralogy or the practice of physic; also persons cunning in all kinds of customs; riding-masters, dancing-masters, teachers of good behaviour, examiners, tasters, mimics, mountebanks, and others, who all attended the court and awaited the king's commands. He here pronounced judgment in suits of appeal. His poets wrote about him:

The lord of lone splendour an instant suspends His course at midnoon, ere he westward descends; And brief are the moments our young monarch knows, Devoted to pleasure or paid to repose!

Before the second sandhya, or noon, about the beginning of the third watch, he recited the names of the gods, bathed, and broke his fast in his private room; then rising from food, he was amused by singers and dancing girls. The labours of the day now became lighter. After eating he retired, repeating the name of his guardian deity, visited the temples, saluted the gods conversed with the priests, and proceeded to receive and to distribute presents. Fifthly, he discussed political questions with his ministers and councillors.

On the announcement of the herald that it was the sixth watch—about 2 or 3 P.M.—Vikram allowed himself to follow his own inclinations, to regulate his family, and to transact business of a private and personal nature.

After gaining strength by rest, he proceeded to review his troops, examining the men, saluting the officers, and holding military councils. At sunset he bathed a third time and performed the five sacraments of listening to a prelection of the Veda; making oblations to the manes; sacrificing to Fire in honour of the deities; giving rice to dumb creatures; and receiving guests with due ceremonies. He spent the evening amidst a select company of wise, learned, and pious men, conversing on different subjects, and reviewing the business of the day.

The night was distributed with equal care. During the first portion Vikram received the reports which his spies and envoys, dressed in every disguise, brought to him about his enemies. Against the latter he ceased not to use the five arts, namely—dividing the kingdom, bribes, mischief-making, negotiations, and brute-force—especially preferring the first two and the last. His forethought and prudence taught him to regard all his nearest neighbours and their allies as hostile. The powers beyond those natural enemies he considered friendly because they were the foes of his foes. And all the remoter nations he looked upon as neutrals, in a transitional or provisional state as it were, till they became either his neighbours' neighbours, or his own neighbours, that is to say, his friends or his foes.

This important duty finished he supped, and at the end of the third watch he retired to sleep, which was not allowed to last beyond three hours. In the sixth watch he arose and purified himself. The seventh was devoted to holding private consultations with his ministers, and to furnishing the officers of government with requisite instructions. The eighth or last watch was spent with the Purohita or priest, and with Brahmans, hailing the dawn with its appropriate rites; he then bathed, made the customary offerings, and prayed in some unfrequented place near pure water.

And throughout these occupations he bore in mind the duty of kings, namely—to pursue every object till it be accomplished; to succour all dependents, and hospitably to receive guests, however numerous. He was generous to his subjects respecting taxes, and kind of speech; yet he was inexorable as death in the punishment of offences. He rarely hunted, and he visited his pleasure gardens only on stated days. He acted in his own dominions with justice; he chastised foreign foes with rigour; he behaved generously to Brahmans, and he avoided favouritism amongst his friends. In war he never slew a suppliant, a spectator, a person asleep or undressed, or anyone that showed fear. Whatever country he conquered, offerings were presented to its gods, and effects and money were given to the reverends. But what benefited him most was his attention to the creature comforts of the nine Gems of Science: those eminent men ate and drank themselves into fits of enthusiasm, and ended by immortalizing their patron's name.

Become Vikram the Great he established his court at a delightful and beautiful location rich in the best of water. The country was difficult of access, and artificially made incapable of supporting a host of invaders, but four great roads met near the city. The capital was surrounded with durable ramparts, having gates of defence, and near it was a mountain fortress, under the especial charge of a great captain.

The metropolis was well garrisoned and provisioned, and it surrounded the royal palace, a noble building without as well as within. Grandeur seemed embodied there, and Prosperity had made it her own. The nearer ground, viewed from the terraces and pleasure pavilions, was a lovely mingling of rock and mountain, plain and valley, field and fallow, crystal lake and glittering stream. The banks of the winding Lavana were fringed with meads whose herbage, pearly with morning dew, afforded choicest grazing for the sacred cow, and were dotted with perfumed clumps of Bo-trees, tamarinds, and holy figs: in one place Vikram planted 100,000 in a single orchard and gave them to his spiritual advisers. The river valley separated the stream from a belt of forest growth which extended to a hill range, dark with impervious jungle, and cleared here and there for the cultivator's village. Behind it, rose another sub-range, wooded with a lower bush and already blue with air, whilst in the background towered range upon range, here rising abruptly into points and peaks, there ramp-shaped or wall-formed, with sheer descents, and all of light azure hue adorned with glories of silver and gold.

After reigning for some years, Vikram the Brave found himself at the age of thirty, a staid and sober middle-aged man, He had several sons—daughters are naught in India—by his several wives, and he had some paternal affection for nearly all—except of course, for his eldest son, a youth who seemed to conduct himself as though he had a claim to the succession. In fact, the king seemed to have taken up his abode for life at Ujjayani, when suddenly he be thought himself, "I must visit those countries of whose names I am ever hearing." The fact is, he had determined to spy out in disguise the lands of all his foes, and to find the best means of bringing against them his formidable army.

We now learn how Bhartari Raja becomes Regent of Ujjayani.

Having thus resolved, Vikram the Brave gave the government into the charge of a younger brother, Bhartari Raja, and in the garb of a religious mendicant, accompanied by Dharma Dhwaj, his second son, a youth bordering on the age of puberty, he began to travel from city to city, and from forest to forest.

The Regent was of a settled melancholic turn of mind, having lost in early youth a very peculiar wife. One day, whilst out hunting, he happened to pass a funeral pyre, upon which a Brahman's widow had just become Sati (a holy woman) with the greatest fortitude. On his return home he related the adventure to Sita Rani, his spouse, and she at once made reply that virtuous women die with their husbands, killed by the fire of grief, not by the flames of the pile. To prove her truth the prince, after an affectionate farewell, rode forth to the chase, and presently sent back the suite with his robes torn and stained, to report his accidental death. Sita perished upon the spot, and the widower remained inconsolable—for a time.

He led the dullest of lives, and took to himself sundry spouses, all equally distinguished for birth, beauty, and modesty. Like his brother, he performed all the proper devoirs of a Raja, rising before the day to finish his ablutions, to worship the gods, and to do due obeisance to the Brahmans. He then ascended the throne, to judge his people according to the Shastra, carefully keeping in subjection lust, anger, avarice, folly, drunkenness, and pride; preserving himself from being seduced by the love of gaming and of the chase; restraining his desire for dancing, singing, and playing on musical instruments, and refraining from sleep during daytime, from wine, from molesting men of worth, from dice, from putting human beings to death by artful means, from useless travelling, and from holding any one guilty without the commission of a crime.

His levees were in a hall decently splendid, and he was distinguished only by an umbrella of peacock's feathers; he received all complainants, petitioners, and presenters of offences with kind looks and soft words. He united to himself the seven or eight wise councillors, and the sober and virtuous secretary that formed the high cabinet of his royal brother, and they met in some secret lonely spot, as a mountain, a terrace, a bower or a forest, whence women, parrots, and other talkative birds were carefully excluded.

And at the end of this useful and somewhat laborious day, he retired to his private apartments, and, after listening to spiritual songs and to soft music, he fell asleep. Sometimes he would summon his brother's "Nine Gems of Science," and give ear to their learned discourses. But it was observed that the viceroy reserved this exercise for nights when he was troubled with insomnia—the words of wisdom being to him an infallible remedy for that disorder.

Thus passed onwards his youth, doing nothing that it could desire, forbidden all pleasures because they were unprincely, and working in the palace harder than in the pauper's hut.

Having, however, fortunately for himself, few predilections and no imagination, he began to pride himself upon being a philosopher.

Much business from an early age had dulled his wits, which were never of the most brilliant; and in the steadily increasing torpidity of his spirit, he traced the germs of that quietude which forms the highest happiness of man in this storm of matter called the world. He therefore allowed himself but one friend of his soul. He retained, I have said, his brother's seven or eight ministers; he was constant in attendance upon the Brahman priests who officiated at the palace, and who kept the impious from touching sacred property; and he was courteous to the commander-in-chief who directed his warriors, to the officers of justice who inflicted punishment upon offenders, and to the lords of towns, varying in number from one to a thousand. But he placed an intimate of his own in the high position of confidential councillor, the ambassador to regulate war and peace.

Mahipala was a person of noble birth, endowed with shining abilities, popular, dexterous in business, acquainted with foreign parts, famed for eloquence and intrepidity, and as Menu the Lawgiver advises, remarkably handsome.

Bhartari Raja, as I have said, became a quietist and a philosopher. But Kama, the bright god who exerts his sway over the three worlds, heaven and earth and grewsome Hades, had marked out the prince once more as the victim of his blossom-tipped shafts and his flowery bow. How, indeed, could he hope to escape the doom which has fallen equally upon Brahma the Creator, Vishnu the Preserver, and dreadful Shiva the Three-eyed Destroyer?

By reason of her exceeding beauty, her face was a full moon shining in the clearest sky; her hair was the purple cloud of autumn when, gravid with rain, it hangs low over earth; and her complexion mocked the pale waxen hue of the large-flowered jasmine. Her eyes were those of the timid antelope; her lips were as red as those of the pomegranate's bud, and when they opened, from them distilled a fountain of ambrosia. Her neck was like a pigeon's; her hand the pink lining of the conch-shell;

her waist a leopard's; her feet the softest lotuses. In a word, a model of grace and loveliness was Dangalah Rani, Raja Bhartari's last and youngest wife.

The warrior laid down his arms before her; the politician spoke out every secret in her presence. The religious prince would have slaughtered a cow—that sole unforgivable sin—to save one of her eyelashes: the absolute king would not drink a cup of water without her permission; the staid philosopher, the sober quietist, to win from her the shadow of a smile, would have danced before her like a singing-girl. So desperately enamoured became Bhartari Raja.

It is written, however, that love, alas! breeds not love; and so it happened to the Regent. The warmth of his affection, instead of animating his wife, annoyed her; his protestations wearied her; his vows gave her the headache; and his caresses were a colic that made her blood run cold. Of course, the prince perceived nothing, being lost in wonder and admiration of the beauty's coyness and coquetry.

And as women must give away their hearts, whether asked or not, so the lovely Dangalah Rani lost no time in lavishing all the passion of her idle soul upon Mahipala, the handsome ambassador of peace and war. By this means the three were happy and were contented; their felicity, however, being built on a rotten foundation, could not long endure. It soon ended in the following extraordinary way.

In the city of Ujjayani, within sight of the palace, dwelt a Brahman and his wife, who, being old and poor, and having nothing else to do, had applied themselves to the practice of austere devotion. They fasted and refrained from drink, they stood on their heads and held their arms for weeks in the air; they prayed till their knees were like pads; they disciplined themselves with scourges of wire; and they walked about unclad in the cold season, and in summer they sat within a circle of flaming wood, till they became the envy and admiration of all the plebeian gods that inhabit the lower heavens.

In fine, as a reward for their exceeding piety, the venerable pair received at the hands of a celestial messenger an apple of the tree Kalpavriksha—a fruit which has the virtue of conferring eternal life upon him that tastes it.

Scarcely had the god disappeared, when the Brahman, opening his toothless mouth, prepared to eat the fruit of immortality. Then his wife addressed him in these words, shedding copious tears the while:

> *"To die, O man, is a passing pain; to be poor is an interminable anguish. Surely our present lot is the penalty of some great crime committed by us in a past state of being. Callest thou this state life? Better we die at once, and so escape the woes of the world!"*

Hearing these words, the Brahman sat undecided, with open jaws and eyes fixed upon the apple. Presently he found tongue: "I have accepted the fruit, and have brought it here; but having heard thy speech, my intellect hath wasted away; now I will do whatever thou pointest out."

The wife resumed her discourse, which had been interrupted by a more than usually copious flow of tears. "Moreover, O husband, we are old, and what are the enjoyments of the stricken in years? Truly quoth the poet:

> *Die loved in youth, not hated in age.*

If that fruit could have restored thy dimmed eyes, and deaf ears, and blunted taste, and warmth of love, I had not spoken to thee thus."

After which the Brahman threw away the apple, to the great joy of his wife, who felt a natural indignation at the prospect of seeing her goodman become immortal, whilst she still remained subject to the laws of death; but she concealed this motive in the depths of her thought, enlarging, as women are apt to do, upon everything but the truth. And she spoke with such success, that the priest was about to toss in his rage the heavenly fruit into the fire, reproaching the gods as if by sending it they had done him an injury. Then the wife snatched it out of his hand, and telling him it was too precious to be wasted, bade him arise and gird his loins and wend him to the Regent's palace, and offer him the fruit—as King Vikram was absent—with a right reverend brahmanical benediction. She concluded with impressing upon her unworldly husband the necessity of requiring a large sum of money as a return for his inestimable gift. "By this means, "she said, "thou mayst promote thy present and future welfare."

Then the Brahman went forth, and standing in the presence of the Raja, told him all things touching the fruit, concluding with "O, mighty prince! vouchsafe to accept this tribute, and bestow wealth upon me. I shall be happy in your living long!"

Bhartari Raja led the supplicant into an inner strongroom, where stood heaps of the finest gold-dust, and bade him carry away all that he could; this the priest did, not forgetting to fill even his eloquent and toothless mouth with the precious metal. Having dismissed the devotee groaning under the burden, the Regent entered the apartments of his wives, and having summoned the beautiful Queen Dangalah Rani, gave her the fruit, and said, "Eat this, light of my eyes! This fruit—joy of my heart!—will make thee everlastingly young and beautiful."

The pretty queen, placing both hands upon her husband's bosom, kissed his eyes and lips, and sweetly smiling on his face—for great is the guile of women—whispered, "Eat it thyself, dear one, or at least share it with me; for what is life and what is youth without the presence of those we love?" But the Raja, whose heart was melted by these unusual words, put her away tenderly, and, having explained that the fruit would serve for only one person, departed.

Whereupon the pretty queen, sweetly smiling as before, slipped the precious present into her pocket. When the Regent was transacting business in the hall of audience she sent for the ambassador who regulated war and peace, and presented him with the apple in a manner at least as tender as that with which it had been offered to her.

Then the ambassador, after slipping the fruit into his pocket also, retired from the presence of the pretty queen, and meeting Lakha, one of the maids of honour, explained to her its wonderful power, and gave it to her as a token of his love. But the maid of honour, being an ambitious girl, determined that the fruit was a fit present to set before the Regent in the absence of the

King. Bhartari Raja accepted it, bestowed on her great wealth, and dismissed her with many thanks.

He then took up the apple and looked at it with eyes brimful of tears, for he knew the whole extent of his misfortune. His heart ached, he felt a loathing for the world, and he said with sighs and groans:

> *"Of what value are these delusions of wealth and affection, whose sweetness endures for a moment and becomes eternal bitterness? Love is like the drunkard's cup: delicious is the first drink, palling are the draughts that succeed it, and most distasteful are the dregs. What is life but a restless vision of imaginary pleasures and of real pains, from which the only waking is the terrible day of death? The affection of this world is of no use, since, in consequence of it, we fall at last into hell. For which reason it is best to practice the austerities of religion, that the Deity may bestow upon us hereafter that happiness which he refuses to us here!"*

Thus did Bhartari Raja determine to abandon the world. But before setting out for the forest, he could not refrain from seeing the queen once more, so hot was the flame which Kama had kindled in his heart. He therefore went to the apartments of his women, and having caused Dangalah Rani to be summoned, he asked her what had become of the fruit which he had given to her. She answered that, according to his command, she had eaten it. Upon which the Regent showed her the apple, and she beholding it stood aghast, unable to make any reply. The Raja gave careful orders for her beheading; he then went out, and having had the fruit washed, ate it. He quitted the throne to be a jogi, or religious mendicant, and without communicating with any one departed into the jungle. There he became such a devotee that death had no power over him, and he is wandering still. But some say that he was duly absorbed into the essence of the Deity.

We are next told how the valiant Vikram returned to his own country.

Thus Vikram's throne remained empty. When the news reached King Indra, Regent of the Lower Firmament and

Protector of Earthly Monarchs, he sent Prithwi Pala, a fierce giant, to defend the city of Ujjayani till such time as its lawful master might reappear, and the guardian used to keep watch and ward night and day over his trust.

In less than a year the valorous Raja Vikram became thoroughly tired of wandering about the woods half dressed: now suffering from famine, then exposed to the attacks of wild beasts, and at all times very ill at ease. He reflected also that he was not doing his duty to his wives and children; that the heir-apparent would probably make the worst use of the parental absence; and finally, that his subjects, deprived of his fatherly care, had been left in the hands of a man who, for ought he could say, was not worthy of the high trust. He had also spied out all the weak points of friend and foe. Whilst these and other equally weighty considerations were hanging about the Raja's mind, he heard a rumour of the state of things spread abroad; that Bhartari, the regent, having abdicated his throne, had gone away into the forest. Then quoth Vikram to his son, "We have ended our wayfarings, now let us turn our steps homewards!"

The gong was striking the mysterious hour of midnight as the king and the young prince approached the principal gate. And they were pushing through it when a monstrous figure rose up before them and called out with a fearful voice, "Who are ye, and where are ye going ? Stand and deliver your names!"

"I am Raja Vikram," rejoined the king, half choked with rage, "and I am come to mine own city. Who art thou that darest to stop or stay me?"

"That question is easily answered," cried Prithwi Pala the giant, in his roaring voice; "the gods have sent me to protect Ujjayani. If thou be really Raja Vikram, prove thyself a man: first fight with me, and then return to thine own."

The warrior king cried "Sadhu!" wanting nothing better. He girt his girdle tight round his loins, summoned his opponent into the empty space beyond the gate, told him to stand on guard, and presently began to devise some means of closing with or running in upon him. The giant's fists were large as watermelons, and his knotted arms whistled through the air like falling trees, threatening fatal blows. Besides which the Raja's head scarcely reached the giant's stomach, and the latter, each time he struck out, whooped so abominably loud, that no human nerves could remain unshaken.

At last Vikram's good luck prevailed. The giant's left foot slipped, and the hero, seizing his antagonist's other leg, began to trip him up. At the same moment the young prince, hastening to his parent's assistance, jumped viciously upon the enemy's naked toes. By their united exertions they brought him to the ground, when the son sat down upon his stomach, making himself as weighty as he well could, whilst the father, climbing up to the monster's throat, placed himself astride upon it, and pressing both thumbs upon his eyes, threatened to blind him if he would not yield.

Then the giant, modifying the bellow of his voice, cried out:

"O Raja, thou hast overthrown me, and I grant thee thy life."

"Surely thou art mad, monster," replied the king, in jeering tone, half laughing, half angry. "To whom grantest thou life? If I desire it I can kill thee; how, then, cost thou talk about granting me my life?"

"Vikram of Ujjayani," said the giant, "be not too proud! I will save thee from a nearly impending death. Only hearken to the tale which I have to tell thee, and use thy judgment, and act upon it. So shalt thou rule the world free from care, and live without danger, and die happily."

"Proceed," quoth the Raja, after a moment's thought, dismounting from the giant's throat, and beginning to listen with all his ears.

The giant raised himself from the ground, and when in a sitting posture, began in solemn tones to speak as follows:

"In short, the history of the matter is, that three men were born in this same city of Ujjayani, in the same lunar mansion, in the same division of the great circle described upon the ecliptic, and in the same period of time. You, the first, were born in the house of a king. The second was an oilman's son, who was slain by the third, a jogi, or anchorite, who kills all he can, wafting the sweet scent of human sacrifice to the nostrils of Durga, goddess of destruction. Moreover, the holy man, after compassing the death of the oilman's son, has suspended him head downwards from a mimosa tree in a cemetery. He is now anxiously plotting thy destruction. He hath murdered his own child:"

"And how came an anchorite to have a child?" asked Raja Vikram, incredulously.

"That is what I am about to tell thee," replied the giant. "In the good days of thy generous father, Gandharba-Sena, as the court was taking its pleasure in the forest, they saw a devotee, or rather a devotee's head, protruding from a hole in the ground. The white ants had surrounded his body with a case of earth, and had made their home upon his skin. All kinds of insects and small animals crawled up and down the face, yet not a muscle moved. Wasps had hung their nests to its temples, and scorpions wandered in and out of the matted and clotted hair; yet the hermit felt them not. He spoke to no one; he received no gifts; and had it not been for the opening of his nostrils, as he continually inhaled the pungent smoke of a thorn fire, man would have deemed him dead. Such were his religious austerities.

"Thy father marvelled much at the sight, and rode home in profound thought. That evening, as he sat in the hall of audience, he could speak of nothing but the devotee; and his curiosity soon rose to such a pitch, that he proclaimed about the city a reward of one hundred gold pieces to any one that could bring to court this anchorite of his own free will."

"Shortly afterwards, Vasantasena, a singing and dancing girl more celebrated for wit and beauty than for sagesse or discretion; appeared before thy sire, and offered for the petty inducement of a gold bangle to bring the anchorite into the palace, carrying a baby on his shoulder."

"The king hearing her speak was astonished, gave her a betel leaf in token that he held her to her promise, and permitted her to depart, which she did with a laugh of triumph."

"Vasantasena went directly to the jungle, where she found the pious man faint with thirst, shriveled with hunger, and half dead with heat and cold. She cautiously put out the fire. Then, having prepared a confection, she approached from behind and rubbed upon his lips a little of the sweetmeat, which he licked up with great relish. Thereupon she made more and gave it to him. After two days of this generous diet he gained some strength, and on the third, as he felt a finger upon his mouth, he opened his eyes and said, "Why hast thou come here?"

"The girl, who had her story in readiness, replied: "I am the daughter of a deity, and have practised religious observances in the heavenly regions. I have now come into this forest!" And the devotee, who began to think how much more pleasant is such society than solitude, asked her where her hut was, and requested to be led there."

"Then Vasantasena, having unearthed the holy man and compelled him to purify himself, led him to the abode which she had caused to be built for herself in the wood. She explained its luxuries by the nature of her vow, which bound her to indulge in costly apparel, in food with six flavours, and in every kind of indulgence. In course of time the hermit learned to follow her example; he gave up inhaling smoke, and he began to eat and drink as a daily occupation."

"At length Kama began to trouble him. Briefly the saint and saintess were made man and wife, by the simple form of matrimony called the Gandharba-vivaha, and about ten months afterwards a son was born to them. Thus the anchorite came to have a child."

"Remained Vasantasena's last feat. Some months passed: then she said to the devotee her husband, 'Oh saint! let us now, having finished our devotions, perform a pilgrimage to some sacred place, that all the sins of our bodies may be washed away, after which we will die and depart into everlasting happiness.' Cajoled by these speeches, the hermit mounted his child upon his shoulder and followed her where she went—directly into Raja Gandharba-Sena's palace."

"When the king and the ministers and the officers and the courtiers saw Vasantasena, and her spouse carrying the baby, they recognized her from afar. The Raja exclaimed, 'Lo!' this is the very singing girl who went forth to bring back the devotee. 'And all replied: 'O great monarch! thou speakest truly; this is the very same woman. And be pleased to observe that whatever things she, having asked leave to undertake, went forth to do, all these she hath done!' Then gathering around her they asked her all manner of questions, as if the whole matter had been the lightest and the most laughable thing in the world.

"But the anchorite, having heard the speeches of the king and his courtiers, thought to himself, 'They have done this for the purpose of taking away the fruits of my penance.' Cursing them all with terrible curses, and taking up his child, he left the hall. Thence he went to the forest, slaughtered the innocent, and began to practice austerities with a view to revenge that hour, and having slain his child, he will attempt thy life. His prayers have been heard. In the first place they deprived thee of thy father. Secondly, they cast enmity between thee and thy brother, thus dooming him to an untimely end. Thirdly, they are now working thy ruin. The anchorite's design is to offer up a king and a king's son to his patroness Durga, and by virtue of such devotional act he will obtain the sovereignty of the whole world!

"But I have promised, O Vikram, to save thee, if such be the will of Fortune, from impending destruction. Therefore hearken well unto my words. Distrust them that dwell amongst the dead, and remember that it is lawful and right to strike off his head that would slay thee. So shalt thou rule the universal earth, and leave behind thee an immortal name!"

Suddenly Prithwi Pala, the giant, ceased speaking, and disappeared. Vikram and his son then passed through the city gates, feeling their limbs to be certain that no bones were broken, and thinking over the scene that had occurred.

We now are informed how the valiant King Vikram met with the Vampire.

It was the spring season when the Raja returned, and the Holi festival caused dancing and singing in every house. Ujjayani was extraordinarily happy and joyful at the return of her ruler, who joined in her gladness with all his kingly heart. The faces and dresses of the public were red and yellow with gulal and abir,—perfumed powders,—which were sprinkled upon one another in token of merriment. Musicians deafened the citizens' ears, dancing girls performed till ready to faint with fatigue, the manufacturers of comfits made their fortunes, and the Nine Gems of Science celebrated the auspicious day with the most long-winded odes.

The royal hero, decked in regal attire, and attended by many thousands of state palanquins glittering with their various ornaments, and escorted by a suite of a hundred kingly personages, with their martial array of the four hosts, of cavalry, elephants, chariots, and infantry, and accompanied by Amazon girls, lovely as the suite of the gods, himself a personification of majesty, bearing the white parasol of dominion, with a golden staff and tassels, began once more to reign.

After the first pleasures of return, the king applied himself unremittingly to good government and to eradicating the abuses which had crept into the administration during the period of his wanderings. Mindful of the wise saying, "if the Rajadid not punish the guilty, the stronger would roast the weaker like a fish on the spit," he began the work of reform with an iron hand. He confiscated the property of a councillor who had the reputation of taking bribes; he branded the forehead of a sudra or servile man whose breath smelt of ardent spirits, and a goldsmith having been detected in fraud he ordered him to be cut in shreds with razors as the law in its mercy directs.

In the case of a notorious evil-speaker he opened the back of his head and had his tongue drawn through the wound. A few murderers he burned alive on iron beds, praying the while that Vishnu might have mercy upon their souls. His spies were ordered, as the shastra called "The Prince" advises, to mix with robbers and thieves with a view of leading them into situations where they might most easily be entrapped, and once or twice when the fellows were too wary, he seized them and their relations and impaled them all, thereby conclusively proving, without any mistake, that he was king of earth.

With the sex feminine he was equally severe. A woman convicted of having poisoned an elderly husband in order to marry a younger man was thrown to the dogs, which speedily devoured her. He punished simple infidelity by cutting off the offender's nose—an admirable practice, which is not only a severe penalty to the culprit, but also a standing warning to others, and an efficient preventative to any recurrence of the fault. Faithlessness combined with bad example or brazen-facedness was further treated by being led in solemn procession through the bazar mounted on a diminutive and crop-eared donkey, with the face turned towards the crupper. After a few such examples the women of Ujjayani became almost modest; it is the fault of man when they are not tolerably well behaved in one point at least.

Every day as Vikram sat upon the judgment-seat, trying causes and punishing offences, he narrowly observed the speech, the gestures, and the countenances of the various criminals and litigants and their witnesses. Ever suspecting women, as I have said, and holding them to be the root of all evil, he never failed when some sin or crime more horrible than usual came before him, to ask the accused, "Who is she?" and the suddenness of the question often elicited the truth by accident. For there can be nothing thoroughly and entirely bad unless a woman is at the bottom of it; and, knowing this, Raja Vikram made certain notable hits under the most improbable circumstances, which had almost given him a reputation for omniscience. But this is easily explained: a man intent upon squaring the circle will see squares in circles wherever he looks, and sometimes he will find them.

In disputed cases of money claims, the king adhered strictly to established practice, and consulted persons learned in the law. He seldom decided a cause on his own judgment, and he showed great temper and patience in bearing with rough language from irritated plaintiffs and defendants, from the infirm, and from old men beyond eighty. That humble petitioners might not be baulked in having access to the "fountain of justice," he caused an iron box to be suspended by a chain from the windows of his sleeping apartment. Every morning he ordered the box to be opened before him, and listened to all the placets at full length. Even in this simple process he displayed abundant cautiousness. For, having forgotten what little of the humanities he had mastered in his youth, he would hand the paper to a secretary whose business it was to read it out before him; after which operation the man of letters was sent into an inner room, and the petition was placed in the hands of a second scribe. Once it so happened by the bungling of the deceitful kayasths (clerks) that an important difference was found to occur in the same sheet. So upon strict inquiry one secretary lost his ears and the other his right hand. After this petitions were rarely if ever falsified.

The Raja Vikram also lost no time in attacking the cities and towns and villages of his enemies, but the people rose to a man against him, and hewing his army to pieces with their weapons, vanquished him. This took place so often that he despaired of bringing all the earth under the shadow of his umbrella.

At length on one occasion when near a village he listened to a conversation of the inhabitants. A woman having baked some cakes was giving them to her child, who leaving the edges would eat only the middle. On his asking for another cake, she cried, "This boy's way is like Vikram's in his attempt to conquer the world!" On his inquiring "Mother, why, what am I doing; and what has Vikram done?" "Thou, my boy," she replied, "throwing away the outside of the cake eatest the middle only. Vikram also in his ambition, without subduing the frontiers before attacking the towns, invades the heart of the country and lays it waste. On that account, both the townspeople and others rising, close upon him from the frontiers to the centre, and destroy his army. That is his folly."

Vikram took notice of the woman's words. He strengthened his army and resumed his attack on the provinces and cities, beginning with the frontiers, reducing the outer towns and stationing troops in the intervals. Thus he proceeded regularly with his invasions. After a respite, adopting the same system and marshalling huge armies, he reduced in regular course each kingdom and province till he became monarch of the whole world.

It so happened that one day as Vikram the Brave sat upon the judgment-seat, a young merchant, by name Mal Deo, who had lately arrived at Ujjayani with loaded camels and elephants, and with the reputation of immense wealth, entered the palace court. Having been received with extreme condescension, he gave into the king's hand a fruit which he had brought in his own, and then spreading a prayer carpet on the floor he sat down. Presently, after a quarter of an hour, he arose and went away. When he had gone the king reflected in his mind: "Under this disguise, perhaps, is the very man of whom the giant spoke." Suspecting this, he did not eat the fruit, but calling the master of the household he gave the present to him, ordering him to keep it in a very careful manner. The young merchant, however, continued every day to court the honour of an interview, each time presenting a similar gift.

By chance one morning Raja Vikram went, attended by his ministers, to see his stables. At this time the young merchant also arrived there, and in the usual manner placed a fruit in the royal hand. As the king was thoughtfully tossing it in the air, it accidentally fell from his fingers to the ground. Then the monkey, who was tethered amongst the horses to draw calamities from their heads, snatched it up and tore it to pieces. Whereupon a ruby of such size and water came forth that the king and his ministers, beholding its brilliancy, gave vent to expressions of wonder.

Quoth Vikram to the young merchant severely—for his suspicions were now thoroughly roused—"Why hast thou given to us all this wealth?"

"O great king," replied Mal Deo, demurely, "it is written in the scriptures (shastra) 'Of Ceremony' that 'we must not go empty-handed into the presence of the following persons, namely, Rajas, spiritual teachers, judges, young maidens, and old women whose daughters we would marry.' But why, O Vikram, cost thou speak of one ruby only, since in each of the fruits which I have laid at thy feet there is a similar jewel?"

Having heard this speech, the king said to the master of his household, "Bring all the fruits which I have entrusted to thee."

The treasurer, on receiving the royal command, immediately brought them, and having split them, there was found in each one a ruby, one and all equally perfect in size and water. Raja Vibram beholding such treasures was excessively pleased. Having sent for a lapidary, he ordered him to examine the rubies, saying, "We cannot take anything with us out of this world. Virtue is a noble quality to possess here below—so tell justly what is the value of each of these gems."

To so moral a speech the lapidary replied, " Maha-Raja! thou hast said truly; whoever possesses virtue, possesses everything; virtue indeed accompanies us always, and is of advantage in both worlds. Hear, O great king! each gem is perfect in colour, quality and beauty. If I were to say that the value of each was ten million millions of suvarnas (gold pieces), even then thou couldst not understand its real worth. In fact, each ruby would buy one of the seven regions into which the earth is divided."

The king on hearing this was delighted, although his suspicions were not satisfied; and, having bestowed a robe of honour upon the lapidary, dismissed him. Thereon, taking the young merchant's hand, he led him into the palace, seated him upon his own carpet in presence of the court, and began to say, "My entire kingdom is not worth one of these rubies: tell me how it is that thou who buyest and sellest hast given me such and so many pearls?"

Mal Deo replied: "O great king, the speaking of matters like the following in public is not right; these things—prayers, spells, drugs, good qualities, household affairs, the eating of forbidden food, and the evil we may have heard of our neighbour—should not be discussed in full assembly. Privately I will disclose to thee my wishes. This is the way of the world; when an affair comes to six ears, it does not remain secret; if a matter is confided to four ears it may escape further hearing; and if to two ears even Brahma the Creator does not know it; how then can any rumour of it come to man?"

Having heard this speech, Raja Vikram took Mal Deo aside, and began to ask him, saying, "O generous man! you have given me so many rubies, and even for a single day you have not eaten food with me; I am exceedingly ashamed, tell me what you desire."

"Raja," said the young merchant, "I am not Mal Deo, but Shanta-Shil, a devotee. I am about to perform spells, incantations and magical rites on the banks of the river Godavari, in a large smashana, a cemetery where bodies are burned. By this means the Eight Powers of Nature will all become mine. This thing I ask of you as alms, that you and the young prince Dharma Dhwaj will pass one night with me, doing my bidding. By you remaining near me my incantations will be successful."

The valiant Vikram nearly started from his seat at the word cemetery, but, like a ruler of men, he restrained his face from expressing his feelings, and he presently replied, "Good, we will come, tell us on what day!"

"You are to come to me," said the devotee, "armed, but without followers, on the Monday evening the 14th of the dark half of the month Bhadra." The Raja said: "Do you go your ways, we will certainly come."

In this manner, having received a promise from the king, and having taken leave, the devotee returned to his house: thence he repaired to the temple, and having made preparations, and taken all the necessary things, he went back into the cemetery and sat down to his ceremonies.

The valiant Vikram, on the other hand, retired into an inner apartment, to consult his own judgment about an adventure with which, for fear of ridicule, he was unwilling to acquaint even the most trustworthy of his ministers.

In due time came the evening moon's day, the 14th of the dark half of the month Bhadra. As the short twilight fell gloomily on earth, the warrior king accompanied by his son, with turband-ends tied under their chins, and with trusty blades tucked under their arms ready for foes, human, bestial, or devilish, slipped out unseen through the palace wicket, and took the road leading to the cemetery on the river bank.

Dark and drear was the night. Urged by the furious blast of the lingering winter-rains, masses of bistre-coloured cloud, like the forms of unwieldy beasts, rolled heavily over the firmament plain.

Whenever the crescent of the young moon, rising from an horizon sable as the sad Tamala's hue, glanced upon the wayfarers, it was no brighter than the fine tip of an elephant's tusk protruding from the muddy wave. A heavy storm was impending; big drops fell in showers from the forest trees as they groaned under the blast, and beneath the gloomy avenue the clayey ground gleamed ghastly white. As the Raja and his son advanced, a faint ray of light, like the line of pure gold streaking the dark surface of the touchstone, caught their eyes, and directed their footsteps towards the cemetery.

When Vikram came upon the open space on the riverbank where corpses were burned, he hesitated for a moment to tread its impure ground. But seeing his son undismayed, he advanced boldly, trampling upon remnants of bones, and only covering his mouth with his turband-end.

Presently, at the further extremity of the smashana, or burning ground, appeared a group. By the lurid flames that flared and flickered round the half-extinguished funeral pyres, with remnants of their dreadful loads, Raja Vikram and Dharma Dhwaj could note the several features of the ill-omened spot. There was an outer circle of hideous bestial forms; tigers were roaring, and elephants were trumpeting; wolves, whose foul hairy coats blazed with sparks of bluish phosphoric light, were devouring the remnants of human bodies; foxes, jackals, and hyenas were disputing over their prey; whilst bears were chewing the livers of children.

The space within was peopled by a multitude of fiends. There were the subtle bodies of men that had escaped their grosser frames prowling about the charnel ground, where their corpses had been reduced to ashes, or hovering in the air, waiting till the new bodies which they were to animate were made ready for their reception. The spirits of those that had been foully slain wandered about with gashed limbs; and skeletons, whose mouldy bones were held together by bits of blackened sinew, followed them as the murderer does his victim. Malignant witches with shriveled skins, horrid eyes and distorted forms, crawled and crouched over the earth; whilst spectres and goblins now stood motionless, and tall as lofty palm trees; then, as if in fits, leaped, danced, and tumbled before their evocator.

The air was filled with shrill and strident cries, with the fitful moaning of the storm-wind, with the hooting of the owl, with the jackal's long wild cry, and with the hoarse gurgling of the swollen river, from whose banks the earth-slip thundered in its fall.

In the midst of all, close to the fire which lit up his evil countenance, sat Shanta-Shil, the jogi, with the banner that denoted his calling and his magic staff planted in the ground behind him. He was clad in the ochre-coloured loin-wrap of his class; from his head streamed long tangled locks of hair like horsehair; his black body was striped with lines of chalk, and a girdle of thighbones encircled his waist.

His face was smeared with ashes from a funeral pyre, and his eyes, fixed as those of a statue, gleamed from this mask with an infernal light of hate. His cheeks were shaven, and he had not forgotten to draw the horizontal sectarian mark. But this was of blood; and Vikram, as he drew near saw that he was playing upon a human skull with two shank bones, making music for the horrid revelry.

Now Raja Vibram, as has been shown by his encounter with Indra's watchman, was a bold prince, and he was cautious as he was brave. The sight of a human being in the midst of these terrors raised his mettle; he determined to prove himself a hero, and feeling that the critical moment was now come, he hoped to rid himself and his house forever of the family curse that hovered over them.

For a moment he thought of the giant's words, "And remember that it is lawful and right to strike off his head that would slay thee." A stroke with his good sword might at once and effectually put an end to the danger. But then he remembered that he had passed his royal word to do the devotee's bidding that night. Besides, he felt assured that the hour for action had not yet sounded.

These reflections having passed through his mind with the rapid course of a star that has lost its honours, Vikram courteously saluted Shanta-Shil. The jogi briefly replied, "Come sit down, both of ye." The father and son took their places, by no means surprised or frightened by the devil dances before and around them. Presently the valiant Raja reminded the devotee that he was come to perform his promise, and lastly asked, "What commands are there for us?"

The jogi replied, "O king, since you have come, just perform one piece of business. About two kos hence, in a southerly direction, there is another place where dead bodies are burned; and in that place is a mimosa tree, on which a body is hanging. Bring it to me immediately."

Raja Vikram took his son's hand, unwilling to leave him in such company; and, catching up a fire-brand, went rapidly away in the proper direction. He was now certain that Shanta-Shil was the anchorite who, enraged by his father, had resolved his destruction; and his uppermost thought was a firm resolve "to breakfast upon his enemy, ere his enemy could dine upon him." He muttered this old saying as he went, whilst the tom-toming of the anchorite upon the skull resounded in his ears, and the devil-crowd, which had held its peace during his meeting with Shanta-Shil, broke out again in an infernal din of whoops and screams, yells and laughter.

The darkness of the night was frightful, the gloom deepened till it was hardly possible to walk. The clouds opened their fountains, raining so that you would say they could never rain again. Lightning blazed forth with more than the light of day, and the roar of the thunder caused the earth to shake. Baleful gleams tipped the black cones of the trees and fitfully scampered like fireflies over the waste. Unclean goblins dogged the travellers and threw themselves upon the ground in their path and obstructed them in a thousand different ways. Huge snakes, whose mouths distilled blood and black venom, kept clinging around their legs in the roughest part of the road, till they were persuaded to loose their hold either by the sword or by reciting a spell. In fact, there were so many horrors and such a tumult and noise that even a brave man would have faltered, yet the king kept on his way.

At length having passed over, somehow or other, a very difficult road, the Raja arrived at the smashana, or burning place pointed out by the jogi. Suddenly he sighted the tree where from root to top every branch and leaf was in a blaze of crimson flame. And when he, still dauntless, advanced towards it, a clamour continued to be raised, and voices kept crying, "Kill them! kill them! seize them! seize them! take care that they do not get away! let them scorch themselves to cinders! let them suffer the pains of Patala."

Far from being terrified by this state of things the valiant Raja increased in boldness, seeing a prospect of an end to his adventure. Approaching the tree he felt that the fire did not burn him, and so he sat there for a while to observe the body, which hung, head downwards, from a branch a little above him.

Its eyes, which were wide open, were of a greenish-brown, and never twinkled; its hair also was brown, and brown was its face—three several shades which, notwithstanding, approached one another in an unpleasant way, as in an over-dried cocoanut. Its body was thin and ribbed like a skeleton or a bamboo framework, and as it held on to a bough, like a flying fox, by the toe-tips, its drawn muscles stood out as if they were ropes of coin. Blood it appeared to have none, or there would have been a decided determination of that curious juice to the head; and as the Raja handled its skin it felt icy cold and clammy as might a snake. The only sign of life was the whisking of a ragged little tail much resembling a goat's.

Judging from these signs the brave king at once determined the creature to be a Baital—a Vampire. For a short time he was puzzled to reconcile the appearance with the words of the giant, who informed him that the anchorite had hung the oilman's son to a tree. But soon he explained to himself the difficulty, remembering the exceeding cunning of jogis and other reverend men, and determining that his enemy, the better to deceive him, had doubtless altered the shape and form of the young oilman's body.

With this idea, Vikram was pleased, saying, "My trouble has been productive of fruit." Remained the task of carrying the Vampire to Shanta-Shil the devotee. Having taken his sword, the Raja fearlessly climbed the tree, and ordering his son to stand away from below, clutched the Vampire's hair with one hand, and with the other struck such a blow of the sword, that the bough was cut and the thing fell heavily upon the ground. Immediately on falling it gnashed its teeth and began to utter a loud wailing cry like the screams of an infant in pain. Vikram having heard the sound of its lamentations, was pleased, and began to say to himself, "This devil must be alive." Then nimbly sliding down the trunk, he made a captive of the body, and asked " Who art thou?"

Scarcely, however, had the words passed the royal lips, when the Vampire slipped through the fingers like a worm, and uttering a loud shout of laughter, rose in the air with its legs uppermost, and as before suspended itself by its toes to another bough. And there it swung to and fro, moved by the violence of its cachinnation.

"Decidedly this is the young oilman!" exclaimed the Raja, after he had stood for a minute or two with mouth open, gazing upwards and wondering what he should do next. Presently he directed Dharma Dhwaj not to lose an instant in laying hands upon the thing when it next might touch the ground, and then he again swarmed up the tree. Having reached his former position, he once more seized the Baital's hair, and with all the force of his arms—for he was beginning to feel really angry—he tore it from its hold and dashed it to the ground, saying, "O wretch, tell me who thou art?"

Then, as before, the Raja slid deftly down the trunk, and hurried to the aid of his son, who in obedience to orders, had fixed his grasp upon the Vampire's neck. Then, too, as before, the Vampire, laughing aloud, slipped through their fingers and returned to its dangling-place.

To fail twice was too much for Raja Vikram's temper, which was right kingly and somewhat hot. This time he bade his son strike the Baital's head with his sword. Then, more like a wounded bear of Himalaya than a prince who had established an era, he hurried up the tree, and directed a furious blow with his sabre at the Vampire's lean and calfless legs. The violence of the stroke made its toes loose their hold of the bough, and when it touched the ground, Dharma Dhwaj's blade fell heavily upon its matted brown hair. But the blows appeared to have lighted on iron-wood—to judge at least from the behaviour of the Baital, who no sooner heard the question, "O wretch, who art thou?" than it returned in loud glee and merriment to its old position.

Five mortal times did Raja Vikram repeat this profitless labour. But so far from losing heart, he quite entered into the spirit of the adventure. Indeed he would have continued climbing up that tree and taking that corpse under his arm—he found his sword useless—and bringing it down, and asking it who it was, and seeing it slip through his fingers, six times sixty times, or till the end of the fourth and present age, had such extreme resolution been required.

However, it was not necessary. On the seventh time of falling, the Baital, instead of eluding its capturer's grasp, allowed itself to be seized, merely remarking that "even the gods cannot resist a thoroughly obstinate man." And seeing that the stranger, for the better protection of his prize, had stripped off his waistcloth and was making it into a bag, the Vampire thought proper to seek the most favourable conditions for himself, and asked his conqueror who he was, and what he was about to do?

"Vile wretch," replied the breathless hero, "know me to be Vikram the Great, Raja of Ujjayani, and I bear thee to a man who is amusing himself by drumming to devils on a skull."

"Remember the old saying, mighty Vikram!" said the Baital, with a sneer, "that many a tongue has cut many a throat. I have yielded to thy resolution and I am about to accompany thee, bound to thy back like a beggar's wallet. But hearken to my words, ere we set out upon the way. I am of a loquacious disposition, and it is well nigh an hour's walk between this tree and the place where thy friend sits, favouring his friends with the peculiar music which they love. Therefore, I shall try to distract my thoughts, which otherwise might not be of the most pleasing nature, by means of sprightly tales and profitable reflections. Sages and men of sense spend their days in the delights of light and heavy literature, whereas dolts and fools waste time in sleep and idleness. And I purpose to ask thee a number of questions, concerning which we will, if it seems fit to thee, make this covenant:

> "*Whenever thou answerest me, either compelled by Fate or entrapped by my cunning into so doing, or thereby gratifying thy vanity and conceit, I leave thee and return to my favourite place and position in the siras-tree, but when thou shalt remain silent, confused, and at a loss to reply, either through humility or thereby confessing thine ignorance, and impotence, and want of comprehension, then will I allow thee, of mine own free will, to place me before thine employer. Perhaps I should not say so; it may sound like bribing thee, but—take my counsel, and mortify thy pride, and assumption, and arrogance, and haughtiness, as soon as possible. So shalt thou derive from me a benefit which none but myself can bestow.*"

Raja Vikram hearing these rough words, so strange to his royal ear, winced; then he rejoiced that his heir apparent was not near; then he looked round at his son Dharma Dhwaj, to see if he was impertinent enough to be amused by the Baital. But the first glance showed him the young prince busily employed in pinching and screwing the monster's legs, so as to make it fit better into the cloth.

Vikram then seized the ends of the waistcloth, twisted them into a convenient form for handling, stooped, raised the bundle with a jerk, tossed it over his shoulder, and bidding his son not to lag behind, set off at a round pace towards the western end of the cemetery.

The shower had ceased, and, as they gained ground, the weather greatly improved.

The Vampire asked a few indifferent questions about the wind and the rain and the mud. When he received no answer, he began to feel uncomfortable, and he broke out with these words: "O King Vikram, listen to the true story which I am about to tell thee."

First Story

In which a Man deceives a Woman

In Benares once reigned a mighty prince, by name Pratapamukut, to whose eighth son Vajramukut happened the strangest adventure.

One morning, the young man, accompanied by the son of his father's pradhan or prime minister, rode out hunting, and went far into the jungle. At last the twain unexpectedly came upon a beautiful "tank " of a prodigious size. It was surrounded by short thick walls of fine baked brick; and flights and ramps of cut-stone steps, half the length of each face, and adorned with turrets, pendants, and finials, led down to the water. The substantial plaster work and the masonry had fallen into disrepair, and from the crevices sprang huge trees, under whose thick shade the breeze blew freshly, and on whose balmy branches the birds sang sweetly; the grey squirrels chirruped joyously as they coursed one another up the gnarled trunks, and from the pendent llianas the longtailed monkeys were swinging sportively.

The bountiful hand of Sravana had spread the earthen rampart with a carpet of the softest grass and many-hued wild flowers, in which were buzzing swarms of bees and myriads of bright winged insects; and flocks of water fowl, wild geese Brahmini ducks, bitterns, herons, and cranes, male and female, were feeding on the narrow strip of brilliant green that belted the long deep pool, amongst the broad-leaved lotuses with the lovely blossoms, splashing through the pellucid waves, and basking happily in the genial sun.

The prince and his friend wondered when they saw the beautiful tank in the midst of a wild forest, and made many vain conjectures about it. They dismounted, tethered their horses, and threw their weapons upon the ground; then, having washed their hands and faces, they entered a shrine dedicated to Mahadeva, and there began to worship the presiding deity.

Whilst they were making their offerings, a bevy of maidens, accompanied by a crowd of female slaves, descended the opposite flight of steps. They stood there for a time, talking and laughing and looking about them to see if any alligators infested the waters. When convinced that the tank was safe, they disrobed themselves in order to bathe. It was truly a splendid spectacle

"Concerning which the less said the better," interrupted Raja Vikram in an offended tone.

—but did not last long. The Raja's daughter—for the principal maiden was a princess—soon left her companions, who were scooping up water with their palms and dashing it over one another's heads, and proceeded to perform the rites of purification, meditation, and worship. Then she began strolling with a friend under the shade of a small mango grove.

The prince also left his companion sitting in prayer, and walked forth into the forest. Suddenly the eyes of the Raja's son and the Raja's daughter met. She started back with a little scream. He was fascinated by her beauty, and began to say to himself, " O thou vile Karma, why worriest thou me?"

Hearing this, the maiden smiled encouragement, but the poor youth, between palpitation of the heart and hesitation about what to say, was so confused that his tongue crave to his teeth. She raised her eyebrows a little. There is nothing which women despise in a man more than modesty, for mo-desty—

A violent shaking of the bag which hung behind Vikram's royal back broke off the end of this offensive sentence. And the warrior king did not cease that discipline till the Baital promised him to preserve more decorum in his observations.

Still the prince stood before her with downcast eyes and suffused cheeks: even the spur of contempt failed to arouse his energies. Then the maiden called to her friend, who was picking jasmine flowers so as not to witness the scene, and angrily asked why that strange man was allowed to stand and stare at her? The friend, in hot wrath, threatened to call the slave, and throw Vajramukut into the pond unless he instantly went away with his impudence. But as the prince was rooted to the spot, and really had not heard a word of what had been said to him, the two women were obliged to make the first move.

As they almost reached the tank, the beautiful maiden turned her head to see what the poor modest youth was doing.

Vajramukut was formed in every way to catch a woman's eye. The Raja's daughter therefore half forgave him his offence of mod. Again she sweetly smiled, disclosing two rows of little opals. Then descending to the water's edge, she stooped down and plucked a lotus This she worshipped; next she placed it in her hair, then she put it in her ear, then she bit it with her teeth, then she trod upon it with her foot, then she raised it up again, and lastly she stuck it in her bosom. After which she mounted her conveyance and went home to her friends; whilst the prince, having become thoroughly desponding and drowned in grief at separation from her, returned to the minister's son.

"Females!" ejaculated the minister's son, speaking to himself in a careless tone, when, his prayer finished, he left the temple, and sat down upon the tank steps to enjoy the breeze. He presently drew a roll of paper from under his waist-belt, and in a short time was engrossed with his study. The women seeing this conduct, exerted themselves in every possible way of wile to attract his attention and to distract his soul. They succeeded only so far as to make him roll his head with a smile, and to remember that such is always the custom of man's bane; after which he turned over a fresh page of manuscript. And although he presently began to wonder what had become of the prince his master, he did not look up even once from his study.

He was a philosopher, that young man. But after all, Raja Vikram, what is mortal philosophy? Nothing but another name for indifference! Who was ever philosophical about a thing truly loved or really hated?—no one! Philosophy, says Shankharacharya, is either a gift of nature or the reward of study. But I, the Baital, the devil, ask you, what is a born philosopher, save a man of cold desires? And what is a bred philosopher but a man who has survived his desires? A young philosopher?—a cold-blooded youth! An elderly philosopher?—a leuco-phlegmatic old man! Much nonsense, of a verity, ye hear in praise of nothing from your Rajaship's Nine Gems of Science, and from sundry other such wise fools.

Then the prince began to relate the state of his case, saying, " O friend, I have seen a damsel, but whether she be a musician from Indra's heaven, a maiden of the sea, a daughter of the serpent kings, or the child of an earthly Raja, I cannot say."

"Describe her," said the statesman in embryo.

"Her face," quoth the prince, "was that of the full moon, her hair like a swarm of bees hanging from the blossoms of the acacia, the corners of her eyes touched her ears, her lips were sweet with lunar ambrosia, her waist was that of a lion, and her walk the walk of a king goose. As a garment, she was white; as a season, the spring; as a flower, the jasmine; as a speaker, the kokila bird; as a perfume, musk; as a beauty, Kamadeva; and as a being, Love. And if she does not come into my possession I will not live; this I have certainly determined upon."

The young minister, who had heard his prince say the same thing more than once before, did not attach great importance to these awful words. He merely remarked that, unless they mounted at once, night would surprise them in the forest. Then the two young men returned to their horses, untethered them, drew on their bridles, saddled them, and catching up their weapons, rode slowly towards the Raja's palace. During the three hours of return hardly a word passed between the pair. Vajramukut not only avoided speaking; he never once replied till addressed thrice in the loudest voice.

The young minister put no more questions, "for," quoth he to himself, "when the prince wants my counsel, he will apply for it." In this point he had borrowed wisdom from his father, who held in peculiar horror the giving of unasked-for advice. So, when he saw that conversation was irksome to his master, he held his peace and meditated upon what he called his "day-thought." It was his practice to choose every morning some tough food for reflection, and to chew the cud of it in his mind at times when, without such employment, his wits would have gone woolgathering. You may imagine, Raja Vikram, that with a few years of this head work, the minister's son became a very crafty young person.

After the second day the Prince Vajramukut, being restless from grief at separation, fretted himself into a fever. Having given up writing, reading, drinking, sleeping, the affairs entrusted to him by his father, and everything else, he sat down, as he said, to die. He used constantly to paint the portrait of the beautiful lotus gatherer, and to lie gazing upon it with tearful eyes; then he would start up and tear it to pieces and beat his forehead, and begin another picture of a yet more beautiful face.

At last, as the pradhan's son had foreseen, he was summoned by the young Raja, whom he found upon his bed, looking yellow and complaining bitterly of headache. Frequent discussions upon the subject of the tender passion had passed between the two youths, and one of them had ever spoken of it so very disrespectfully that the other felt ashamed to introduce it. But when his friend, with a view to provoke communicativeness, advised a course of boiled and bitter herbs and great attention to diet, quoting the hemistich attributed to the learned physician Charndatta.

A fever starve, but feed a cold,

the unhappy Vajramukut's fortitude abandoned him; he burst into tears, and exclaimed," Whosoever enters upon the path of love cannot survive it; and if (by chance) he should live, what is life to him but a prolongation of his misery?"

"Yea," replied the minister's son, "the sage hath said—

The road of love is that which hath no beginning nor end;
Take thou heed of thyself, man I ere thou place foot upon it.

And the wise, knowing that there are three things whose effect upon himself no man can foretell—namely, desire of woman, the dice-box, and the drinking of ardent spirits—find total abstinence from them the best of rules. Yet, after all, if there is no cow, we must milk the bull."

The advice was, of course, excellent, but the hapless lover could not help thinking that on this occasion it came a little too late. However, after a pause he returned to the subject and said, "I have ventured to tread that dangerous way, be its end pain or pleasure, happiness or destruction." He then hung down his head and sighed from the bottom of his heart.

"She is the person who appeared to us at the tank?" asked the pradhan's son, moved to compassion by the state of his master.

The prince assented.

"O great king," resumed the minister's son, "at the time of going away had she said anything to you? or had you said anything to her?"

"Nothing!" replied the other laconically, when he found his friend beginning to take an interest in the affair.

"Then," said the minister's son, "it will be exceedingly difficult to get possession of her."

"Then," repeated the Raja's son, "I am doomed to death; to an early and melancholy death!"

"Humph!" ejaculated the young statesman rather impatiently, "did she make any sign, or give any hint? Let me know all that happened: half confidences are worse than none."

Upon which the prince related everything that took place by the side of the tank, bewailing the false shame which had made him dumb, and concluding with her pantomime.

The pradhan's son took thought for a while. He thereupon seized the opportunity of representing to his master all the evil effects of bashfulness when women are concerned, and advised him, as he would be a happy lover, to brazen his countenance for the next interview.

Which the young Raja faithfully promised to do.

"And, now," said the other, "be comforted, O my master! I know her name and her dwelling-place. When she suddenly plucked the lotus flower and worshipped it, she thanked the gods for having blessed her with a sight of your beauty."

Vajramukut smiled, the first time for the last month.

"When she applied it to her ear, it was as if she would have explained to thee, 'I am a daughter of the Carnatic: and when she bit it with her teeth, she meant to say that 'My father is Raja Dantawat, ' who, by-the-bye, has been, is, and ever will be, a mortal foe to thy father."

Vajramukut shuddered.

"When she put it under her foot it meant, 'My name is Padmavati. "

Vajramukut uttered a cry of joy.

"And when she placed it in her bosom, 'You are truly dwelling in my heart' was meant to be understood."

At these words the young Raja started up full of new life, and after praising with enthusiasm the wondrous sagacity of his dear friend, begged him by some contrivance to obtain the permission of his parents, and to conduct him to her city. The minister's son easily got leave for Vajramukut to travel, under pretext that his body required change of water, and his mind change of scene. They both dressed and armed themselves for the journey, and having taken some jewels, mounted their horses and followed the road in that direction in which the princess had gone.

Arrived after some days at the capital of the Carnatic, the minister's son having disguised his master and himself in the garb of travelling traders, alighted and pitched his little tent upon a clear bit of ground in one of the suburbs. He then proceeded to inquire for a wise woman, wanting, he said, to have his fortune told. When the prince asked him what this meant, he replied that elderly dames who professionally predict the future are never above [ministering to the present, and therefore that, in such circumstances, they are the properest persons to be consulted.

"Is this a treatise upon the subject of immorality, devil?" demanded the King Vikram ferociously. The Baital declared that it was not, but that he must tell his story.

The person addressed pointed to an old woman who, seated before the door of her hut, was spinning at her wheel. Then the young men went up to her with polite salutations and said, "Mother, we are travelling traders, and our stock is coming after us; we have come on in advance for the purpose of finding a place to live in. If you will give us a house, we will remain there and pay you highly."

The old woman, who was a physiognomist as well as a fortune-teller, looked at the faces of the young men and liked them, because their brows were wide, and their mouths denoted generosity. Having listened to their words, she took pity upon them and said kindly, "This hovel is yours, my masters, remain here as long as you please." Then she led them into an inner room, again welcomed them, lamented the poorness of her abode, and begged them to lie down and rest themselves.

After some interval of time the old woman came to them once more, and sitting down began to gossip. The minister's son upon this asked her, "How is it with thy family, thy relatives, and connections; and what are thy means of subsistence?" She replied, ``My son is a favourite servant in the household of our great king Dantawat, and your slave is the wet-nurse of the Princess Padmavati, his eldest child. From the coming on of old age," she added, "I dwell in this house, but the king provides for my eating and drinking. I go once a day to see the girl, who is a miracle of beauty and goodness, wit and accomplishments, and returning thence, I bear my own griefs at home. "

In a few days the young Vajramukut had, by his liberality, soft speech, and good looks, made such progress in nurse Lakshmi's affections that, by the advice of his companion, he ventured to broach the subject ever nearest his heart. He begged his hostess, when she went on the morrow to visit the charming Padmavati, that she would be kind enough to slip a bit of paper into the princess's hand.

"Son," she replied, delighted with the proposal—and what old woman would not be?—"there is no need for putting off so urgent an affair till the morrow. Get your paper ready, and I will immediately give it."

Trembling with pleasure, the prince ran to find his friend, who was seated in the garden reading, as usual, and told him what the old nurse had engaged to do. He then began to debate about how he should write his letter, to cull sentences and to weigh phrases; whether "light of my eyes" was not too trite, and "blood of my liver" rather too forcible. At this the minister's son smiled, and bade the prince not trouble his head with composition. He then drew his inkstand from his waist shawl, nibbed a reed pen, and choosing a piece of pink and flowered paper, he wrote upon it a few lines. He then folded it, gummed it, sketched a lotus flower upon the outside, and handing it to the young prince, told him to give it to their hostess, and that all would be well.

The old woman took her staff in her hand and hobbled straight to the palace. Arrived there, she found the Raja's daughter sitting alone in her apartment. The maiden, seeing her nurse, immediately arose, and making a respectful bow, led her to a seat and began the most affectionate inquiries. After giving her blessing and sitting for some time and chatting about indifferent matters, the nurse said, "O daughter! in infancy I reared and nourished thee, now the Bhagwan (Deity) has rewarded me by giving thee stature, beauty, health, and goodness. My heart only longs to see the happiness of thy womanhood, after which I shall depart in peace. I implore thee read this paper, given to me by the handsomest and the properest young man that my eyes have ever seen."

The princess, glancing at the lotus on the outside of the note, slowly unfolded it and perused its contents, which were as follows:

1. She was to me the pearl that clings To sands all hid from mortal sight, Yet fit for diadems of kings, The pure and lovely light.
2. She was to me the gleam of sun That breaks the gloom of wintry day; One moment shone my soul upon, Then passed—how soon!—away.
3. She was to me the dreams of bliss That float the dying eyes before, For one short hour shed happiness, And fly to bless no more.

4. O light, again upon me shine; O pearl, again delight my eyes; O dreams of bliss, again be mine!—No! earth may not be Paradise.

I must not forget to remark, parenthetically, that the minister's son, in order to make these lines generally useful, had provided them with a last stanza in triplicate. "For lovers," he said sagely," are either in the optative mood, the desperative, or the exultative." This time he had used the optative. For the desperative he would substitute:

The joys of life lie dead, lie dead, The light of day is quenched in gloom The spark of hope my heart hath fled—What now witholds me from the tomb?

And this was the termination exultative, as he called it:

O joy I the pearl is mine again, Once more the day is bright and clear, And now 'tis real, then 'twas vain, My dream of bliss—O heaven is here!

The Princess Padmavati having perused this doggrel with a contemptuous look, tore off the first word of the last line, and said to the nurse, angrily, "Get thee gone, O mother of Yama, O unfortunate creature, and take back this answer"—giving her the scrap of paper—"to the fool who writes such bad verses. I wonder where he studied the humanities. Begone, and never do such an action again!"

The old nurse, distressed at being so treated, rose up and returned home. Vajramukut was too agitated to await her arrival, so he went to meet her on the way. Imagine his disappointment when she gave him the fatal word and repeated to him exactly what happened, not forgetting to describe a single look! He felt tempted to plunge his sword into his bosom; but Fortune interfered, and sent him to consult his confidant.

"Be not so hasty and desperate, my prince," said the pradhan's son, seeing his wild grief; "you have not understood her meaning. Later in life you will be aware of the fact that, in nine cases out of ten, a woman's 'no' is a distinct 'yes.' This morning's work has been good; the maiden asked where you learnt the humanities, which being interpreted signifies 'Who are you?'"

On the next day the prince disclosed his rank to old Lakshmi, who naturally declared that she had always known it. The trust they reposed in her made her ready to address Padmavati once more on the forbidden subject. So she again went to the palace, and having lovingly greeted her nursling, said to her, "The Raja's son, whose heart thou didst fascinate on the brim of the tank, on the fifth day of the moon, in the light half of the month Yeth, has come to my house, and sends this message to thee: "Perform what you promised; we have now come"; and I also tell thee that this prince is worthy of thee: just as thou art beautiful, so is he endowed with all good qualities of mind and body."

When Padmavati heard this speech she showed great anger, and, rubbing sandal on her beautiful hands, she slapped the old woman's cheeks, and cried, "Wretch, Daina (witch)! get out of my house; did I not forbid thee to talk such folly in my presence?"

The lover and the nurse were equally distressed at having taken the advice of the young minister, till he explained what the crafty damsel meant. "When she smeared the sandal on her ten fingers," he explained, "and struck the old woman on the face, she signified that when the remaining ten moonlight nights shall have passed away she will meet you in the dark." At the same time he warned his master that to all appearances the lady Padmavati was far too clever to make a comfortable wife. The minister's son especially hated talented intellectual, and strong-minded women; he had been heard to describe the torments of Naglok as the compulsory companionship of a polemical divine and a learned authoress, well stricken in years and of forbidding aspect, as such persons mostly are.

Amongst womankind he admired—theoretically, as became a philosopher—the small, plump, laughing, chattering, unintellectual, and material-minded. And therefore—excuse the digression, Raja Vikram—he married an old maid, tall, thin, yellow, strictly proper, cold-mannered, a conversationist, and who prided herself upon spirituality. But more wonderful still, after he did marry her, he actually loved her—what an incomprehensible being is man in these matters!

To return, however. The pradhan's son, who detected certain symptoms of strong-mindedness in the Princess Padmavati, advised his lord to be wise whilst wisdom availed him. This sage counsel was, as might be guessed, most ungraciously rejected by him for whose benefit it was intended. Then the sensible young statesman rated himself soundly for having broken his father's rule touching advice, and atoned for it by blindly forwarding the views of his master.

After the ten nights of moonlight had passed, the old nurse was again sent to the palace with the usual message. This time Padmavati put saffron on three of her fingers, and again left their marks on the nurse's cheek. The minister's son explained that this was to crave delay for three days, and that on the fourth the lover would have access to her.

When the time had passed the old woman again went and inquired after her health and well-being. The princess was as usual very wroth, and having personally taken her nurse to the western gate, she called her "Mother of the elephant's trunk," and drove her out with threats of the bastinado if she ever came back. This was reported to the young statesman, who, after a few minutes' consideration, said, "The explanation of this matter is, that she has invited you tomorrow, at nighttime, to meet her at this very gate.

"When brown shadows fell upon the face of earth, and here and there a star spangled the pale heavens, the minister's son called Vajramukut, who had been engaged in adorning himself at least half that day. He had carefully shaved his cheeks and chin; his mustachio was trimmed and curled; he had arched his eyebrows by plucking out with tweezers the fine hairs around them; he had trained his curly musk-coloured love-locks to hang gracefully down his face; he had drawn broad lines of antimony along his eyelids, a most brilliant sectarian mark was affixed to his forehead, the colour of his lips had been heightened by chewing betel-nut:

"One would imagine that you are talking of a silly girl, not of a prince, fiend!" interrupted Vikram, who did not wish his son to hear what he called these fopperies and frivolities.

—and whitened his neck by having it shaved (continued the Baital, speaking quickly, as if determined not to be interrupted), and reddened the tips of his ears by squeezing them, and made his teeth shine by rubbing copper powder into the roots, and set off the delicacy of his fingers by staining the tips with henna.

He had not been less careful with his dress: he wore a well-arranged turband, which had taken him at least two hours to bind, and a rich suit of brown stuff chosen for the adventure he was about to attempt, and he hung about his person a number of various weapons, so as to appear a hero—which young damsels admire.

Vajramukut asked his friend how he looked, and smiled happily when the other replied "Admirable!" His happiness was so great that he feared it might not last, and he asked the minister's son how best to conduct himself?

"As a conqueror, my prince!" answered that astute young man, "if it so be that you would be one. When you wish to win a woman, always impose upon her. Tell her that you are her master, and she will forthwith believe herself to be your servant. Inform her that she loves you, and forthwith she will adore you. Show her that you care nothing for her, and she will think of nothing but you. Prove to her by your demeanour that you consider her a slave, and she will become your pariah. But above all things—excuse me if I repeat myself too often—beware of the fatal virtue which men call modesty and women sheepishness. Recollect the trouble it has given us, and the danger which we have incurred: all this might have been managed at a tank within fifteen miles of your royal father's palace. And allow me to say that you may still thank your stars: in love a lost opportunity is seldom if ever recovered. The time to woo a woman is the moment you meet her, before she has had time to think; allow her the use of reflection and she may escape the net. And after avoiding the rock of Modesty, fall not, I conjure you, into the gulf of Security. I fear the lady Padmavati, she is too clever and too prudent. When damsels of her age draw the sword of Love, they throw away the scabbard of

Precaution. But you yawn—I weary you—it is time for us to move."

Two watches of the night had passed, and there was profound stillness on earth. The young men then walked quietly through the shadows, till they reached the western gate of the palace, and found the wicket ajar. The minister's son peeped in and saw the porter dozing, stately as a Brahman deep in the Vedas, and behind him stood a veiled woman seemingly waiting for somebody. He then returned on tiptoe to the place where he had left his master, and with a parting caution against modesty and security, bade him fearlessly glide through the wicket. Then having stayed a short time at the gate listening with anxious ear, he went back to the old woman's house.

Vajramukut penetrating to the staircase, felt his hand grasped by the veiled figure, who motioning him to tread lightly, led him quickly forwards. They passed under several arches, through dim passages and dark doorways, till at last running up a flight of stone steps they reached the apartments of the princess.

Vajramukut was nearly fainting as the flood of splendour broke upon him. Recovering himself he gazed around the rooms, and presently a tumult of delight invaded his soul, and his body bristled with joy. The scene was that of fairyland. Golden censers exhaled the most costly perfumes, and gemmed vases bore the most beautiful flowers; silver lamps containing fragrant oil illuminated doors whose panels were wonderfully decorated, and walls adorned with pictures in which such figures were formed that on seeing them the beholder was enchanted.

On one side of the room stood a bed of flowers and a couch covered with brocade of gold, and strewed with freshly-culled jasmine flowers. On the other side, arranged in proper order, were attar holders, betel-boxes, rose-water bottles, trays, and silver cases with four partitions for essences compounded of rose leaves, sugar, and spices, prepared sandal wood, saffron, and pods of musk. Scattered about a stuccoed floor white as crystal, were coloured caddies of exquisite confections, and in others sweetmeats of various kinds. Female attendants clothed in dresses of various colours were standing each according to her rank, with hands respectfully joined. Some were reading plays and beautiful poems, others danced and others performed with glittering fingers and flashing arms on various instruments—the ivory lute, the ebony pipe and the silver kettledrum. In short, all the means and appliances of pleasure and enjoyment were there; and any description of the appearance of the apartments, which were the wonder of the age, is impossible.

Then another veiled figure, the beautiful Princess Padmavati, came up and disclosed herself, and dazzled the eyes of her delighted Vajramukut. She led him into an alcove, made him sit down, rubbed sandal powder upon his body, hung a garland of jasmine flowers round his neck, sprinkled rose-water over his dress, and began to wave over his head a fan of peacock feathers with a golden handle.

Said the prince, who despite all efforts could not entirely shake off his unhappy habit of being modest, "Those very delicate hands of yours are not fit to ply the pankha. Why do you take so much trouble? I am cool and refreshed by the sight of you. Do give the fan to me and sit down."

"Nay, great king!" replied Padmavati, with the most fascinating of smiles, "you have taken so much trouble for my sake in coming here, it is right that I perform service for you."

Upon which her favourite slave, taking the pankha from the hand of the princess, exclaimed, "This is my duty. I will perform the service; do you two enjoy yourselves!"

The lovers then began to chew betel, which, by the bye, they disposed of in little agate boxes which they drew from their pockets, and they were soon engaged in the tenderest conversation.

Here the Baital paused for a while, probably to take breath. Then he resumed his tale as follows:

In the meantime, it became dawn; the princess concealed him; and when night returned they again engaged in the same innocent pleasures. Thus day after day sped rapidly by. Imagine, if you can, the youth's felicity; he was of an ardent temperament, deeply enamoured, barely a score of years old, and he had been strictly brought up by serious parents. He therefore resigned himself entirely to the siren for whom he willingly forgot the world, and he wondered at his good fortune, which had thrown in his way a conquest richer than all the mines of Meru. He could not sufficiently admire his Padmavati's grace, beauty, bright wit, and numberless accomplishments. Every morning, for vanity's sake, he learned from her a little useless knowledge in verse as well as prose, for instance, the saying of the poet—

Enjoy the present hour, 'tis shine; be this, O man, thy law;
Who e'er resew the yester? Who the morrow e'er foresaw?

And this highly philosophical axiom:

Eat, drink, and love—the rest's not worth a fillip.

"By means of which he hoped, Raja Vikram!" said the demon, not heeding his royal carrier's "ughs" and "poohs," "to become in course of time almost as clever as his mistress."

Padmavati, being, as you have seen, a maiden of superior mind, was naturally more smitten by her lover's dulness than by any other of his qualities; she adored it, it was such a contrast to herself. At first she did what many clever women do—she invested him with the brightness of her own imagination. Still water, she pondered, runs deep; certainly under this disguise must lurk a brilliant fancy, a penetrating but a mature and ready judgment—are they not written by nature's hand on that broad high brow?

With such lovely mustachios can he be aught but generous, noble-minded, magnanimous? Can such eyes belong to any but a hero? And she fed the delusion. She would smile upon him with intense fondness, when, after wasting hours over a few lines of poetry, he would misplace all the adjectives and barbarously entreat the metre. She laughed with gratification, when, excited by the bright sayings that fell from her lips, the youth put forth some platitude, dim as the lamp in the expiring fire-fly. When he slipped in grammar she saw malice under it, when he retailed a borrowed jest she called it a good one, and when he used—as princes sometimes will—bad language, she discovered in it a charming simplicity.

At first she suspected that the stratagems which had won her heart were the results of a deep-laid plot proceeding from her lover. But clever women are apt to be rarely sharp-sighted in every matter which concerns themselves. She frequently determined that a third was in the secret. She therefore made no allusion to it. Before long the enamoured Vajramukut had told her everything, beginning with the diatribe against love pronounced by the minister's son, and ending with the solemn warning that she, the pretty princess, would some day or other play her husband a foul trick.

"If I do not revenge myself upon him," thought the beautiful Padmavati, smiling like an angel as she listened to the youth's confidence, "may I become a gardener's ass in the next birth!"

Having thus registered a vow, she broke silence, and praised to the skies the young pradhan's wisdom and sagacity; professed herself ready from gratitude to become his slave, and only hoped that one day or other she might meet that true friend by whose skill her soul had been gratified in its dearest desire. "Only," she concluded, "I am convinced that now my Vajramukut knows every corner of his little Padmavati's heart, he will never expect her to do anything but love, admire, adore and kiss him!" Then suiting the action to the word, she convinced him that the young minister had for once been too crabbed and cynic in his philosophy.

But after the lapse of a month Vajramukut, who had eaten and drunk and slept a great deal too much, and who had not once hunted, became bilious in body and in mind melancholic. His face turned yellow, and so did the whites of his eyes; he yawned, as liver patients generally do, complained occasionally of sick headaches, and lost his appetite: he became restless and anxious, and once when alone at night he thus thought aloud: "I have given up country, throne, home, and everything else, but the friend by means of whom this happiness was obtained I have not seen for the long length of thirty days. What will he say to himself, and how can I know what has happened to him?"

In this state of things he was sitting, and in the meantime the beautiful princess arrived. She saw through the matter, and lost not a moment in entering upon it. She began by expressing her astonishment at her lover's fickleness and fondness for change, and when he was ready to wax wroth, and quoted the words of the sage, "A barren wife may be superseded by another in the eighth year; she whose children all die, in the tenth; she who brings forth only daughters, in the eleventh; she who scolds, without delay," thinking that she alluded to his love, she smoothed his temper by explaining that she referred to his forgetting his friend. "How is it possible, O my soul," she asked with the softest of voices, that thou canst happiness here whilst thy heart is wandering there? Why didst thou conceal this from me, O astute one? Was it for fear of distressing me? Think better of thy wife than to suppose that she would ever separate thee from one to whom we both owe so much!

"After this Padmavati advised, nay ordered, her lover to go forth that night, and not to return till his mind was quite at ease, and she begged him to take a few sweetmeats and other trifles as a little token of her admiration and regard for the clever young man of whom she had heard so much.

Vajramukut embraced her with a transport of gratitude, which so inflamed her anger, that fearing lest the cloak of concealment might fall from her countenance, she went away hurriedly to find the greatest delicacies which her comfit boxes contained. Presently she returned, carrying a bag of sweetmeats of every kind for her lover, and as he rose up to depart, she put into his hand a little parcel of sugarplums especially intended for the friend; they were made up with her own delicate fingers, and they would please, she flattered herself, even his discriminating palate.

The young prince, after enduring a number of farewell embraces and hopings for a speedy return, and last words ever beginning again, passed safely through the palace gate, and with a relieved aspect walked briskly to the house of the old nurse. Although it was midnight his friend was still sitting on his mat.

The two young men fell upon one another's bosoms and embraced affectionately. They then began to talk of matters nearest their hearts. The Raja's son wondered at seeing the jaded and haggard looks of his companion, who did not disguise that they were caused by his anxiety as to what might have happened to his friend at the hand of so talented and so superior a princess. Upon which Vajramukut, who now thought Padmavati an angel, and his late abode a heaven, remarked with formality—and two blunders to one quotation—that abilities properly directed win for a man the happiness of both worlds.

The pradhan's son rolled his head.

"Again on your hobbyhorse, nagging at talent whenever you find it in others! " cried the young prince with a pun, which would have delighted Padmavati. "Surely you are jealous of her!" he resumed, anything but pleased with the dead silence that had received his joke; "jealous of her cleverness, and of her love for me. She is the very best creature in the world. Even you, woman-hater as you are, would own it if you only knew all the kind messages she sent, and the little pleasant surprise that she has prepared for you. There! take and eat; they are made by her own dear hands!" cried the young Raja, producing the sweetmeats. "As she herself taught me to say-

Thank God I am a man, Not a philosopher!"

"The kind messages she sent me! The pleasant surprise she has prepared for me!" repeated the minister's son in a hard, dry tone. "My lord will be pleased to tell me how she heard of my name?"

"I was sitting one night," replied the prince, "in anxious thought about you, when at that moment the princess coming in and seeing my condition, asked, 'Why are you thus sad? Explain the cause to me.' I then gave her an account of your cleverness, and when she heard it she gave me permission to go and see you, and sent these sweetmeats for you: eat them and I shall be pleased."

"Great king!" rejoined the young statesman, "one thing vouchsafe to hear from me. You have not done well in that you have told my name. You should never let a woman think that your left hand knows the secret which she confided to your right, much less that you have shared it to a third person. Secondly, you did evil in allowing her to see the affection with which you honour your unworthy servant—a woman ever hates her lover's or husband's friend."

"What could I do?" rejoined the young Raja, in a querulous tone of voice. "When I love a woman I like to tell her everything—to have no secrets from her—to consider her another self—"

"Which habit," interrupted the pradhan's son, "you will lose when you are a little older, when you recognize the fact that love is nothing but a bout, a game of skill between two individuals of opposite sexes: the one seeking to gain as much, and the other striving to lose as little as possible; and that the sharper of the twain thus met on the chessboard must, in the long run, win. And reticence is but a habit. Practise it for a year, and you will find it harder to betray than to conceal your thoughts. It hath its joy also. Is there no pleasure, think you, when suppressing an outbreak of tender but fatal confidence in saying to yourself, 'O, if she only knew this?' 'O, if she did but suspect that?' Returning, however, to the sugarplums, my life to a pariah's that they are poisoned!"

"Impossible!" exclaimed the prince, horror-struck at the thought; "what you say, surely no one ever could do. If a mortal fears not his fellow-mortal, at least he dreads the Deity."

"I never yet knew," rejoined the other, "what a woman in love does fear. However, prince, the trial is easy. Come here, Muti!" cried he to the old woman's dog, "and off with thee to that three-headed kinsman of shine, that attends upon his amiable-looking master." Having said this, he threw one of the sweetmeats to the dog; the animal ate it, and presently writhing and falling down, died.

"The wretch! O the wretch!" cried Vajramukut, transported with wonder and anger. " And I loved her! But now it is all over. I dare not associate with such a calamity!"

"What has happened, my lord, has happened!" quoth the minister's son calmly. "I was prepared for something of this kind from so talented a princess. None commit such mistakes, such blunders, such follies as your clever women; they cannot even turn out a crime decently executed. O give me dulness with one idea, one aim, one desire. O thrice blessed dulness that combines with happiness, power."

This time Vajramukut did not defend talent.

"And your slave did his best to warn you against perfidy. But now my heart is at rest. I have tried her strength. She has attempted and failed; the defeat will prevent her attempting again—just yet. But let me ask you to put to yourself one question. Can you be happy without her?"

"Brother!" replied the prince, after a pause, "I cannot"; and he blushed as he made the avowal.

"Well," replied the other, "better confess then conceal that fact; we must now meet her on the battlefield, and beat her at her own weapons—cunning. I do not willingly begin treachery with women, because, in the first place, I don't like it; and secondly, I know that they will certainly commence practising it upon me, after which I hold myself justified in deceiving them. And probably this will be a good wife; remember that she intended to poison me, not you. During the last month my fear has been lest my prince had run into the tiger's brake. Tell me, my lord, when does the princess expect you to return to her?"

"She bade me," said the young Raja, "not to return till my mind was quite at ease upon the subject of m talented friend."

"This means that she expects you back tomorrow night, as you cannot enter the palace before. And now I will retire to my cot, as it is there that I am wont to ponder over my plans. Before dawn my thought shall mature one which must place the beautiful Padmavati in your power."

"A word before parting," exclaimed the prince "you know my father has already chosen a spouse for me; what will he say if I bring home a second? "

"In my humble opinion," said the minister's son rising to retire, "woman is a monogamous, man a polygamous, creature, a fact scarcely established in physiological theory, but very observable in everyday practice For what said the poet?—Divorce, friend! Re-wed thee! The spring draweth near, And a wife's but an almanac—good for the year.

If your royal father say anything to you, refer him to what he himself does."

Reassured by these words, Vajramukut bade his friend a cordial good-night and sought his cot, where he slept soundly, despite the emotions of the last few hours. The next day passed somewhat slowly. In the evening, when accompanying his master to the palace, the minister's son gave him the following directions.

"Our object, dear my lord, is how to obtain possession of the princess. Take, then, this trident, and hide it carefully when you see her show the greatest love and affection. Conceal what has happened, and when she, wondering at your calmness, asks about me, tell her that last night I was weary and out of health, that illness prevented my eating her sweetmeats, but that I shall eat them for supper tonight. When she goes to sleep, then, taking off her jewels and striking her left leg with the trident, instantly come away to me. But should she lie awake, rub upon your thumb a little of this—do not fear, it is only a powder of grubs fed on verdigris—and apply it to her nostrils. It would make an elephant senseless, so be careful how you approach it to your own face."

Vajramukut embraced his friend, and passed safely through the palace gate. He found Padmavati awaiting him; she fell upon his bosom and looked into his eyes, and deceived herself, as clever women will do. Overpowered by her joy and satisfaction, she now felt certain that her lover was hers eternally, and that her treachery had not been discovered; so the beautiful princess fell into a deep sleep.

Then Vajramukut lost no time in doing as the minister's son had advised, and slipped out of the room, carrying off Padmavati's jewels and ornaments. His counsellor having inspected them, took up a sack and made signs to his master to follow him. Leaving the horses and baggage at the nurse's house, they walked to a burning-place outside the city. The minister's son there buried his dress, together with that of the prince, and drew from the sack the costume of a religious ascetic: he assumed this himself, and gave to his companion that of a disciple. Then quoth the guru (spiritual preceptor) to his chela (pupil), "Go, youth, to the bazar, and sell these jewels, remembering to let half the jewellers in the place see the things, and if any one lay hold of thee, bring him to me."

Upon which, as day had dawned, Vajramukut carried the princess's ornaments to the market, and entering the nearest goldsmith's shop, offered to sell them, and asked what they were worth. As your majesty well knows, gardeners, tailors, and goldsmiths are proverbially dishonest, and this man was no exception to the rule. He looked at the pupil's face and wondered, because he had brought articles whose value he did not appear to know. A thought struck him that he might make a bargain which would fill his coffers, so he offered about a thousandth part of the price.

This the pupil rejected, because he wished the affair to go further. Then the goldsmith, seeing him about to depart, sprang up and stood in the door way, threatening to call the officers of justice if the young man refused to give up the valuables which he said had lately been stolen from his shop. As the pupil only laughed at this, the goldsmith thought seriously of executing his threat, hesitating only because he knew that the officers of justice would gain more than he could by that proceeding. As he was still in doubt a shadow darkened his shop, and in entered the chief jeweller of the city. The moment the ornaments were shown to him he recognized them, and said, "These jewels belong to Raja Dantawat's daughter; I know them well, as I set them only a few months ago!" Then he turned to the disciple, who still held the valuables in his hand, and cried, "Tell me truly whence you received them?"

While they were thus talking, a crowd of ten or twenty persons had collected, and at length the report reached the superintendent of the archers. He sent a soldier to bring before him the pupil, the goldsmith, and the chief jeweller, together with the ornaments. And when all were in the hall of justice, he looked at the jewels and said to the young man, "Tell me truly, whence have you obtained these?"

"My spiritual preceptor," said Vajramukut, pretending great fear, "who is now worshipping in the cemetery outside the town, gave me these white stones, with an order to sell them. How know I whence he obtained them? Dismiss me, my lord, for I am an innocent man."

"Let the ascetic be sent for," commanded the kotwal. Then, having taken both of them, along with the jewels, into the presence of King Dantawat, he related the whole circumstances.

"Master," said the king on hearing the statement, "whence have you obtained these jewels?"

The spiritual preceptor, before deigning an answer, pulled from under his arm the hide of a black antelope, which he spread out and smoothed deliberately before using it as an asan. He then began to finger a rosary of beads each as large as an egg, and after spending nearly an hour in mutterings and in rollings of the head, he looked fixedly at the Raja, and repined:

> *"By Shiva! great king, they are mine own. On the fourteenth of the dark half of the moon at night, I had gone into a place where dead bodies are burned, for the purpose of accomplishing a witch's incantation. After long and toilsome labour she appeared, but her demeanour was so unruly that I was forced to chastise her. I struck her with this, my trident, on the left leg, if memory serves me. As she continued to be refractory, in order to punish her I took off all her jewels and clothes, and told her to go where she pleased. Even this had little effect upon her—never have I looked upon so perverse a witch. In this way the jewels came into my possession."*

Raja Dantawat was stunned by these words. He begged the ascetic not to leave the palace for a while, and forthwith walked into the private apartments of the women. Happening first to meet the queen dowager, he said to her, "Go, without losing a minute, O my mother, and look at Padmavati's left leg, and see if there is a mark or not, and what sort of a mark!" Presently she returned, and coming to the king said, "Son, I find thy daughter lying upon her bed, and complaining that she has met with an accident; and indeed Padmavati must be in great pain. I found that some sharp instrument with three points had wounded her. The girl says that a nail hurt her, but I never yet heard of a nail making three holes. However, we must all hasten, or there will be erysipelas, tumefaction, gangrene, mortification, amputation, and perhaps death in the house," concluded the old queen, hurrying away in the pleasing anticipation of these ghastly consequences.

For a moment King Dantawat's heart was ready to break. But he was accustomed to master his feelings; he speedily applied the reins of reflection to the wild steed of passion. He thought to himself, "the affairs of one's household, the intentions of one's heart, and whatever one's losses may be, should not be disclosed to any one. Since Padmavati is a witch, she is no longer my daughter. I will verily go forth and consult the spiritual preceptor."

With these words the king went outside, where the guru was still sitting upon his black hide, making marks with his trident on the floor. Having requested that the pupil might be sent away, and having cleared the room, he said to the jogi, "O holy man! what punishment for the heinous crime of witchcraft is awarded to a woman in the Dharma-Shastra ?"

"Greet king!" replied the devotee, "in the Dharma Shastra it is thus written: 'If a Brahman, a cow, a woman, a child, or any other person whatsoever who may be dependent on us, should be guilty of a perfidious act, their punishment is that they be banished the country.' However much they may deserve death, we must not spill their blood, as Lakshmi flies in horror from the deed."

Hearing these words the Raja dismissed the guru with many thanks and large presents. He waited till nightfall and then ordered a band of trusty men to seize Padmavati without alarming the household, and to carry her into a distant jungle full of fiends, tigers, and bears, and there to abandon her.

In the meantime, the ascetic and his pupil hurrying to the cemetery resumed their proper dresses; they then went to the old nurse's house, rewarded her hospitality till she wept bitterly, girt on their weapons, and mounting their horses, followed the party which issued from the gate of King Dantawat's palace. And it may easily be believed that they found little difficulty in persuading the poor girl to exchange her chance in the wild jungle for the prospect of becoming Vajramukut's wife—lawfully wedded at Benares. She did not even ask if she was to have a rival in the house,—a question which women, you know, never neglect to put under usual circumstances. After some days the two pilgrims of one love arrived at the house of their fathers, and to all, both great and small, excess in joy came.

"Now, Raja Vikram!" said the Baital, "you have not spoken much; doubtless you are engrossed by the interest of a story wherein a man beats a woman at her own weapon—deceit. But I warn you that you will assuredly fall into Narak (the infernal regions) if you do not make up your mind upon and explain this matter. Who was the most to blame amongst these four? the lover the lover's friend, the girl, or the father?"

"For my part I think Padmavati was the worst, she being at the bottom of all their troubles," cried Dharma Dhwaj. The king said something about young people and the two senses of seeing and hearing, but his son's sentiment was so sympathetic that he at once pardoned the interruption. At length, determined to do justice despite himself, Vikram said, "Raja Dantawat is the person most at fault."

"In what way was he at fault? " asked the Baital curiously.

King Vikram gave him this reply: "The Prince Vajramukut being tempted of the love-god was insane, and therefore not responsible for his actions. The minister's son performed his master's business obediently, without considering causes or asking questions—a very excellent quality in a dependent who is merely required to do as he is bid. With respect to the young woman, I have only to say that she was a young woman, and thereby of necessity a possible murderess. But the Raja, a prince, a man of a certain age and experience, a father of eight! He ought never to have been deceived by so shallow a trick, nor should he, without reflection, have banished his daughter from the country."

"Gramercy to you!" cried the Vampire, bursting into a discordant shout of laughter, "I now return to my tree. By my tail! I never yet heard a Raja so readily condemn a Raja." With these words he slipped out of the cloth, leaving it to hang empty over the great king's shoulder.

Vikram stood for a moment, fixed to the spot with blank dismay. Presently, recovering himself, he retraced his steps, followed by his son, ascended the sires-tree, tore down the Baital, packed him up as before, and again set out upon his way.

Soon afterwards a voice sounded behind the warrior king's back, and began to tell another true story.

Second Story

Of the Relative Villany of Men and Women

In the great city of Bhogavati dwelt, once upon a time, a young prince, concerning whom I may say that he strikingly resembled this amiable son of your majesty.

Raja Vikram was silent, nor did he acknowledge the Baital's indirect compliment. He hated flattery, but he liked, when flattered, to be flattered in his own person; a feature in their royal patron's character which the Nine Gems of Science had turned to their own account.

Now the young prince Raja Ram (continued the tale teller) had an old father, concerning whom I may say that he was exceedingly unlike your Rajaship, both as a man and as a parent. He was fond of hunting, dicing, sleeping by day, drinking at night, and eating perpetual tonics, while he delighted in the idleness of watching nautch girls, and the vanity of falling in love. But he was adored by his children because he took the trouble to win their hearts. He did not lay it down as a law of heaven that his offspring would assuredly go to Patala if they neglected the duty of bestowing upon him without cause all their affections, as your moral, virtuous, and highly respectable fathers are only too apt——. Aie! Aie!

These sounds issued from the Vampire's lips as the warrior king, speechless with wrath, passed his hand behind his back, and viciously twisted up a piece of the speaker's skin. This caused the Vampire to cry aloud, more however, it would appear, in derision than in real suffering, for he presently proceeded with the same subject.

Fathers, great king, may be divided into three kinds; and be it said aside, that mothers are the same. Firstly, we have the parent of many ideas, amusing, pleasant, of course poor, and the idol of his children. Secondly, there is the parent with one idea and a half. This sort of man would, in your place, say to himself, "That demon fellow speaks a manner of truth. I am not above learning from him, despite his position in life. I will carry out his theory, just to see how far it goes"; and so saying, he wends his way home, and treats his young ones with prodigious kindness for a time, but it is not lasting. Thirdly, there is the real one-idea'd type of parent-yourself, O warrior king Vikram, an admirable example. You learn in youth what you are taught: for instance, the blessed precept that the green stick is of the trees of Paradise; and in age you practice what you have learned. You cannot teach yourselves anything before your beards sprout, and when they grow stiff you cannot be taught by others. If any one attempt to change your opinions you cry,

What is new is not true, What is true is not new and you rudely pull his hand from the subject. Yet have you your uses like other things of earth. In life you are good working camels for the mill-track, and when you die your ashes are not worse compost than those of the wise.

Your Rajaship will observe (continued the Vampire, as Vikram began to show symptoms of ungovernable anger) that I have been concise in treating this digression. Had I not been so, it would have led me far indeed from my tale. Now to return.

When the old king became air mixed with air, the young king, though he found hardly ten pieces of silver in the paternal treasury and legacies for thousands of golden ounces, yet mourned his loss with the deepest grief. He easily explained to himself the reckless emptiness of the royal coffers as a proof of his dear kind parent's goodness, because he loved him.

But the old man had left behind him, as he could not carry it off with him, a treasure more valuable than gold and silver: one Churaman, a parrot, who knew the world, and who besides discoursed in the most correct Sanscrit. By sage counsel and wise guidance this admirable bird soon repaired his young master's shattered fortunes.

One day the prince said, "Parrot, thou knowest everything: tell me where there is a mate fit for me. The shastras inform us, respecting the choice of a wife, 'She who is not descended from his paternal or maternal ancestors within the sixth degree is eligible by a high caste man for nuptials. In taking a wife let him studiously avoid the following families, be they ever so great, or ever so rich in kine, goats, sheep, gold, or grain: the family which has omitted prescribed acts of devotion; that which has produced no male children; that in which the Veda (scripture) has not been read; that which has thick hair on the body; and that in which members have been subject to hereditary disease. Let a person choose for his wife a girl whose person has no defect; who has an agreeable name; who walks gracefully, like a young elephant; whose hair and teeth are moderate in quantity and in size; and whose body is of exquisite softness.'"

"Great king," responded the parrot Churaman, "there is in the country of Magadh a Raja, Magadheshwar by name, and he has a daughter called Chandravati. You will marry her; she is very learned, and, what is better far, very fait. She is of yellow colour, with a nose like the flower of the sesamum; her legs are taper, like the plantain-tree; her eyes are large, like the principal leaf of the lotus; her eye-brows stretch towards her ears; her lips are red, like the young leaves of the mango-tree; her face is like the full moon; her voice is like the sound of the cuckoo; her arms reach to her knees; her throat is like the pigeon's; her flanks are thin, like those of the lion; her hair hangs in curls only down to her waist; her teeth are like the seeds of the pomegranate; and her gait is that of the drunken elephant or the goose."

On hearing the parrot's speech, the king sent for an astrologer, and asked him, "Whom shall I marry?" The wise man, having consulted his art, replied, "Chandravati is the name of the maiden, and your marriage with her will certainly take place." Thereupon the young Raja, though he had never seen his future queen, became incontinently enamoured of her. He summoned a Brahman, and sent him to King Magadheshwar, saying, "If you arrange satisfactorily this affair of our marriage we will reward you amply"-a promise which lent wings to the priest.

Now it so happened that this talented and beautiful princess had a jay, whose name was Madan-manjari or Love-garland. She also possessed encyclopaedic knowledge after her degree, and, like the parrot, she spoke excellent Sanscrit.

Be it briefly said, O warrior king-for you think that I am talking fables—that in the days of old, men had the art of making birds discourse in human language. The invention is attributed to a great philosopher, who split their tongues, and after many generations produced a selected race born with those members split. He altered the shapes of their skulls by fixing ligatures behind the occiput, which caused the sinciput to protrude, their eyes to become prominent, and their brains to master the art of expressing thoughts in words.

But this wonderful discovery, like those of great philosophers generally, had in it a terrible practical flaw The birds beginning to speak, spoke wisely and so well, they told the truth so persistently, they rebuked their brethren of the featherless skins so openly, they flattered them so little and they counselled them so much, that mankind presently grew tired of hearing them discourse. Thus the art gradually fell into desuetude, and now it is numbered with the things that were.

One day the charming Princess Chandravati was sitting in confidential conversation with her jay. The dialogue was not remarkable, for maidens in all ages seldom consult their confidantes or speculate upon the secrets of futurity, or ask to have dreams interpreted, except upon one subject. At last the princess said, for perhaps the hundredth time that month, "Where, O jay, is there a husband worthy of me?"

"Princess," replied Madan-manjari, "I am happy at length to be able as willing to satisfy your just curiosity. For just it is, though the delicacy of our sex—"

"Now, no preaching!" said the maiden; "or thou shalt have salt instead of sugar for supper."

Jays, your Rajaship, are fond of sugar. So the confidante retained a quantity of good advice which she was about to produce, and replied,

"I now see clearly the ways of Fortune. Raja Ram, king of Bhogavati, is to be thy husband. He shall be happy in thee and thou in him, for he is young and handsome, rich and generous, good-tempered, not too clever, and without a chance of being an invalid."

Thereupon the princess, although she had never seen her future husband, at once began to love him. In fact, though neither had set eyes upon the other, both were mutually in love.

"How can that be, sire?" asked the young Dharma Dhwaj of his father. " I always thought that—"

The great Vikram interrupted his son, and bade him not to ask silly questions. Thus he expected to neutralize the evil effects of the Baital's doctrine touching the amiability of parents unlike himself.

Now, as both these young people (resumed the Baital) were of princely family and well to do in the world, the course of their love was unusually smooth. When the Brahman sent by Raja Ram had reached Magadh, and had delivered his King's homage to the Raja Magadheshwar, the latter received him with distinction, and agreed to his proposal. The beautiful princess's father sent for a Brahman of his own, and charging him with nuptial gifts and the customary presents, sent him back to Bhogavati in company with the other envoy, and gave him this order, "Greet Raja Ram, on my behalf, and after placing the tilak or mark upon his forehead, return here with all speed. When you come back I will get all things ready for the marriage."

Raja Ram, on receiving the deputation, was greatly pleased, and after generously rewarding the Brahmans and making all the necessary preparations, he set out in state for the land of Magadha, to claim his betrothed.

In due season the ceremony took place with feasting and bands of music, fireworks and illuminations, rehearsals of scripture, songs, entertainments, processions, and abundant noise. And hardly had the turmeric disappeared from the beautiful hands and feet of the bride, when the bridegroom took an affectionate leave of his new parents—he had not lived long in the house—and receiving the dowry and the bridal gifts, set out for his own country.

Chandravati was dejected by leaving her mother, and therefore she was allowed to carry with her the jay, Madanmanian. She soon told her husband the wonderful way in which she had first heard his name, and he related to her the advantage which he had derived from confabulation with Churaman, his parrot.

"Then why do we not put these precious creatures into one cage, after marrying them according to the rites of the angelic marriage (Gandharva-lagana)?" said the charming queen. Like most brides, she was highly pleased to find an opportunity of making a match.

"Ay! why not, love ? Surely they cannot live happy in what the world calls single blessedness," replied the young king. As bridegrooms sometimes are for a short time, he was very warm upon the subject of matrimony.

Thereupon, without consulting the parties chiefly concerned in their scheme, the master and mistress, after being comfortably settled at the end of their journey, caused a large cage to be brought, and put into it both their favourites.

Upon which Churaman the parrot leaned his head on one side and directed a peculiar look at the jay. But Madan-manjari raised her beak high in the air, puffed through it once or twice, and turned away her face in extreme disdain.

"Perhaps," quoth the parrot, at length breaking silence, "you will tell me that you have no desire to be married?"

"Probably," replied the jay.

"And why?" asked the male bird.

"Because I don't choose," replied the female.

"Truly a feminine form of resolution this," ejaculated the parrot. "I will borrow my master's words and call it a woman's reason, that is to say, no reason at all. Have you any objection to be more explicit?"

"None whatever," retorted the jay, provoked by the rude innuendo into telling more plainly than politely exactly what she thought; "none whatever, sir parrot. You he-things are all of you sinful, treacherous, deceitful, selfish, devoid of conscience, and accustomed to sacrifice us, the weaker sex, to your smallest desire or convenience."

"Of a truth, fair lady," quoth the young Raja Ram to his bride, "this pet of thine is sufficiently impudent."

"Let her words be as wind in thine ear, master," interrupted the parrot. "And pray, Mistress Jay, what are you she-things but treacherous, false, ignorant, and avaricious beings, whose only wish in this world is to prevent life being as pleasant as it might be?"

"Verily, my love," said the beautiful Chandravati to her bridegroom, "this thy bird has a habit of expressing his opinions in a very free and easy way."

"I can prove what I assert," whispered the jay in the ear of the princess.

"We can confound their feminine minds by an anecdote," whispered the parrot in the ear of the prince.

Briefly, King Vikram, it was settled between the twain that each should establish the truth of what it had advanced by an illustration in the form of a story.

Chandravati claimed, and soon obtained, precedence for the jay. Then the wonderful bird, Madan-manjari, began to speak as follows:

I have often told thee, O queen, that before coming to thy feet, my mistress was Ratnawati, the daughter of a rich trader, the dearest, the sweetest, the:

Here the jay burst into tears, and the mistress was sympathetically affected. Presently the speaker resumed: However, I anticipate. In the city of Ilapur there was a wealthy merchant, who was without offspring; on this account he was continually fasting and going on pilgrimage, and when at home he was ever engaged in reading the Puranas and in giving alms to the Brahmans. At length, by favour of the Deity, a son was born to this merchant, who celebrated his birth with great pomp and rejoicing, and gave large gifts to Brahmans and to bards, and distributed largely to the hungry, the thirsty, and the poor. When the boy was five years old he had him taught to read, and when older he was sent to a guru, who had formerly himself been a student, and who was celebrated as teacher and lecturer.

In the course of time the merchant's son grew up. Praise be to Brahma! what a wonderful youth it was, with a face like a monkey's, legs like a stork's, and a back like a camel's. You know the old proverb:

Expect thirty-two villanies from the limping, and eighty from the one-eyed man, But when the hunchback comes, say "Lord defend us!"

Instead of going to study, he went to gamble with other ne'er-do-weels, to whom he talked loosely, and whom he taught to be bad-hearted as himself. He made love to every woman, and despite his ugliness, he was not unsuccessful. For they are equally fortunate who are very handsome or very ugly, in so far as they are both remarkable and remarked. But the latter bear away the palm. Beautiful men begin well with women, who do all they can to attract them, love them as the apples of their eyes, discover them to be fools, hold them to be their equals, deceive them, and speedily despise them. It is otherwise with the ugly man, who, in consequence of his homeliness, must work his wits and take pains with himself, and become as pleasing as he is capable of being, till women forget his ape's face, bird's legs, and bunchy back.

The hunchback, moreover, became a Tantri, so as to complete his villanies. He was duly initiated by an apostate Brahman, made a declaration that he renounced all the ceremonies of his old religion, and was delivered from their yoke, and proceeded to perform in token of joy an abominable rite. In company with eight men and eight women-a Brahman female, a dancing girl, a weaver's daughter, a woman of ill fame, a washerwoman, a barber's wife, a milkmaid, and the daughter of a land-owner-choosing the darkest time of night and the most secret part of the house, he drank with them, was sprinkled and anointed, and went through many ignoble ceremonies, such as sitting nude upon a dead body.

The teacher informed him that he was not to indulge shame, or aversion to anything, nor to prefer one thing to another, nor to regard caste, ceremonial cleanness or uncleanness, but freely to enjoy all the pleasures of sense-that is, of course, wine and us, since we are the representatives of the wife of Cupid, and wine prevents the senses from going astray. And whereas holy men, holding that the subjugation or annihilation of the passions is essential to final beatitude, accomplish this object by bodily austerities, and by avoiding temptation, he proceeded to blunt the edge of the passions with excessive indulgence. And he jeered at the pious, reminding them that their ascetics are safe only in forests, and while keeping a perpetual fast; but that he could subdue his passions in the very presence of what they most desired.

Presently this excellent youth's father died, leaving him immense wealth. He blunted his passions so piously and so vigorously, that in very few years his fortune was dissipated. Then he turned towards his neighbour's goods and prospered for a time, till being discovered robbing, he narrowly escaped the stake. At length he exclaimed, "Let the gods perish! the rascals send me nothing but ill luck!" and so saying he arose and fled from his own country.

Chance led that villain hunchback to the city of Chandrapur, where, hearing the name of my master Hemgupt, he recollected that one of his father's wealthiest correspondents was so called. Thereupon, with his usual audacity, he presented himself at the house, walked in, and although he was clothed in tatters, introduced himself, told his father's name and circumstances, and wept bitterly.

The good man was much astonished, and not less grieved, to see the son of his old friend in such woful plight. He rose up, however, embraced the youth, and asked the reason of his coming.

"I freighted a vessel," said the false hunchback, "for the purpose of trading to a certain land. Having gone there, I disposed of my merchandise, and, taking another cargo, I was on my voyage home. Suddenly a great storm arose, and the vessel was wrecked, and I escaped on a plank, and after a time arrived here. But I am ashamed, since I have lost all my wealth, and I cannot show my face in this plight in my own city. My excellent father would have consoled me with his pity. But now that I have carried him and my mother to Ganges, every one will turn against me; they will rejoice in my misfortunes, they will accuse me of folly and recklessness—alas! alas! I am truly miserable."

My dear master was deceived by the cunning of the wretch. He offered him hospitality, which was readily enough accepted, and he entertained him for some time as a guest. Then, having reason to be satisfied with his conduct, Hemgupt admitted him to his secrets, and finally made him a partner in his business. Briefly, the villain played his cards so well, that at last the merchant said to himself:

> *"I have had for years an anxiety and a calamity in my house. My neighbours whisper things to my disadvantage, and those who are bolder speak out with astonishment amongst themselves, saying, 'At seven or eight, people marry their daughters, and this indeed is*

the appointment of the law: that period is long since gone; she is now thirteen or fourteen years old, and she is very tall and lusty, resembling a married woman of thirty. How can her father eat his rice with comfort and sleep with satisfaction, whilst such a disreputable thing exists in his house? At present he is exposed to shame, and his deceased friends are suffering through his retaining a girl from marriage beyond the period which nature has prescribed.' And now, while I am sitting quietly at home, the Bhagwan (Deity) removes all my uneasiness: by his favour such an opportunity occurs. It is not right to delay. It is best that I shall give my daughter in marriage to him. Whatever can be done today is best; who knows what may happen tomorrow?

"Thus thinking, the old man went to his wife and said to her, "Birth, marriage, and death are all under the direction of the gods; can anyone say when they will be ours? We want for our daughter a young man who is of good birth, rich and handsome, clever and honourable. But we do not find him. If the bridegroom be faulty, thou sayest, all will go wrong. I cannot put a string round the neck of our daughter and throw her into the ditch. If, however, thou think well of the merchant's son, now my partner, we will celebrate Ratnawati's marriage with him."

The wife, who had been won over by the hunchback's hypocrisy, was also pleased, and replied, "My lord! when the Deity so plainly indicates his wish, we should do it; since, though we have sat quietly at home, the desire of our hearts is accomplished. It is best that no delay be made: and, having quickly summoned the family priest, and having fixed upon a propitious planetary conjunction, that the marriage be celebrated."

Then they called their daughter—ah, me! what a beautiful being she was, and worthy the love of a Gandharva (demigod). Her long hair, purple with the light of youth, was glossy as the bramra's wing; her brow was pure and clear as the agate; the ocean-coral looked pale beside her lips, and her teeth were as two chaplets of pearls. Everything in her was formed to be loved. Who could look into her eyes without wishing to do it again? Who could hear her voice without hoping that such music would sound once more? And she was good as she was fair. Her father adored her; her mother, though a middle-aged woman, was not envious or jealous of her; her relatives doted on her, and her friends could find no fault with her. I should never end were I to tell her precious qualities. Alas, alas ! my poor Ratnawati!

So saying, the jay wept abundant tears; then she resumed:

When her parents informed my mistress of their resolution, she replied, "Sadhu-it is well!" She was not like most young women, who hate nothing so much as a man whom their seniors order them to love. She bowed her head and promised obedience, although, as she afterwards told her mother, she could hardly look at her intended, on account of his prodigious ugliness. But presently the hunchback's wit surmounted her disgust. She was grateful to him for his attention to her father and mother; she esteemed him for his moral and religious conduct; she pitied him for his misfortunes, and she finished with forgetting his face, legs, and back in her admiration of what she supposed to be his mind.

She had vowed before marriage faithfully to perform all the duties of a wife, however distasteful to her they might be; but after the nuptials, which were not long deferred, she was not surprised to find that she loved her husband. Not only did she omit to think of his features and figure; I verily believe that she loved him the more for his repulsiveness. Ugly, very ugly men prevail over women for two reasons. Firstly, we begin with repugnance, which in the course of nature turns to affection; and we all like the most that which, when unaccustomed to it, we most disliked. Hence the poet says, with as much truth as is in the male:

Never despair, O man! when woman's spite Detests thy name and sickens at thy sight: Sometime her heart shall learn to love thee more For the wild hatred which it felt before, &c.

Secondly, the very ugly man appears, deceitfully enough, to think little of his appearance, and he will give himself the trouble to pursue a heart because he knows that the heart will not follow after him. Moreover, we women (said the jay) are by nature pitiful, and this our enemies term a "strange perversity." A widow is generally disconsolate if she loses a little, wizen-faced, shrunken shanked, ugly, spiteful, distempered thing that scolded her and quarrelled with her, and beat her and made her hours bitter; whereas she will follow her husband to Ganges with exemplary fortitude if he was brave, handsome, generous:

"Either hold your tongue or go on with your story," cried the warrior king, in whose mind these remarks awakened disagreeable family reflections.

"Hi! hi! hi!" laughed the demon; "I will obey your majesty, and make Madan-manjari, the misanthropical jay, proceed."

Yes, she loved the hunchback; and how wonderful is our love! quoth the jay. A light from heaven which rains happiness on this dull, dark earth! A spell falling upon the spirit, which reminds us of a higher existence! A memory of bliss! A present delight! An earnest of future felicity! It makes hideousness beautiful and stupidity clever, old age young and wickedness good, moroseness amiable, and low-mindedness magnanimous, perversity pretty and vulgarity piquant. Truly it is sovereign alchemy and excellent flux for blending contradictions is our love, exclaimed the jay.

And so saying, she cast a triumphant look at the parrot, who only remarked that he could have desired a little more originality in her remarks.

For some months (resumed Madan-manjari), the bride and the bridegroom lived happily together in Hemgupt's house. But it is said:

Never yet did the tiger become a lamb; and the hunchback felt that the edge of his passions again wanted blunting. He reflected, "Wisdom is exemption from attachment, and affection for children, wife, and home." Then he thus addressed my poor young mistress:

"I have been now in thy country some years, and I have heard no tidings of my own family, hence my mind is sad, I have told thee everything about myself; thou must now ask thy mother leave for me to go to my own city, and, if thou wishest, thou mayest go with me."

Ratnawati lost no time in saying to her mother, "My husband wishes to visit his own country; will you so arrange that he may not be pained about this matter?"

The mother went to her husband, and said, "Your son-in-law desires leave to go to his own country."

Hemgupt replied, " Very well; we will grant him leave. One has no power over another man's son. We will do what he wishes."

The parents then called their daughter, and asked her to tell them her real desire-whether she would go to her father-in-law's house, or would remain in her mother's home. She was abashed at this question, and could not answer; but she went back to her husband, and said, "As my father and mother have declared that you should do as you like, do not leave me behind."

Presently the merchant summoned his son-in-law, and having bestowed great wealth upon him, allowed him to depart. He also bade his daughter farewell, after giving her a palanquin and a female slave. And the parents took leave of them with wailing and bitter tears; their hearts were like to break. And so was mine.

For some days the hunchback travelled quietly along with his wife, in deep thought. He could not take her to his city, where she would find out his evil life, and the fraud which he had passed upon her father. Besides which, although he wanted her money, he by no means wanted her company for life. After turning on many projects in his evil-begotten mind, he hit upon the following:

He dismissed the palanquin-bearers when halting at a little shed in the thick jungle through which they were travelling, and said to his wife, "This is a place of danger; give me thy jewels, and I will hide them in my waist-shawl. When thou reachest the city thou canst wear them again." She then gave up to him all her ornaments, which were of great value. Thereupon he inveigled the slave girl into the depths of the forest, where he murdered her, and left her body to be devoured by wild beasts. Lastly, returning to my poor mistress, he induced her to leave the hut with him, and pushed her by force into a dry well, after which exploit he set out alone with his ill-gotten wealth, walking towards his own city.

In the meantime, a wayfaring man, who was passing through that jungle, hearing the sound of weeping, stood still, and began to say to himself, "How came to my ears the voice of a mortal's grief in this wild wood?" then followed the direction of the noise, which led him a pit, and peeping over the side, he saw a woman crying at the bottom. The traveller at once loosened his gird cloth, knotted it to his turband, and letting down the line pulled out the poor bride. He asked her who she was and how she came to fall into that well. She replied, "I am the daughter of Hemgupt, the wealthiest merchant in the city of Çhandrapur; and I was journeying wit my husband to his own country, when robbers set upon us and surrounded us. They slew my slave girl, the threw me into a well, and having bound my husband they took him away, together with my jewels. I have no tidings of him, nor he of me." And so saying, she burst into tears and lamentations.

The wayfaring man believed her tale, and conducted her to her home, where she gave the same account of the accident which had befallen her, ending with, "beyond this, I know not if they have killed my husband, or have let him go." The father thus soothed her grief "Daughter! have no anxiety; thy husband is alive, and by the will of the Deity he will come to thee in a few days. Thieves take men's money, not their lives." Then the parents presented her with ornaments more precious than those which she had lost; and summoning their relations and friends, they comforted her to the best of their power.

And so did I. The wicked hunchback had, meanwhile, returned to his own city, where he was excellently well received, because he brought much wealth with him. His old associates flocked around him rejoicing; and he fell into the same courses which had beggared him before. Gambling and debauchery soon blunted his passions, and emptied his purse. Again his boon companions, finding him without a broken cowrie, drove him from their doors, he stole and was flogged for theft; and lastly, half famished, he fled the city. Then he said to himself, "I must go to my father-in-law, and make the excuse that a grandson has been born to him, and that I have come to offer him congratulations on the event."

Imagine, however, his fears and astonishment, when, as he entered the house, his wife stood before him. At first he thought it was a ghost, and turned to run away, but she went out to him and said, "Husband, be not troubled ! I have told my father that thieves came upon us, and killed the slave girl and robbed me and threw me into a well, and bound thee and carried thee off. Tell the same story, and put away all anxious feelings. Come up and change thy tattered garments-alas! some misfortune hath befallen thee. But console thyself; all is now well, since thou art returned to me, and fear not, for the house is shine, and I am thy slave."

The wretch, with all his hardness of heart, could scarcely refrain from tears. He followed his wife to her room, where she washed his feet, caused him to bathe, dressed him in new clothes, and placed food before him. When her parents returned, she presented him to their embrace, saying in a glad way, "Rejoice with me, O my father and mother! the robbers have at length allowed him to come back to us." Of course the parents were deceived, they are mostly a purblind race; and Hemgupt, showing great favour to his worthless son-in-law, exclaimed, "Remain with us, my son, and be happy!"

For two or three months the hunchback lived quietly with his wife, treating her kindly and even affectionately. But this did not last long. He made acquaintance with a band of thieves, and arranged his plans with them.

After a time, his wife one night came to sleep by his side, having put on all her jewels. At midnight, when he saw that she was fast asleep, he struck her with a knife so that she died. Then he admitted his accomplices, who savagely murdered Hemgupt and his wife; and with their assistance he carried off any valuable article upon which he could lay his hands. The ferocious wretch! As he passed my cage he looked at it, and thought whether he had time to wring my neck. The barking of a dog saved my life; but my mistress, my poor Ratnawati-ah, me! ah, me!:

> *"Queen," said the jay, in deepest grief, "all this have I seen with mine own eyes, and have heard with mine own ears. It affected me in early life, and gave me a dislike for the society of the other sex. With due respect to you, I have resolved to remain an old maid. Let your majesty reflect, what crime had my poor mistress committed? A male is of the same disposition as a highway robber; and she who forms friendship with such an one, cradles upon her bosom a black and venomous snake."*

"Sir Parrot," said the jay, turning to her wooer, "I have spoken. I have nothing more to say, but that you he-things are all a treacherous, selfish, wicked race, created for the express purpose of working our worldly woe, and—"

"When a female, O my king, asserts that she has nothing more to say, but," broke in Churaman, the parrot with a loud dogmatical voice, "I know that what she has said merely whets her tongue for what she is about to say. This person has surely spoken long enough and drearily enough."

"Tell me, then, O parrot," said the king, "what faults there may be in the other sex."

"I will relate," quoth Churaman, "an occurrence which in my early youth determined me to live and to die an old bachelor."

When quite a young bird, and before my schooling began, I was caught in the land of Malaya, and was sold to a very rich merchant called Sagardati, a widower with one daughter, the lady Jayashri. As her father spent all his days and half his nights in his counting-house, conning his ledgers and scolding his writers, that young woman had more liberty than is generally allowed to those of her age, and a mighty bad use she made of it.

O king! men commit two capital mistakes in rearing the "domestic calamity," and these are over-vigilance and under-vigilance. Some parents never lose sight of their daughters, suspect them of all evil intentions, and are silly enough to show their suspicions, which is an incentive to evildoing. For the weak-minded things do naturally say, "I will be wicked at once. What do I now but suffer all the pains and penalties of badness, without enjoying its pleasures?" And so they are guilty of many evil actions; for, however vigilant fathers and mothers may be, the daughter can always blind their eyes.

On the other hand, many parents take no trouble whatever with their charges: they allow them to sit in idleness, the origin of badness; they permit them to communicate with the wicked, and they give them liberty which breeds opportunity. Thus they also, falling into the snares of the unrighteous, who are ever a more painstaking race than the righteous, are guilty of many evil actions.

What, then, must wise parents do? The wise will study the characters of their children, and modify their treatment accordingly. If a daughter be naturally good, she will be treated with a prudent confidence. If she be vicious, an apparent trust will be reposed in her; but her father and mother will secretly ever be upon their guard. The one-idea'd:

> *"All this parrot-prate, I suppose, is only intended to vex me," cried the warrior king, who always considered himself, and very naturally, a person of such consequence as ever to be uppermost in the thoughts and minds of others. "If thou must tell a tale, then tell one, Vampire! or else be silent, as I am sick to the death of thy psychics."*

"It is well, O warrior king," resumed the Baital.

After that Churaman the parrot had given the young Raja Ram a golden mine full of good advice about the management of daughters, he proceeded to describe Jayashri.

She was tall, stout, and well made, of lymphatic temperament, and yet strong passions. Her fine large eyes had heavy and rather full eyelids, which are to be avoided. Her hands were symmetrical without being small, and the palms were ever warm and damp. Though her lips were good, her mouth was somewhat underhung; and her voice was so deep, that at times it sounded like that of a man. Her hair was smooth as the kokila's plume, and her complexion was that of the young jasmine; and these were the points at which most persons looked. Altogether, she was neither handsome nor ugly, which is an excellent thing in woman. Sita the goddess was lovely to excess; therefore she was carried away by a demon. Raja Bali was exceedingly generous, and he emptied his treasury. In this way, exaggeration, even of good, is exceedingly bad.

Yet must I confess, continued the parrot, that, as a rule, the beautiful woman is more virtuous than the ugly. The former is often tempted, but her vanity and conceit enable her to resist, by the self-promise that she shall be tempted again and again. On the other hand, the ugly woman must tempt instead of being tempted, and she must yield, because her vanity and conceit are gratified by yielding, not by resisting.

"Ho, there!" broke in the jay contemptuously. "What woman cannot win the hearts of the silly things called men? Is it not said that a pig-faced female who dwells in Landanpur has a lover?"

I was about to remark, my king! said the parrot, somewhat nettled, if the aged virgin had not interrupted me, that as ugly women are more vicious than handsome women, so they are most successful. "We love the pretty, we adore the plain," is a true saying amongst the worldly wise. And why do we adore the plain? Because they seem to think less of themselves than of us-a vital condition of adoration.

Jayashri made some conquests by the portion of good looks which she possessed, more by her impudence, and most by her father's reputation for riches. She was truly shameless, and never allowed herself fewer than half a dozen admirers at the time. Her chief amusement was to appoint interviews with them successively, at intervals so short that she was obliged to hurry away one in order to make room for another. And when a lover happened to be jealous, or ventured in any way to criticize her arrangements, she replied at once by showing him the door. Answer unanswerable!

When Jayashri had reached the ripe age of thirteen, the son of a merchant, who was her father's gossip and neighbour, returned home after a long sojourn in far lands, whither he had travelled in the search of wealth. The poor wretch, whose name, by-the-bye, was Shridat (Gift of Fortune), had loved her in her childhood; and he came back, as men are apt to do after absence from familiar scenes, painfully full of affection for house and home and all belonging to it. From his cross, stingy old uncle to the snarling superannuated beast of a watchdog, he viewed all with eyes of love and melting heart. He could not see that his idol was greatly changed, and nowise for the better; that her nose was broader and more club-like, her eyelids fatter and thicker, her under lip more prominent, her voice harsher, and her manner coarser. He did not notice that she was an adept in judging of men's dress, and that she looked with admiration upon all swordsmen, especially upon those who fought upon horses and elephants. The charm of memory, the curious faculty of making past time present caused all he viewed to be enchanting to him.

Having obtained her father's permission, Shridat applied for betrothal to Jayashri, who with peculiar boldness, had resolved that no suitor should come to her through her parent. And she, after leading him on by all the coquetries of which she was a mistress, refused to marry him, saying that she liked him as a friend, but would hate him as a husband.

You see, my king! there are three several states of feeling with which women regard their masters, and these are love, hate, and indifference. Of all, love is the weakest and the most transient, because the essentially unstable creatures naturally fall out of it as readily as they fall into it. Hate being a sister excitement will easily become, if a man has wit enough to effect the change, love; and hate-love may perhaps last a little longer than love-love. Also, man has the occupation, the excitement, and the pleasure of bringing about the change. As regards the neutral state, that poet was not happy in his ideas who sang—

Whene'er indifference appears, or scorn, Then, man, despair! then, hapless lover, mourn!

For a man versed in the Lila Shastra can soon turn a woman's indifference into hate, which I have shown is as easily permuted to love. In which predicament it is the old thing over again, and it ends in the pure Asat or nonentity.

"Which of these two birds, the jay or the parrot, had dipped deeper into human nature, mighty King Vikram?" asked the demon in a wheedling tone of voice.

The trap was this time set too openly, even for the royal personage, to fall into it. He hurried on, calling to his son, and not answering a word. The Vampire therefore resumed the thread of his story at the place where he had broken it off.

Shridat was in despair when he heard the resolve of his idol. He thought of drowning himself, of throwing himself down from the summit of Mount Girnar, of becoming a religious beggar; in short, of a multitude of follies. But he refrained from all such heroic remedies for despair, having rightly judged, when he became somewhat calmer, that they would not be likely to further his suit. He discovered that patience is a virtue, and he resolved impatiently enough to practice it. And by perseverance he succeeded. The worse for him! How vain are men to wish! How wise is the Deity, who is deaf to their wishes!

Jayashri, for potent reasons best known to herself, was married to Shridat six months after his return home. He was in raptures. He called himself the happiest man in existence. He thanked and sacrificed to the Bhagwan for listening to his prayers. He recalled to mind with thrilling heart the long years which he had spent in hopeless exile from all that was dear to him, his sadness and anxiety, his hopes and joys, his toils and troubles his loyal love and his vows to Heaven for the happiness of his idol, and for the furtherance of his fondest desires.

For truly he loved her, continued the parrot, and there is something holy in such love. It becomes not only a faith, but the best of faiths-an abnegation of self which emancipates the spirit from its straightest and earthliest bondage, the "I"; the first step in the regions of heaven; a homage rendered through the creature to the Creator; a devotion solid, practical, ardent, not as worship mostly is, a cold and lifeless abstraction; a merging of human nature into one far nobler and higher the spiritual existence of the supernal world. For perfect love is perfect happiness, and the only perfection of man; and what is a demon but a being without love? And what makes man's love truly divine, is the fact that it is bestowed upon such a thing as woman.

And now, Raja Vikram," said the Vampire, speaking in his proper person, "I have given you Madanmanjari the jay's and Churaman the parrot's definitions of the tender passion, or rather their descriptions of its effects. Kindly observe that I am far from accepting either one or the other. Love is, according to me, somewhat akin to mania, a temporary condition of selfishness, a transient confusion of identity. It enables man to predicate of others who are his other selves, that which he is ashamed to say about his real self.

I will suppose the beloved object to be ugly, stupid, vicious, perverse, selfish, low minded, or the reverse; man finds it charming by the same rule that makes his faults and foibles dearer to him than all the virtues and good qualities of his neighbours. Ye call love a spell, an alchemy, a deity. Why? Because it deifies self by gratifying all man's pride, man's vanity, and man's conceit, under the mask of complete unegotism. Who is not in heaven when he is talking of himself? and, prithee, of what else consists all the talk of lovers?

It is astonishing that the warrior king allowed this speech to last as long as it did. He hated nothing so fiercely, now that he was in middle-age, as any long mention of the "handsome god." Having vainly endeavoured to stop by angry mutterings the course of the Baital's eloquence, he stepped out so vigorously and so rudely shook that inveterate talker, that the latter once or twice nearly bit off the tip of his tongue. Then the Vampire became silent, and Vikram relapsed into a walk which allowed the tale to be resumed.

Jayashri immediately conceived a strong dislike for her husband, and simultaneously a fierce affection for a reprobate who before had been indifferent to her. The more lovingly Shridat behaved to her, the more vexed end annoyed she was. When her friends talked to her, she turned up her nose, raising her eyebrows (in token of displeasure), and remained silent. When her husband spoke words of affection to her, she found them disagreeable, and turning away her face, reclined on the bed. Then he brought dresses and ornaments of various kinds and presented them to her, saying, "Wear these." Whereupon she would become more angry, knit her brows, turn her face away, and in an audible whisper call him "fool."

All day she stayed out of the house, saying to her companions, "Sisters, my youth is passing away, and I have not, up to the present time, tasted any of this world's pleasures." Then she would ascend to the balcony, peep through the lattice, and seeing the reprobate going along, she would cry to her friend, "Bring that person to me." All night she tossed and turned from side to side, reflecting in her heart, "I am puzzled in my mind what I shall say, and whither I shall go. I have forgotten sleep, hunger, and thirst; neither heat nor cold is refreshing to me."

At last, unable any longer to support the separation from her reprobate paramour, whom she adored, she resolved to fly with him. On one occasion, when she thought that her husband was fast asleep, she rose up quietly, and leaving him, made her way fearlessly in the dark night to her lover's abode. A footpad, who saw her on the way, thought to himself, "Where can this woman, clothed in jewels, be going alone at midnight?" And thus he followed her unseen, and watched her.

When Jayashri reached the intended place, she went into the house, and found her lover lying at the door. He was dead, having been stabbed by the footpad; but she, thinking that he had, according to custom, drunk intoxicating hemp, sat upon the floor, and raising his head, placed it tenderly in her lap. Then, burning with the fire of separation from him, she began to kiss his cheeks, and to fondle and caress him with the utmost freedom and affection.

By chance a Pisach (evil spirit) was seated in a large fig-tree opposite the house, and it occurred to him, when beholding this scene, that he might amuse himself in a characteristic way. He therefore hopped down from his branch, vivified the body, and began to return the woman's caresses. But as Jayashri bent down to kiss his lips, he caught the end of her nose in his teeth, and bit it clean off. He then issued from the corpse, and returned to the branch where he had been sitting.

Jayashri was in despair. She did not, however, lose her presence of mind, but sat down and proceeded to take thought; and when she had matured her plan she arose, dripping with blood, and walked straight home to her husband's house. On entering his room she clapped her hand to her nose, and began to gnash her teeth, and to shriek so violently, that all the members of the family were alarmed. The neighbours also collected in numbers at the door, and, as it was bolted inside, they broke it open and rushed in, carrying lights. There they saw the wife sitting upon the ground with her face mutilated, and the husband standing over her, apparently trying to appease her.

"O ignorant, criminal, shameless, pitiless wretch!" cried the people, especially the women; "why hast thou cut off her nose, she not having offended in any way?"

Poor Shridat, seeing at once the trick which had been played upon him, thought to himself: "One should put no confidence in a changeful mind, a black serpent, or an armed enemy, and one should dread a woman's doings. What cannot a poet describe? What is there that a saint (jogi) does not know? What nonsense will not a drunken man talk? What limit is there to a woman's guile? True it is that the gods know nothing of the defects of a horse, of the thundering of clouds, of a woman's deeds, or of a man's future fortunes. How then can we know?" He could do nothing but weep, and swear by the herb basil, by his cattle, by his grain, by a piece of gold, and by all that is holy, that he had not committed the crime.

In the meanwhile, the old merchant, Jayashri's father, ran off, and laid a complaint before the kotwal, and the footmen of the police magistrate were immediately sent to apprehend the husband, and to carry him bound before the judge. The latter, after due examination, laid the affair before the king. An example happening to be necessary at the time, the king resolved to punish the offence with severity, and he summoned the husband and wife to the court.

When the merchant's daughter was asked to give an account of what had happened, she pointed out the state of her nose, and said, "Maharaj! why inquire of me concerning what is so manifest?" The king then turned to the husband, and bade him state his defence. He said, "I know nothing of it," and in the face of the strongest evidence he persisted in denying his guilt.

Thereupon the king, who had vainly threatened to cut off Shridat's right hand, infuriated by his refusing to confess and to beg for mercy, exclaimed, "How must I punish such a wretch as thou art?" The unfortunate man answered, "Whatever your majesty may consider just, that be pleased to do." Thereupon the king cried, "Away with him, and impale him"; and the people, hearing the command, prepared to obey it.

Before Shridat had left the court, the footpad, who had been looking on, and who saw that an innocent man was about to be unjustly punished, raised a cry for justice and, pushing through the crowd, resolved to make himself heard. He thus addressed the throne: "Great king, the cherishing of the good, and the punishment of the bad, is the invariable duty of kings." The ruler having caused him to approach, asked him who he was, and he replied boldly, " Maharaj! I am a thief, and this man is innocent and his blood is about to be shed unjustly. Your majesty has not done what is right in this affair." Thereupon the king charged him to tell the truth according to his religion; and the thief related explicitly the whole circumstances, omitting of course, the murder.

"Go ye," said the king to his messengers, "and look in the mouth of the woman's lover who has fallen dead. If the nose be there found, then has this thief-witness told the truth, and the husband is a guiltless man."

The nose was presently produced in court, and Shridat escaped the stake. The king caused the wicked Jayashri's face to be smeared with oily soot, and her head and eyebrows to be shaved; thus blackened and disfigured, she was mounted upon a little ragged-limbed ass and was led around the market and the streets, after which she was banished for ever from the city. The husband and the thief were then dismissed with betel and other gifts, together with much sage advice which neither of them wanted.

"My king," resumed the misogyne parrot, "of such excellencies as these are women composed. It is said that 'wet cloth will extinguish fire and bad food will destroy strength; a degenerate son ruins a family, and when a friend is in wrath he takes away life. But a woman is an inflicter of grief in love and in hate, whatever she does turns out to be for our ill. Truly the Deity has created woman a strange being in this world.' And again, 'The beauty of the nightingale is its song, science is the beauty of an ugly man, forgiveness is the beauty of a devotee, and the beauty of a woman is virtue-but where shall we find it?' And again, 'Among the sages, Narudu; among the beasts, the jackal; among the birds, the crow; among men, the barber; and in this world woman-is the most crafty.'

"What I have told thee, my king, I have seen with mine own eyes, and I have heard with mine own ears. At the time I was young, but the event so affected me that I have ever since held female kind to be a walking pest, a two-legged plague, whose mission on earth, like flies and other vermin, is only to prevent our being too happy. O, why do not children and young parrots sprout in crops from the ground-from budding trees or vinestocks?"

"I was thinking, sire," said the young Dharma Dhwaj to the warrior king his father, "what women would say of us if they could compose Sanskrit verses!"

"Then keep your thoughts to yourself," replied the Raja, nettled at his son daring to say a word in favour of the sex. "You always take the part of wickedness and depravity—"

"Permit me, your majesty," interrupted the Baital, "to conclude my tale."

When Madan-manjari, the jay, and Churaman, the parrot, had given these illustrations of their belief, they began to wrangle, and words ran high. The former insisted that females are the salt of the earth, speaking, I presume, figuratively. The latter went so far as to assert that the opposite sex have no souls, and that their brains are in a rudimental and inchoate state of development. Thereupon he was tartly taken to task by his master's bride, the beautiful Chandravati, who told him that those only have a bad opinion of women who have associated with none but the vicious and the low, and that he should be ashamed to abuse feminine parrots, because his mother had been one.

This was truly logical.

On the other hand, the jay was sternly reproved for her mutinous and treasonable assertions by the husband of her mistress, Raja Ram, who, although still a bridegroom, had not forgotten the gallant rule of his syntax:

The masculine is more worthy than the feminine; till Madan-manjari burst into tears and declared that her life was not worth having. And Raja Ram looked at her as if he could have wrung her neck.

In short, Raja Vikram, all the four lost their tempers, and with them what little wits they had. Two of them were but birds, and the others seem not to have been much better, being young, ignorant, inexperienced, and lately married. How then could they decide so difficult a question as that of the relative wickedness and villany of men and women? Had your majesty been there, the knot of uncertainty would soon have been undone by the trenchant edge of your wit and wisdom; your knowledge and experience. You have, of course, long since made up your mind upon the subject? Dharma Dhwaj would have prevented his father's reply. But the youth had been twice reprehended in the course of this tale, and he thought it wisest to let things take their own way.

"Women," quoth the Raja, oracularly, "are worse than we are; a man, however depraved he may be, ever retains some notion of right and wrong, but a woman does not. She has no such regard whatever."

"The beautiful Bangalah Rani for instance?" said the Baital, with a demonaic sneer.

At the mention of a word, the uttering of which was punishable by extirpation of the tongue, Raja Vikram's brain whirled with rage. He staggered in the violence of his passion, and putting forth both hands to break his fall, he dropped the bundle from his back. Then the Baital, disentangling himself and laughing lustily, ran off towards the tree as fast as his thin brown legs would carry him. But his activity availed him little.

The king, puffing with fury, followed him at the top of his speed, and caught him by his tail before he reached the siras-tree, hurled him backwards with force, put foot upon his chest, and after shaking out the cloth, rolled him up in it with extreme violence, bumped his back half a dozen times against the stony ground, and finally, with a jerk, threw him on his shoulder, as he had done before.

The young prince, afraid to accompany his father whilst he was pursuing the fiend, followed slowly in the rear, and did not join him for some minutes.

But when matters were in their normal state, the Vampire, who had endured with exemplary patience the penalty of his impudence, began in honeyed accents,

"Listen, O warrior king, whilst thy servant recounts unto thee another true tale."

Third Story

Of a High-minded Family

In the venerable city of Bardwan, O warrior king! (quoth the Vampire) during the reign of the mighty Rupsen, flourished one Rajeshwar, a Rajput warrior of distinguished fame. By his valour and conduct he had risen from the lowest ranks of the army to command it as its captain. And arrived at that dignity, he did not put a stop to all improvements, like other chiefs, who rejoice to rest and return thanks. On the contrary, he became such a reformer that, to some extent, he remodelled the art of war.

Instead of attending to rules and regulations, drawn up in their studies by pandits and Brahmans, he consulted chiefly his own experience and judgment. He threw aside the systematic plans of campaigns laid down in the Shastras or books of the ancients, and he acted upon the spur of the moment. He displayed a skill in the choice of ground, in the use of light troops, and in securing his own supplies whilst he cut off those of the enemy, which Kartikaya himself, God of War, might have envied.

Finding that the bows of his troops were clumsy and slow to use, he had them all changed before compelled so to do by defeat; he also gave his attention to the sword handles, which cramped the men's grasp but which having been used for eighteen hundred years were considered perfect weapons. And having organized a special corps of warriors using fire arrows, he soon brought it to such perfection that, by using it against the elephants of his enemies, he gained many a campaign.

One instance of his superior judgment I am about to quote to thee, O Vikram, after which I return to my tale; for thou art truly a warrior king, very likely to imitate the innovations of the great general Rajeshwar. (A grunt from the monarch was the result of the Vampire's sneer.)

He found his master's armies recruited from Northern Hindustan, and officered by Kshatriya warriors, who grew great only because they grew old and—fat. Thus the energy and talent of the younger men were wasted in troubles and disorders; whilst the seniors were often so ancient that they could not mount their chargers unaided, nor, when they were mounted, could they see anything a dozen yards before them.

But they had served in a certain obsolete campaign, and until Rajeshwar gave them pensions and dismissals, they claimed a right to take first part in all campaigns present and future. The commander-in-chief refused to use any captain who could not stand steady on his legs, or endure the sun for a whole day. When a soldier distinguished himself in action, he raised him to the powers and privileges of the warrior caste. And whereas it had been the habit to lavish circles and bars of silver and other metals upon all those who had joined in the war, whether they had sat behind a heap of sand or had been foremost to attack the foe, he broke through the pernicious custom, and he rendered the honour valuable by conferring it only upon the deserving. I need hardly say that, in an inordinately short space of time, his army beat every king and general that opposed it.

One day the great commander-in-chief was seated in a certain room near the threshold of his gate, when the voices of a number of people outside were heard. Rajeshwar asked, "Who is at the door, and what is the meaning of the noise I hear?" The porter replied, "It is a fine thing your honour has asked. Many persons come sitting at the door of the rich for the purpose of obtaining a livelihood and wealth. When they meet together they talk of various things: it is these very people who are now making this noise."

Rajeshwar, on hearing this, remained silent.

In the meantime a traveller, a Rajput, Birbal by name, hoping to obtain employment, came from the southern quarter to the palace of the chief. The porter having listened to his story, made the circumstance known to his master, saying, "O chief! an armed man has arrived here, hoping to obtain employment, and is standing at the door. If I receive a command he shall be brought into your honour's presence."

"Bring him in," cried the commander-in-chief.

The porter brought him in, and Rajeshwar inquired, "O Rajput, who and what art thou?"

Birbal submitted that he was a person of distinguished fame for the use of weapons, and that his name for fidelity and velour had gone forth to the utmost ends of Bharat-Kandha.

The chief was well accustomed to this style of self introduction, and its only effect upon his mind was a wish to shame the man by showing him that he had not the least knowledge of weapons. He therefore bade him bare his blade and perform some feat.

Birbal at once drew his good sword. Guessing the thoughts which were hovering about the chief's mind, he put forth his left hand, extending the forefinger upwards, waved his blade like the arm of a demon round his head, and, with a dexterous stroke, so shaved off a bit of nail that it fell to the ground, and not a drop of blood appeared upon the finger-tip.

"Live for ever!" exclaimed Rajeshwar in admiration. He then addressed to the recruit a few questions concerning the art of war, or rather concerning his peculiar views of it. To all of which Birbal answered with a spirit and a judgment which convinced the hearer that he was no common sworder.

Whereupon Rajeshwar bore off the new man at arms to the palace of the king Rupsen, and recommended that he should be engaged without delay.

The king, being a man of few words and many ideas, after hearing his commander-in-chief, asked, "O Rajput, what shall I give thee for thy daily expenditure?"

"Give me a thousand ounces of gold daily," said Birbal, "and then I shall have wherewithal to live on."

"Hast thou an army with thee?" exclaimed the king in the greatest astonishment.

"I have not," responded the Rajput somewhat stiffly. "I have first, a wife; second, a son; third, a daughter; fourth, myself; there is no fifth person with me."

All the people of the court on hearing this turned aside their heads to laugh, and even the women, who were peeping at the scene, covered their mouths with their veils. The Rajput was then dismissed the presence.

It is, however, noticeable amongst you humans, that the world often takes you at your own valuation. Set a high price upon yourselves, and each man shall say to his neighbour, "In this man there must be something." Tell everyone that you are brave, clever, generous, or even handsome, and after a time they will begin to believe you. And when thus you have attained success, it will be harder to unconvince them than it was to convince them. Thus:

"Listen not to him, sirrah," cried Raja Vikram to Dharma Dhwaj, the young prince, who had fallen a little way

behind, and was giving ear attentively to the Vampire's ethics. "Listen to him not. And tell me, villain, with these ignoble principles of shine, what will become of modesty, humility, self-sacrifice, and a host of other Guna or good qualities which—which are good qualities?"

"I know not," rejoined the Baital, "neither do I care. But my habitually inspiriting a succession of human bodies has taught me one fact. The wise man knows himself, and is, therefore, neither unduly humble nor elated, because he had no more to do with making himself than with the cut of his cloak, or with the fitness of his loin-cloth. But the fool either loses his head by comparing himself with still greater fools, or is prostrated when he finds himself inferior to other and lesser fools. This shyness he calls modesty, humility, and so forth. Now, whenever entering a corpse, whether it be of man, woman, or child, I feel peculiarly modest; I know that my tenement lately belonged to some conceited ass. And:"

"Wouldst thou have me bump thy back against the ground?" asked Raja Vikram angrily.

(The Baital muttered some reply scarcely intelligible about his having this time stumbled upon a metaphysical thread of ideas, and then continued his story.)

Now Rupsen, the king, began by inquiring of himself why the Rajput had rated his services so highly. Then he reflected that if this recruit had asked so much money, it must have been for some reason which would afterwards become apparent. Next, he hoped that if he gave him so much, his generosity might some day turn out to his own advantage. Finally, with this idea in his mind, he summoned Birbal and the steward of his household, and said to the latter, "Give this Rajput a thousand ounces of gold daily from our treasury."

It is related that Birbal made the best possible use of his wealth. He used every morning to divide it into two portions, one of which was distributed to Brahmans and Parohitas. Of the remaining moiety, having made two parts, he gave one as alms to pilgrims, to Bairagis or Vishnu's mendicants, and to

Sanyasis or worshippers of Shiva, whose bodies, smeared with ashes, were hardly covered with a narrow cotton cloth and a rope about their loins, and whose heads of artificial hair, clotted like a rope, besieged his gate. With the remaining fourth, having caused food to be prepared, he regaled the poor, while he himself and his family ate what was left.

Every evening, arming himself with sword and buckler, he took up his position as guard at the royal bedside, and walked round it all night sword in hand. If the king chanced to wake and asked who was present, Birbal immediately gave reply that "Birbal is here; whatever command you give, that he will obey." And oftentimes Rupsen gave him unusual commands, for it is said, "To try thy servant, bid him do things in season and out of season: if he obey thee willingly, know him to be useful; if he reply, dismiss him at once. Thus is a servant tried, even as a wife by the poverty of her husband, and brethren and friends by asking their aid."

In such manner, through desire of money, Birbal remained on guard all night; and whether eating, drinking, sleeping, sitting, going or wandering about, during the twenty-four hours, he held his master in watchful remembrance. This, indeed, is the custom; if a man sell another the latter is sold, but a servant by doing service sells himself, and when a man has become dependent, how can he be happy?

Certain it is that however intelligent, clever, or learned a man may be, yet, while he is in his master's presence, he remains silent as a dumb man, and struck with dread. Only while he is away from his lord can he be at ease. Hence, learned men say that to do service aright is harder than any religious study.

On one occasion it is related that there happened to be heard at night-time the wailing of a woman in a neighbouring cemetery. The king on hearing it called out, "Who is in waiting?"

"I am here," replied Birbal; "what command is there?"

"Go," spoke the king, "to the place whence proceeds this sound of woman's wail, and having inquired the cause of her grief, return quickly."

On receiving this order the Rajput went to obey it; and the king, unseen by him, and attired in a black dress, followed for the purpose of observing his courage.

Presently Birbal arrived at the cemetery. And what sees he there? A beautiful woman of a light yellow colour, loaded with jewels from head to foot, holding a horn in her right and a necklace in her left hand. Sometimes she danced, sometimes she jumped, and sometimes she ran about. There was not a tear in her eye, but beating her head and making lamentable cries, she kept dashing herself on the ground.

Seeing her condition, and not recognizing the goddess born of sea foam, and whom all the host of heaven loved, Birbal inquired, "Why art thou thus beating thyself and crying out? Who art thou? And what grief is upon thee?"

"I am the Royal-Luck," she replied.

"For what reason," asked Birbal, "art thou weeping?"

The goddess then began to relate her position to the Rajput. She said, with tears, "In the king's palace Shudra (or low caste acts) are done, and hence misfortune will certainly fall upon it, and I shall forsake it. After a month has passed, the king, having endured excessive affliction, will die. In grief for this, I weep. I have brought much happiness to the king's house, and hence I am full of regret that this my prediction cannot in any way prove untrue."

"Is there," asked Birbal, "any remedy for this trouble, so that the king may be preserved and live a hundred years?"

"Yes," said the goddess, "there is. About eight miles to the east thou wilt find a temple dedicated to my terrible sister Devi. Offer to her thy son's head, cut off with shine own hand, and the reign of thy king shall endure for an age." So saying Raj-Lakshmi disappeared.

Birbal answered not a word, but with hurried steps he turned towards his home. The king, still in black so as not to be seen, followed him closely, and observed and listened to everything he did.

The Rajput went straight to his wife, awakened her, and related to her everything that had happened. The wise have said, "she alone deserves the name of wife who always receives her husband with affectionate and submissive words." When she heard the circumstances, she at once aroused her son, and her daughter also awoke. Then Birbal told them all that they must follow him to the temple of Devi in the wood.

On the way the Rajput said to his wife, "If thou wilt give up thy son willingly, I will sacrifice him for our master's sake to Devi the Destroyer."

She replied, "Father and mother, son and daughter, brother and relative, have I now none. You are everything to me. It is written in the scripture that a wife is not made pure by gifts to priests, nor by performing religious rites; her virtue consists in waiting upon her husband, in obeying him and in loving him—yea! though he be lame, maimed in the hands, dumb, deaf, blind, one eyed, leprous, or humpbacked.

It is a true saying that 'a son under one's authority, a body free from sickness, a desire to acquire knowledge, an intelligent friend, and an obedient wife; whoever holds these five will find them bestowers of happiness and dispellers of affliction. An unwilling servant, a parsimonious king, an insincere friend, and a wife not under control; such things are disturbers of ease and givers of trouble.'"

Then the good wife turned to her son and said "Child by the gift of thy head, the king's life may be spared, and the kingdom remain unshaken."

"Mother," replied that excellent youth, "in my opinion we should hasten this matter. Firstly, I must obey your command; secondly, I must promote the interests of my master; thirdly, if this body be of any use to a goddess, nothing better can be done with it in this world."

("Excuse me, Raja Vikram," said the Baital, interrupting himself, "if I repeat these fair discourses at full length; it is interesting to hear a young person, whose throat is about to be cut, talk so like a doctor of laws.")

Then the youth thus addressed his sire: "Father, whoever can be of use to his master, the life of that man in this world has been lived to good purpose, and by reason of his usefulness he will be rewarded in other worlds."

His sister, however, exclaimed, "If a mother should give poison to her daughter, and a father sell his son, and a king seize the entire property of his subjects, where then could one look for protection?" But they heeded her not, and continued talking as they journeyed towards the temple of Devi—the king all the while secretly following them.

Presently they reached the temple, a single room, surrounded by a spacious paved area; in front was an immense building capable of seating hundreds of people. Before the image there were pools of blood, where victims had lately been slaughtered. In the sanctum was Devi, a large black figure with ten arms. With a spear in one of her right hands she pierced the giant Mahisha; and with one of her left hands she held the tail of a serpent, and the hair of the giant, whose breast the serpent was biting. Her other arms were all raised above her head, and were filled with different instruments of war; against her right leg leaned a lion.

Then Birbal joined his hands in prayer, and with Hindu mildness thus addressed the awful goddess: "O mother, let the king's life be prolonged for a thousand years by the sacrifice of my son. O Devi, mother! destroy, destroy his enemies! Kill! kill! Reduce them to ashes! Drive them away! Devour them! devour them! Cut them in two! Drink! drink their blood! Destroy them root and branch! With thy thunderbolt, spear, scymitar, discus, or rope, annihilate them! Spheng! Spheng!"

The Rajput, having caused his son to kneel before the goddess, struck him so violent a blow that his head rolled upon the ground. He then threw the sword down, when his daughter, frantic with grief, snatched it up and struck her neck with such force that her head, separated from her body, fell. In her turn the mother, unable to survive the loss of her children, seized the weapon and succeeded in decapitating herself. Birbal, beholding all this slaughter, thus reflected: "My children are dead why, now, should I remain in servitude, and upon whom shall I bestow the gold I receive from the king?" He then gave himself so deep a wound in the neck, that his head also separated from his body.

Rupsen, the king, seeing these four heads on the ground, said in his heart, "For my sake has the family of Birbal been destroyed. Kingly power, for the purpose of upholding which the destruction of a whole household is necessary, is a mere curse, and to carry on government in this manner is not just." He then took up the sword and was about to slay himself, when the Destroying Goddess, probably satisfied with bloodshed, stayed his hand, bidding him at the same time ask any boon he pleased.

The generous monarch begged, thereupon, that his faithful servant might be restored to life, together with all his high-minded family; and the goddess Devi in the twinkling of an eye fetched from Patala, the regions below the earth, a vase full of Amrita, the water of immortality, sprinkled it upon the dead, and raised them all as before. After which the whole party walked leisurely home, and in due time the king divided his throne with his friend Birbal.

Having stopped for a moment, the Baital proceeded to remark, in a sententious tone, "Happy the servant who grudges not his own life to save that of his master! And happy, thrice happy the master who can annihilate all greedy longing for existence and worldly prosperity. Raja, I have to ask thee one searching question—Of these five, who was the greatest fool?"

"Demon!" exclaimed the great Vikram, all whose cherished feelings about fidelity and family affection, obedience, and high-mindedness, were outraged by this Vampire view of the question; "if thou meanest by the greatest fool the noblest mind, I reply without hesitating Rupsen, the king."

"Why, prithee?" asked the Baital.

"Because, dull demon," said the king, "Birbal was bound to offer up his life for a master who treated him so generously; the son could not disobey his father, and the women naturally and instinctively killed themselves, because the example was set to them. But Rupsen the king gave up his throne for the sake of his retainer, and valued not a straw his life and his high inducements to live. For this reason I think him the most meritorious."

"Surely, mighty Vikram," laughed the Vampire, "you will be tired of ever clambering up yon tall tree, even had you the legs and arms of Hanuman himself."

And so saying he disappeared from the cloth, although it had been placed upon the ground.

But the poor Baital had little reason to congratulate himself on the success of his escape. In a short time he was again bundled into the cloth with the usual want of ceremony, and he revenged himself by telling another true story.

Fourth Story

Of a Woman who Told the Truth

"Listen, great king!" again began the Baital.

An unimportant Baniya (trader), Hiranyadatt, had a daughter, whose name was Madansena Sundari, the beautiful army of Cupid. Her face was like the moon; her hair like the clouds; her eyes like those of a muskrat; her eyebrows like a bent bow; her nose like a parrot's bill; her neck like that of a dove; her teeth like pomegranate grains; the red colour of her lips like that of a gourd; her waist lithe and bending like the pards: her hands and feet like softest blossoms; her complexion like the jasmine-in fact, day by day the splendour of her youth increased.

When she had arrived at maturity, her father and mother began often to resolve in their minds the subject of her marriage. And the people of all that country side ruled by Birbar king of Madanpur bruited it abroad that in the house of Hiranyadatt had been born a daughter by whose beauty gods, men, and munis (sages) were fascinated.

Thereupon many, causing their portraits to be painted, sent them by messengers to Hiranyadatt the Baniya, who showed them all to his daughter. But she was capricious, as beauties sometimes are, and when her father said, "Make choice of a husband thyself," she told him that none pleased her, and moreover she begged of him to find her a husband who possessed good looks, good qualities, and good sense.

At length, when some days had passed, four suitors came from four different countries. The father told them that he must have from each some indication that he possessed the required qualities; that he was pleased with their looks, but that they must satisfy him about their knowledge.

"I have," the first said, "a perfect acquaintance with the Shastras (or Scriptures); in science there is none to rival me. As for my handsome mien, it may plainly be seen by you."

The second exclaimed, "My attainments are unique in the knowledge of archery. I am acquainted with the art of discharging arrows and killing anything which though not seen is heard, and my fine proportions are plainly visible to you."

The third continued, "I understand the language of land and water animals, of birds and of beasts, and I have no equal in strength. Of my comeliness you yourself may judge."

"I have the knowledge," quoth the fourth, "how to make a certain cloth which can be sold for five rubies: having sold it I give the proceeds of one ruby to a Brahman, of the second I make an offering to a deity, a third I wear on my own person, a fourth I keep for my wife; and, having sold the fifth, I spend it in giving feasts. This is my knowledge, and none other is acquainted with it. My good looks are apparent."

The father hearing these speeches began to reflect, "It is said that excess in anything is not good. Sita was very lovely, but the demon Ravana carried her away; and Bali king of Mahabahpur gave much alms, but at length he became poor. My daughter is too fair to remain a maiden; to which of these shall I give her?"

So saying, Hiranyadatt went to his daughter, explained the qualities of the four suitors, and asked, "To which shall I give thee?" On hearing these words she was abashed; and, hanging down her head, knew not what to reply.

Then the Baniya, having reflected, said to himself, "He who is acquainted with the Shastras is a Brahman, he who could shoot an arrow at the sound was a Kshatriya or warrior, and he who made the cloth was a Shudra or servile. But the youth who understands the language of birds is of our own caste. To him, therefore, will I marry her." And accordingly he proceeded with the betrothal of his daughter.

Meanwhile Madansena went one day, during the spring season into the garden for a stroll. It happened, just before she came out, that Somdatt, the son of the merchant Dharmdatt, had gone for pleasure into the forest, and was returning through the same garden to his home.

He was fascinated at the sight of the maiden, and said to his friend, "Brother, if I can obtain her my life will be prosperous, and if I do not obtain her my living in the world will be in vain."

Having thus spoken, and becoming restless from the fear of separation, he involuntarily drew near to her, and seizing her hand, said—"If thou wilt not form an affection for me, I will throw away my life on thy account."

"Be pleased not to do this," she replied; "it will be sinful, and it will involve me in the guilt and punishment of shedding blood; hence I shall be miserable in this world and in that to be."

"Thy blandishments," he replied, "have pierced my heart, and the consuming thought of parting from thee has burnt up my body, and memory and understanding have been destroyed by this pain; and from excess of love I have no sense of right or wrong. But if thou wilt make me a promise, I will live again."

She replied, "Truly the Kali Yug (iron age) has commenced, since which time falsehood has increased in the world and truth has diminished; people talk smoothly with their tongues, but nourish deceit in their hearts; religion is destroyed, crime has increased, and the earth has begun to give little fruit. Kings levy fines, Brahmans have waxed covetous, the son obeys not his sire's commands, brother distrusts brother; friendship has departed from amongst friends; sincerity has left masters; servants have given up service; man has abandoned manliness; and woman has abandoned modesty. Five days hence, my marriage is to be; but if thou slay not thyself, I will visit thee first, and after that I will remain with my husband." Having given this promise, and having sworn by the Ganges, she returned home. The merchant's son also went his way.

Presently the marriage ceremonies came on, and Hiranyadatt the Baniya expended a lakh of rupees in feasts and presents to the bridegroom. The bodies of the twain were anointed with turmeric, the bride was made to hold in her hand the iron box for eye paint, and the youth a pair of betel scissors. During the night before the wedding there was loud and shrill music, the heads and limbs of the young couple were rubbed with an ointment of oil, and the bridegroom's head was duly shaved. The wedding procession was very grand. The streets were a blaze of flambeaux and torches carried in the hand, fireworks by the ton were discharged as the people passed; elephants, camels, and horses richly caparisoned, were placed in convenient situations; and before the procession had reached the house of the bride half a dozen wicked boys and bad young men were killed or wounded. After the marriage formulas were repeated, the Baniya gave a feast or supper, and the food was so excellent that all sat down quietly, no one uttered a complaint, or brought dishonour on the bride's family, or cut with scissors the garments of his neighbour.

The ceremony thus happily concluded, the husband brought Madansena home to his own house. After some days the wife of her husband's youngest brother, and also the wife of his eldest brother, led her at night by force to her bridegroom, and seated her on a bed ornamented with flowers.

As her husband proceeded to take her hand, she jerked it away, and at once openly told him all that she had promised to Somdatt on condition of his not killing himself.

"All things," rejoined the bridegroom, hearing her words, "have their sense ascertained by speech; in speech they have their basis, and from speech they proceed; consequently a falsifier of speech falsifies everything. If truly you are desirous of going to him, go!

"Receiving her husband's permission, she arose and went off to the young merchant's house in full dress. Upon the road a thief saw her, and in high good humour came up and asked-

"Whither goest thou at midnight in such darkness, having put on all these fine clothes and ornaments?"

She replied that she was going to the house of her beloved.

"And who here," said the thief, "is thy protector?"

"Kama Deva," she replied, "the beautiful youth who by his fiery arrows wounds with love the hearts of the inhabitants of the three worlds, Ratipati, the husband of Rati, accompanied by the kokila bird, the humming bee and gentle breezes." She then told to the thief the whole story, adding-

"Destroy not my jewels: I give thee a promise before I go, that on my return thou shalt have all these ornaments."

Hearing this the thief thought to himself that it would be useless now to destroy her jewels, when she had promised to give them to him presently of her own good will. He therefore let her go, and sat down and thus soliloquized:

> *"To me it is astonishing that he who sustained me in my mother's womb should take no care of me now that I have been born and am able to enjoy the good things of this world. I know not whether he is asleep or dead. And I would rather swallow poison than ask man for money or favour. For these six things tend to lower a man:—friendship with the perfidious; causeless laughter; altercation with women; serving an unworthy master; riding an ass, and speaking any language but Sanskrit. And these five things the deity writes on our fate at the hour of birth:—first, age; secondly, action; thirdly, wealth; fourthly, science; fifthly, fame. I have now done a good deed, and as long as a man's virtue is in the ascendant, all people becoming his servants obey him. But when virtuous deeds diminish, even his friends become inimical to him."*

Meanwhile Madansena had reached the place where Somdatt the young trader had fallen asleep.

She awoke him suddenly, and he springing up in alarm quickly asked her, "Art thou the daughter of a deity? or of a saint? or of a serpent? Tell me truly, who art thou? And whence hast thou come?"

She replied, "I am human—Madansena, the daughter of the Baniya Hiranyadatt. Dost thou not remember taking my hand in that grove, and declaring that thou wouldst slay thyself if I did not swear to visit thee first and after that remain with my husband?"

"Hast thou," he inquired, "told all this to thy husband or not?"

She replied, "I have told him everything; and he, thoroughly understanding the whole affair, gave me permission."

"This matter," exclaimed Somdatt in a melancholy voice, "is like pearls without a suitable dress, or food without clarified butter, or singing without melody; they are all alike unnatural. In the same way, unclean clothes will mar beauty, bad food will undermine strength, a wicked wife will worry her husband to death, a disreputable son will ruin his family, an enraged demon will kill, and a woman, whether she love or hate, will be a source of pain. For there are few things which a woman will not do. She never brings to her tongue what is in her heart, she never speaks out what is on her tongue, and she never tells what she is doing. Truly the Deity has created woman a strange creature in this world." He concluded with these words: "Return thou home with another man's wife I have no concern."

Madansena rose and departed. On her way she met the thief, who, hearing her tale, gave her great praise, and let her go unplundered.

She then went to her husband, and related the whole matter to him. But he had ceased to love her, and he said, "Neither a king nor a minister, nor a wife, nor a person's hair nor his nails, look well out of their places. And the beauty of the kokila is its note, of an ugly man knowledge, of a devotee forgiveness, and of a woman her chastity."

The Vampire having narrated thus far, suddenly asked the king, "Of these three, whose virtue was the greatest?"

Vikram, who had been greatly edified by the tale, forgot himself, and ejaculated, "The Thief's."

"And pray why?" asked the Baital.

"Because," the hero explained, "when her husband saw that she loved another man, however purely, he ceased to feel affection for her. Somdatt let her go unharmed, for fear of being punished by the king. But there was no reason why the thief should fear the law and dismiss her; therefore he was the best."

"Hi! hi! hi!" laughed the demon, spitefully. "Here, then, ends my story."

Upon which, escaping as before from the cloth in which he was slung behind the Raja's back, the Baital disappeared through the darkness of the night, leaving father and son looking at each other in dismay.

"Son Dharma Dhwaj," quoth the great Vikram, "the next time when that villain Vampire asks me a question, I allow thee to take the liberty of pinching my arm even before I have had time to answer his questions. In this way we shall never, of a truth, end our task."

"Your words be upon my head, sire," replied the young prince. But he expected no good from his father's new plan, as, arrived under the sires-tree, he heard the Baital laughing with all his might."

Surely he is laughing at our beards, sire," said the beardless prince, who hated to be laughed at like a young person.

"Let them laugh that win," fiercely cried Raja Vikram, who hated to be laughed at like an elderly person.

Fifth Story

Of the Thief who Laughed and Wept

Your majesty (quoth the demon, with unusual politeness), there is a country called Malaya, on the western coast of the land of Bharat-—you see that I am particular in specifying the place—and in it was a city known as Chandrodaya, whose king was named Randhir.

This Raja, like most others of his semi-deified order, had been in youth what is called a Sarva-rasi; that is, he ate and drank and listened to music, and looked at dancers and made love much more than he studied, reflected, prayed, or conversed with the wise. After the age of thirty he began to reform, and he brought such zeal to the good cause, that in an incredibly short space of time he came to be accounted and quoted as the paragon of correct Rajas. This was very praiseworthy. Many of Brahma's vicegerents on earth, be it observed, have loved food and drink, and music and dancing, and the worship of Kama, to the end of their days.

Amongst his officers was Gunshankar, a magistrate of police, who, curious to say, was as honest as he was just. He administered equity with as much care before as after dinner; he took no bribes even in the matter of advancing his family; he was rather merciful than otherwise to the poor, and he never punished the rich ostentatiously, in order to display his and his law's disrespect for persons. Besides which, when sitting on the carpet of justice, he did not, as some Kotwals do, use rough or angry language to those who cannot reply; nor did he take offence when none was intended.

All the people of the city Chandrodaya, in the province of Malaya, on the western coast of Bharatland, loved and esteemed this excellent magistrate; which did not, however, prevent thefts being committed so frequently and so regularly, that no one felt his property secure. At last the merchants who had suffered most from these depredations went in a body before Gunshankar, and said to him:

> *"O flower of the law! robbers have exercised great tyranny upon us, so great indeed that we can no longer stay in this city."*

Then the magistrate replied, "What has happened, has happened. But in future you shall be free from annoyance. I will make due preparation for these thieves."

Thus saying Gunshankar called together his various delegates, and directed them to increase the number of their people. He pointed out to them how they should keep watch by night; besides which he ordered them to open registers of all arrivals and departures, to make themselves acquainted by means of spies with the movements of every suspected person in the city, and to raise a body of paggis (trackers), who could follow the footprints of thieves even when they wore thieving shoes, till they came up with and arrested them. And lastly, he gave the patrols full power, whenever they might catch a robber in the act, to slay him without asking questions.

People in numbers began to mount guard throughout the city every night, but, notwithstanding this, robberies continued to be committed. After a time all the merchants having again met together went before the magistrate, and said, "O incarnation of justice! you have changed your officers, you have hired watchmen, and you have established patrols: nevertheless the thieves have not diminished, and plundering is ever taking place."

Thereupon Gunshankar carried them to the palace, and made them lay their petition at the feet of the king Randhir. That Raja, having consoled them, sent them home, saying, "Be ye of good cheer. I will tonight adopt a new plan, which, with the blessing of the Bhagwan, shall free ye from further anxiety."

Observe, O Vikram, that Randhir was one of those concerning whom the poet sang—

The unwise run from one end to the other.

Not content with becoming highly respectable, correct, and even unimpeachable in point of character, he reformed even his reformation, and he did much more than he was required to do.

When Canopus began to sparkle gaily in the southern skies, the king arose and prepared for a night's work. He disguised his face by smearing it with a certain paint, by twirling his moustachios up to his eyes, by parting his beard upon his chin, and conducting the two ends towards his ears, and by tightly tying a hair from a horse's tail over his nose, so as quite to change its shape. He then wrapped himself in a coarse outer garment, girt his loins, buckled on his sword, drew his shield upon his arm, and without saying a word to those within the palace, he went out into the streets alone, and on foot.

It was dark, and Raja Randhir walked through the silent city for nearly an hour without meeting anyone. As, however, he passed through a back street in the merchants' quarter, he saw what appeared to be a homeless dog, lying at the foot of a house-wall. He approached it, and up leaped a human figure, whilst a loud voice cried, "Who art thou?"

Randhir replied, "I am a thief; who art thou?"

"And I also am a thief," rejoined the other, much pleased at hearing this; "come, then, and let us make together. But what art thou, a high-loper or a lully-prigger?"

"A little more ceremony between coves in the lorst," whispered the king, speaking as a flash man, "were not out of place. But, look sharp, mind old Oliver, or the lamb-skin man will have the pull of us, and as sure as eggs is eggs we shall be scragged as soon as lagged."

"Well, keep your red rag quiet," grumbled the other, "and let us be working."

Then the pair, king and thief, began work in right earnest. The gang seemed to swarm in the street. They were drinking spirits, slaying victims, rubbing their bodies with oil, daubing their eyes with lamp-black, and repeating incantations to enable them to see in the darkness; others were practicing the lessons of the god with the golden spear, and carrying out the four modes of breaching a house: 1. Picking out burnt bricks. 2.Cutting through unbaked ones when old, when softened by recent damp, by exposure to the sun, or by saline exudations. 3. Throwing water on a mud wall; and 4. Boring through one of wood. The sons of Skanda were making breaches in the shape of lotus blossoms, the sun, the new moon, the lake, and the water jar, and they seemed to be anointed with magic unguents, so that no eye could behold, no weapon harm them.

At length having filled his bag with costly plunder, the thief said to the king, "Now, my rummy cove, we'll be off to the flash ken, where the lads and the morts are waiting to wet their whistles."

Randhir, who as a king was perfectly familiar with "thieves' Latin," took heart, and resolved to hunt out the secrets of the den. On the way, his companion, perfectly satisfied with the importance which the new cove had attached to a rat-hole, and convinced that he was a true robber, taught him the whistle, the word, and the sign peculiar to the gang, and promised him that he should smack the lit that night before "turning in."

So saying the thief rapped twice at the city gate, which was at once opened to him, and preceding his accomplice led the way to a rock about two kos (four miles) distant from the walls. Before entering the dark forest at the foot of the eminence, the robber stood still for a moment and whistled twice through his fingers with a shrill scream that rang through the silent glades. After a few minutes the signal was answered by the hooting of an owl, which the robber acknowledged by shrieking like a jackal. Thereupon half a dozen armed men arose from their crouching places in the grass, and one advanced towards the new comers to receive the sign. It was given, and they both passed on, whilst the guard sank, as it were, into the bowels of the earth. All these things Randhir carefully remarked: besides which he neglected not to take note of all the distinguishable objects that lay on the road, and, when he entered the wood, he scratched with his dagger all the tree trunks within reach.

After a sharp walk the pair reached a high perpendicular sheet of rock, rising abruptly from a clear space in the jungle, and profusely printed over with vermilion hands. The thief, having walked up to it, and made his obeisance, stooped to the ground, and removed a bunch of grass. The two then raised by their united efforts a heavy trap door, through which poured a stream of light, whilst a confused hubbub of voices was heard below.

"This is the ken," said the robber, preparing to descend a thin ladder of bamboo, "follow me!" And he disappeared with his bag of valuables.

The king did as he was bid, and the pair entered together a large hall, or rather a cave, which presented a singular spectacle. It was lighted up by links fixed to the sombre walls, which threw a smoky glare over the place, and the contrast after the deep darkness reminded Randhir of his mother's descriptions of Patal-puri, the infernal city. Carpets of every kind, from the choicest tapestry to the coarsest rug, were spread upon the ground, and were strewed with bags, wallets, weapons, heaps of booty, drinking cups, and all the materials of debauchery.

Passing through this cave the thief led Randhir into another, which was full of thieves, preparing for the pleasures of the night. Some were changing garments, ragged and dirtied by creeping through gaps in the houses: others were washing the blood from their hands and feet; these combed out their long dishevelled, dusty hair: those anointed their skins with perfumed cocoanut oil. There were all manner of murderers present, a villanous collection of Kartikeya's and Bhawani's crew. There were stabbers with their poniards hung to lanyards lashed round their naked waists, Dhaturiya-poisoners distinguished by the little bag slung under the left arm, and Phansigars wearing their fatal kerchiefs round their necks. And Randhir had reason to thank the good deed in the last life that had sent him there in such strict disguise, for amongst the robbers he found, as might be expected, a number of his own people, spies and watchmen, guards and patrols.

The thief, whose importance of manner now showed him to be the chief of the gang, was greeted with applause as he entered the robing room, and he bade all make salam to the new companion. A number of questions concerning the success of the night's work was quickly put and answered: then the company, having got ready for the revel, flocked into the first cave. There they sat down each in his own place, and began to eat and drink and make merry.

After some hours the flaring torches began to burn out, and drowsiness to overpower the strongest heads. Most of the robbers rolled themselves up in the rugs, and covering their heads, went to sleep. A few still sat with their backs to the wall, nodding drowsily or leaning on one side, and too stupefied with opium and hemp to make any exertion.

At that moment a servant woman, whom the king saw for the first time, came into the cave, and looking at him exclaimed,

"O Raja! how came you with these wicked men? Do you run away as fast as you can, or they will surely kill you when they awake."

"I do not know the way; in which direction am I to go?" asked Randhir.

The woman then showed him the road. He threaded the confused mass of snorers, treading with the foot of a tiger-cat, found the ladder, raised the trap-door by exerting all his strength, and breathed once more the open air of heaven. And before plunging into the depths of the wood he again marked the place where the entrance lay and carefully replaced the bunch of grass.

Hardly had Raja Randhir returned to the palace, and removed the traces of his night's occupation, when he received a second deputation of the merchants, complaining bitterly and with the longest faces about their fresh misfortunes.

"O pearl of equity!" said the men of money, "but yesterday you consoled us with the promise of some contrivance by the blessing of which our houses and coffers would be safe from theft; whereas our goods have never yet suffered so severely as during the last twelve hours."

Again Randhir dismissed them, swearing that this time he would either die or destroy the wretches who had been guilty of such violence.

Then having mentally prepared his measures, the Raja warned a company of archers to hold themselves in readiness for secret service, and as each one of his own people returned from the robbers' cave he had him privily arrested and put to death—because the deceased, it is said, do not, like Baitals, tell tales. About nightfall, when he thought that the thieves, having finished their work of plunder, would meet together as usual for wassail and debauchery, he armed himself, marched out his men, and led them to the rock in the jungle.

But the robbers, aroused by the disappearance of the new companion, had made enquiries and had gained intelligence of the impending danger. They feared to flee during the daytime, lest being tracked they should be discovered and destroyed in detail. When night came they hesitated to disperse, from the certainty that they would be captured in the morning. Then their captain, who throughout had been of one opinion, proposed to them that they should resist, and promised them success if they would hear his words. The gang respected him, for he was known to be brave: they all listened to his advice, and they promised to be obedient.

As young night began to cast transparent shade upon the jungle ground, the chief of the thieves mustered his men, inspected their bows and arrows, gave them encouraging words, and led them forth from the cave. Having placed them in ambush he climbed the rock to espy the movements of the enemy, whilst others applied their noses and ears to the level ground. Presently the moon shone full upon Randhir and his band of archers, who were advancing quickly and carelessly, for they expected to catch the robbers in their cave. The captain allowed them to march nearly through the line of ambush. Then he gave the signal, and at that moment the thieves, rising suddenly from the bush fell upon the royal troops and drove them back in confusion.

The king also fled, when the chief of the robbers shouted out, "Hola! thou a Rajput and running away from combat?" Randhir hearing this halted, and the two, confronting each other, bared their blades and began to do battle with prodigious fury.

The king was cunning of fence, and so was the thief. They opened the duel, as skilful swordsmen should, by bending almost double, skipping in a circle, each keeping his eye well fixed upon the other, with frowning brows and contemptuous lips; at the same time executing divers gambados and measured leaps, springing forward like frogs and backward like monkeys, and beating time with their sabres upon their shields, which rattled like drums.

Then Randhir suddenly facing his antagonist, cut at his legs with a loud cry, but the thief sprang in the air, and the blade whistled harmlessly under him. Next moment the robber chief's sword, thrice whirled round his head, descended like lightning in a slanting direction towards the king's left shoulder: the latter, however, received it upon his target and escaped all hurt, though he staggered with the violence of the blow.

And thus they continued attacking each other, parrying and replying, till their breath failed them and their hands and wrists were numbed and cramped with fatigue. They were so well matched in courage, strength, and address, that neither obtained the least advantage, till the robber's right foot catching a stone slid from under him, and thus he fell to the ground at the mercy of his enemy. The thieves fled, and the Raja, himself on his prize, tied his hands behind him, and brought him back to the city at the point of his good sword.

The next morning Randhir visited his prisoner, whom he caused to be bathed, and washed, and covered with fine clothes. He then had him mounted on a camel and sent him on a circuit of the city, accompanied by a crier proclaiming aloud: "Who hears! who hears! who hears! the king commands! This is the thief who has robbed and plundered the city of Chandrodaya. Let all men therefore assemble themselves together this evening in the open space outside the gate leading towards the sea. And let them behold the penalty of evil deeds, and learn to be wise."

Randhir had condemned the thief to be crucified, nailed and tied with his hands and feet stretched out at full length, in an erect posture until death; everything he wished to eat was ordered to him in order to prolong life and misery. And when death should draw near, melted gold was to be poured down his throat till it should burst from his neck and other parts of his body.

In the evening the thief was led out for execution, and by chance the procession passed close to the house of a wealthy landowner. He had a favourite daughter named Shobhani, who was in the flower of her youth and very lovely; every day she improved, and every moment added to her grace and beauty. The girl had been carefully kept out of sight of mankind, never being allowed outside the high walls of the garden, because her nurse, a wise woman much trusted in the neighbourhood, had at the hour of death given a solemn warning to her parents.

The prediction was that the maiden should be the admiration of the city, and should die a Sati-widow before becoming a wife. From that hour Shobhani was kept as a pearl in its casket by her father, who had vowed never to survive her, and had even fixed upon the place and style of his suicide.

But the shaft of Fate strikes down the vulture sailing above the clouds, and follows the worm into the bowels of the earth, and pierces the fish at the bottom of the ocean—how then can mortal man expect to escape it? As the robber chief, mounted upon the camel, was passing to the cross under the old householder's windows, a fire breaking out in the women's apartments, drove the inmates into the rooms looking upon the street.

The hum of many voices arose from the solid pavement of heads: "This is the thief who has been robbing the whole city; let him tremble now, for Randhir will surely crucify him!"

In beauty and bravery of bearing, as in strength and courage, no man in Chandrodaya surpassed the robber, who, being magnificently dressed, looked, despite his disgraceful cavalcade, like the son of a king. He sat with an unmoved countenance, hardly hearing in his pride the scoffs of the mob; calm and steady when the whole city was frenzied with anxiety because of him. But as he heard the word "tremble" his lips quivered, his eyes flashed fire, and deep lines gathered between his eyebrows.

Shobhani started with a scream from the casement behind which she had hid herself, gazing with an intense womanly curiosity into the thoroughfare. The robber's face was upon a level with, and not half a dozen feet from, her pale cheeks. She marked his handsome features, and his look of wrath made her quiver as if it had been a flash of lightning. Then she broke away from the fascination of his youth and beauty, and ran breathless to her father, saying:

"Go this moment and get that thief released!

"The old housekeeper replied: "That thief has been pilfering and plundering the whole city, and by his means the king's archers were defeated; why, then, at

my request, should our most gracious Raja Randhir release him?"

Shobhani, almost beside herself, exclaimed: "If by giving up your whole property, you can induce the Raja to release him, then instantly so do; if he does not come to me, I must give up my life!"

The maiden then covered her head with her veil, and sat down in the deepest despair, whilst her father, hearing her words, burst into a cry of grief, and hastened to present himself before the Raja. He cried out:

"O great king, be pleased to receive four lakhs of rupees, and to release this thief."

But the king replied: "He has been robbing the whole city, and by reason of him my guards have been destroyed. I cannot by any means release him."

Then the old householder finding, as he had expected the Raja inexorable, and not to be moved, either by tears or bribes, or by the cruel fate of the girl, returned home with fire in his heart, and addressed her:

"Daughter, I have said and done all that is possible but it avails me nought with the king. Now, then, we die."

In the mean time, the guards having led the thief all round the city, took him outside the gates, and made him stand near the cross. Then the messengers of death arrived from the palace, and the executioners began to nail his limbs. He bore the agony with the fortitude of the brave; but when he heard what had been done by the old householder's daughter, he raised his voice and wept bitterly, as though his heart had been bursting, and almost with the same breath he laughed heartily as at a feast. All were startled by his merriment; coming as it did at a time when the iron was piercing his flesh, no man could see any reason for it.

When he died, Shobhani, who was married to him in the spirit, recited to herself these sayings:

"There are thirty-five millions of hairs on the human body. The woman who ascends the pile with her husband

will remain so many years in heaven. As the snake-catcher draws the serpent from his hole, so she, rescuing her husband from hell, rejoices with him; aye, though he may have sunk to a region of torment, be restrained in dreadful bonds, have reached the place of anguish, be exhausted of strength, and afflicted and tortured for his crimes. No other effectual duty is known for virtuous women at any time after the death of their lords, except casting themselves into the same fire. As long as a woman in her successive transmigrations, shall decline burning herself, like a faithful wife, in the same fire with her deceased lord, so long shall she not be exempted from springing again to life in the body of some female animal."

Therefore the beautiful Shobhani, virgin and wife, resolved to burn herself, and to make the next life of the thief certain. She showed her courage by thrusting her finger into a torch flame till it became a cinder, and she solemnly bathed in the nearest stream.

A hole was dug in the ground, and upon a bed of green tree-trunks were heaped hemp, pitch, faggots, and clarified butter, to form the funeral pyre. The dead body, anointed, bathed, and dressed in new clothes, was then laid upon the heap, which was some two feet high. Shobhani prayed that as long as fourteen Indras reign, or as many years as there are hairs in her head, she might abide in heaven with her husband, and be waited upon by the heavenly dancers. She then presented her ornaments and little gifts of corn to her friends, tied some cotton round both wrists, put two new combs in her hair, painted her forehead, and tied up in the end of her body-cloth clean parched rice and cowrie-shells.

These she gave to the bystanders, as she walked seven times round the funeral pyre, upon which lay the body. She then ascended the heap of wood, sat down upon it, and taking the thief's head in her lap, without cords or levers or upper layer or faggots, she ordered the pile to be lighted. The crowd standing around set fire to it in several places, drummed their drums, blew their conchs, and raised a loud cry of "Hari bol!

Hari bol! " Straw was thrown on, and pitch and clarified butter were freely poured out. But Shobhani's was a Sahamaran, a blessed easy death: no part of her body was seen to move after the pyre was lighted—in fact, she seemed to die before the flame touched her.

By the blessing of his daughter's decease, the old householder beheaded himself. He caused an instrument to be made in the shape of a half-moon with an edge like a razor, and fitting the back of his neck. At both ends of it, as at the beam of a balance, chains were fastened. He sat down with eyes closed; he was rubbed with the purifying clay of the holy river, Vaiturani; and he repeated the proper incantations. Then placing his feet upon the extremities of the chains, he suddenly jerked up his neck, and his severed head rolled from his body upon the ground. What a happy death was this!

The Baital was silent, as if meditating on the fortunate transmigration which the old householder had thus secured.

"But what could the thief have been laughing at, sire?" asked the young prince Dharma Dhwaj of his father.

"At the prodigious folly of the girl, my son," replied the warrior king, thoughtlessly.

"I am indebted once more to your majesty," burst out the Baital, "for releasing me from this unpleasant position, but the Raja's penetration is again at fault. Not to leave your royal son and heir labouring under a false impression, before going I will explain why the brave thief burst into tears, and why he laughed at such a moment.

"He wept when he reflected that he could not requite her kindness in being willing to give up everything she had in the world to save his life; and this thought deeply grieved him.

Then it struck him as being passing strange that she had begun to love him when the last sand of his life was well nigh run out; that wondrous are the ways of the revolving heavens which bestow wealth upon the niggard that cannot use it, wisdom upon the bad man who will misuse it, a beautiful wife upon the fool who cannot protect her, and fertilizing showers upon the stony hills. And thinking over these things, the gallant and beautiful thief laughed aloud.

"Before returning to my sires-tree," continued the Vampire, "as I am about to do in virtue of your majesty's unintelligent reply, I may remark that men may laugh and cry, or may cry and laugh, about everything in this world, from their neighbours' deaths, which, as a general rule, in no wise concern them, to their own latter ends, which do concern them exceedingly. For my part, I am in the habit of laughing at everything, because it animates the brain, stimulates the lungs, beautifies the countenance, and—for the moment, goodbye, Raja Vikram!

The warrior king, being forewarned this time, shifted the bundle containing the Baital from his back to under his arm, where he pressed it with all his might.

This proceeding, however, did not prevent the Vampire from slipping back to his tree, and leaving an empty cloth with the Raja.

Presently the demon was trussed up as usual; a voice sounded behind Vikram, and the loquacious thing again began to talk.

Sixth Story

In which Three Men Dispute about a Woman

On the lovely banks of Jumna's stream there was a city known as Dharmasthal—the Place of Duty; and therein dwelt a certain Brahman called Keshav. He was a very pious man, in the constant habit of performing penance and worship upon the river Sidi. He modelled his own clay images instead of buying them from others; he painted holy stones red at the top, and made to them offerings of flowers, fruit, water, sweetmeats, and fried peas. He had become a learned man somewhat late in life, having, until twenty years old, neglected his reading, and addicted himself to worshipping the beautiful youth Kama-Deva and Rati his wife, accompanied by the cuckoo, the humming-bee, and sweet breezes.

One day his parents having rebuked him sharply for his ungovernable conduct, Keshav wandered to a neighbouring hamlet, and hid himself in the tall fig-tree which shadowed a celebrated image of Panchanan. Presently an evil thought arose in his head: he defiled the god, and threw him into the nearest tank.

The next morning, when the person arrived whose livelihood depended on the image, he discovered that his god was gone. He returned into the village distracted, and all was soon in an uproar about the lost deity.

In the midst of this confusion the parents of Keshav arrived, seeking for their son; and a man in the crowd declared that he had seen a young man sitting in Panchanan's tree, but what had become of the god he knew not.

The runaway at length appeared, and the suspicions of the villagers fell upon him as the stealer of Panchanan. He confessed the fact, pointed out the place where he had thrown the stone, and added that he had polluted the god. All hands and eyes were raised in amazement at this atrocious crime, and every one present declared that Panchanan would certainly punish the daring insult by immediate death. Keshav was dreadfully frightened; he began to obey his parents from that very hour, and applied to his studies so sedulously that he soon became the most learned man of his country.

Now Keshav the Brahman had a daughter whose name was the Madhumalati or Sweet Jasmine. She was very beautiful. Whence did the gods procure the materials to form so exquisite a face? They took a portion of the most excellent part of the moon to form that beautiful face? Does any one seek a proof of this? Let him look at the empty places left in the moon. Her eyes resembled the full-blown blue nymphaea; her arms the charming stalk of the lotus; her flowing tresses the thick darkness of night.

When this lovely person arrived at a marriageable age, her mother, father, and brother, all three became very anxious about her. For the wise have said, "A daughter nubile but without a husband is ever a calamity hanging over a house." And, "Kings, women, and climbing plants love those who are near them." Also, "Who is there that has not suffered from the sex? for a woman cannot be kept in due subjection, either by gifts or kindness, or correct conduct, or the greatest services, or the laws of morality, or by the terror of punishment, for she cannot discriminate between good and evil."

It so happened that one day Keshav the Brahman went to the marriage of a certain customer of his, and his son repaired to the house of a spiritual preceptor in order to read. During their absence, a young man came to the house, when the Sweet Jasmine's mother, inferring his good qualities from his good looks, said to him, "I will give to thee my daughter in marriage."

The father also had promised his daughter to a Brahman youth whom he had met at the house of his employer; and the brother likewise had betrothed his sister to a fellow student at the place where he had gone to read.

After some days father and son came home, accompanied by these two suitors, and in the house a third was already seated. The name of the first was Tribikram, of the second Baman, and of the third Madhusadan. The three were equal in mind and body, in knowledge, and in age.

Then the father, looking upon them, said to himself, "Ho! there is one bride and three bridegrooms; to whom shall I give, and to whom shall I not give? We three have pledged our word to these three. A strange circumstance has occurred; what must we do?"

He then proposed to them a trial of wisdom, and made them agree that he who should quote the most excellent saying of the wise should become his daughter's husband.

Quoth Tribikram: "Courage is tried in war; integrity in the payment of debt and interest; friendship in distress; and the faithfulness of a wife in the day of poverty."

Baman proceeded: "That woman is destitute of virtue who in her father's house is not in subjection, who wanders to feasts and amusements, who throws off her veil in the presence of men, who remains as a guest in the houses of strangers, who is much devoted to sleep, who drinks inebriating beverages, and who delights in distance from her husband."

"Let none," pursued Madhusadan, "confide in the sea, nor in whatever has claws or horns, or who carries deadly weapons; neither in a woman, nor in a king."

Whilst the Brahman was doubting which to prefer, and rather inclining to the latter sentiment, a serpent bit the beautiful girl, and in a few hours she died.

Stunned by this awful sudden death, the father and the three suitors sat for a time motionless. They then arose, used great exertions, and brought all kinds of sorcerers, wise men and women who charm away poisons by incantations. These having seen the girl said, "She cannot return to life." The first declared, "A person always dies who has been bitten by a snake on the fifth, sixth, eighth, ninth, and fourteenth days of the lunar month." The second asserted, "One who has been bitten on a Saturday or a Tuesday does not survive." The third opined, "Poison infused during certain six lunar mansions cannot be got under." Quoth the fourth, "One who has been bitten in any organ of sense, the lower lip, the cheek, the neck, or the stomach, cannot escape death." The fifth said, "In this case even Brahma, the Creator, could not restore life—of what account, then, are we? Do you perform the funeral rites; we will depart."

Thus saying, the sorcerers went their way. The mourning father took up his daughter's corpse and caused it to be burnt, in the place where dead bodies are usually burnt, and returned to his house. After that the three young men said to one another, "We must now seek happiness elsewhere. And what better can we do than obey the words of Indra, the God of Air, who spake thus?:

"'*For a man who does not travel about there is no felicity, and a good man who stays at home is a bad man. Indra is the friend of him who travels. Travel!*

"'*A traveller's legs are like blossoming branches, and he himself grows and gathers the fruit. All his wrongs vanish, destroyed by his exertion on the roadside. Travel!*

"'*The fortune of a man who sits, sits also; it rises when he rises; it sleeps when he sleeps; it moves well when he moves. Travel!*

"'*A man who sleeps is like the Iron Age. A man who awakes is like the Bronze Age. A man who rises up is like the Silver Age. A man who travels is like the Golden Age. Travel!*

"'*A traveller finds honey; a traveller finds sweet figs. Look at the happiness of the sun, who travelling never tires. Travel!*"'

Before parting they divided the relics of the beloved one, and then they went their way.

Tribikram, having separated and tied up the burnt bones, became one of the Vaisheshikas, in those days a powerful sect. He solemnly forswore the eight great crimes, namely: feeding at night; slaying any animal; eating the fruit of trees that give milk, or pumpkins or young bamboos: tasting honey or flesh; plundering the wealth of others; taking by force a married woman; eating flowers, butter, or cheese; and worshipping the gods of other religions. He learned that the highest act of virtue is to abstain from doing injury to sentient creatures; that crime does not justify the destruction of life; and that kings, as the administrators of criminal justice, are the greatest of sinners.

He professed the five vows of total abstinence from falsehood, eating flesh or fish, theft, drinking spirits, and marriage. He bound himself to possess nothing beyond a white loin-cloth, a towel to wipe the mouth, a beggar's dish, and a brush of woollen threads to sweep the ground for fear of treading on insects. And he was ordered to fear secular affairs; the miseries of a future state; the receiving from others more than the food of a day at once; all accidents; provisions, if connected with the destruction of animal life; death and disgrace; also to please all, and to obtain compassion from all.

He attempted to banish his love. He said to himself, "Surely it was owing only to my pride and selfishness that I ever looked upon a woman as capable of affording happiness; and I thought, 'Ah! ah! thine eyes roll about like the tail of the water-wagtail, thy lips resemble the ripe fruit, thy bosom is like the lotus bud, thy form is resplendent as gold melted in a crucible, the moon wanes through desire to imitate the shadow of thy face, thou resemblest the pleasure-house of Cupid; the happiness of all time is concentrated in thee; a touch from thee would surely give life to a dead image; at thy approach a living admirer would be changed by joy into a lifeless stone; obtaining thee I can face all the horrors of war; and were I pierced by showers of arrows, one glance of thee would heal all my wounds.'

"My mind is now averted from the world. Seeing her I say, 'Is this the form by which men are bewitched? This is a basket covered with skin; it contains bones, flesh, blood, and impurities. The stupid creature who is captivated by this—is there a cannibal feeding in Currim a greater cannibal than he? These persons call a thing made up of impure matter a face, and drink its charms as a drunkard swallows the inebriating liquor from his cup. The blind, infatuated beings! Why should I be pleased or displeased with this body, composed of flesh and blood? It is my duty to seek Him who is the Lord of this body, and to disregard everything which gives rise either to pleasure or to pain.'"

Baman, the second suitor, tied up a bundle of his beloved one's ashes, and followed—somewhat prematurely—the precepts of the great lawgiver Manu. "When the father of a family perceives his muscles becoming flaccid, and his hair grey, and sees the child of his child, let him then take refuge in a forest. Let him take up his consecrated fire and all his domestic implements for making oblations to it, and, departing from the town to the lonely wood, let him dwell in it with complete power over his organs of sense and of action. With many sorts of pure food, such as holy sages used to eat, with green herbs, roots, and fruit, let him perform the five great sacraments, introducing them with due ceremonies.

Let him wear a black antelope-hide, or a vesture of bark; let him bathe evening and morning; let him suffer the hair of his head, his beard and his nails to grow continually. Let him slide backwards and forwards on the ground; or let him stand a whole day on tiptoe; or let him continue in motion, rising and sitting alternately; but at sunrise, at noon, and at sunset, let him go to the waters and bathe In the hot season let him sit exposed to five fires, four blazing around him, with the sun above; in the rains let him stand uncovered, without even a mantle, where the clouds pour the heaviest showers; in the cold season let him wear damp clothes, and let him increase by degrees the austerity of his devotions. Then, having reposited his holy fires, as the law directs, in his mind, let him live without external fire, without a mansion, wholly silent, feeding on roots and fruit."

Meanwhile Madhusadan the third, having taken a wallet and neckband, became a Jogi, and began to wander far and wide, living on nothing but chaff, and practising his devotions. In order to see Brahma he attended to the following duties; 1. Hearing; 2. Meditation; 3. Fixing the Mind; 4. Absorbing the Mind. He combated the three evils, restlessness, injuriousness, voluptuousness by settling the Deity in his spirit, by subjecting his senses, and by destroying desire.

Thus he would do away with the illusion (Maya) which conceals all true knowledge. He repeated the name of the Deity till it appeared to him in the form of a Dry Light or glory. Though connected with the affairs of life, that is, with affairs belonging to a body containing blood, bones, and impurities; to organs which are blind, palsied, and full of weakness and error; to a mind filled with thirst, hunger, sorrow, infatuation; to confirmed habits, and to the fruits of former births: still he strove not to view these things as realities. He made a companion of a dog, honouring it with his own food, so as the better to think on spirit. He practised all the five operations connected with the vital air, or air collected in the body. He attended much to Pranayama, or the gradual suppression of breathing, and he secured fixedness of mind as follows.

By placing his sight and thoughts on the tip of his nose he perceived smell; on the tip of his tongue he realized taste, on the root of his tongue he knew sound, and so forth. He practised the eighty-four Asana or postures, raising his hand to the wonders of the heavens, till he felt no longer the inconveniences of heat or cold, hunger or thirst. He particularly preferred the Padma or lotus-posture, which consists of bringing the feet to the sides, holding the right in the left hand and the left in the right. In the work of suppressing his breath he permitted its respiration to reach at furthest twelve fingers' breadth, and gradually diminished the distance from his nostrils till he could confine it to the length of twelve fingers from his nose, and even after restraining it for some time he would draw it from no greater distance than from his heart. As respects time, he began by retaining inspiration for twenty-six seconds, and he enlarged this period gradually till he became perfect.

He sat cross-legged, closing with his fingers all the avenues of inspiration, and he practised Prityahara, or the power of restraining the members of the body and mind, with meditation and concentration, to which there are four enemies, *viz.*, a sleepy heart, human passions, a confused mind, and attachment to anything but the one Brahma.

He also cultivated Yama, that is, inoffensiveness, truth, honesty, the forsaking of all evil in the world, and the refusal of gifts except for sacrifice, and Nihama, *i.e.*, purity relative to the use of water after defilement, pleasure in everything whether in prosperity or adversity, renouncing food when hungry, and keeping down the body. Thus delivered from these four enemies of the flesh, he resembled the unruffled flame of the lamp, and by Brahmagnana, or meditating on the Deity, placing his mind on the sun, moon, fire, or any other luminous body, or within his heart, or at the bottom of his throat, or in the centre of his skull, he was enabled to ascend from gross images of omnipotence to the works and the divine wisdom of the glorious original.

One day Madhusadan, the Jogi, went to a certain house for food, and the householder having seen him began to say, "Be so good as to take your food here this day!" The visitor sat down, and when the victuals were ready, the host caused his feet and hands to be washed, and leading him to the Chauka, or square place upon which meals are served, seated him and sat by him. And he quoted the scripture: "No guest must be dismissed in the evening by a housekeeper: he is sent by the returning sun, and whether he come in fit season or unseasonably, he must not sojourn in the house without entertainment: let me not eat any delicate food, without asking my guest to partake of it: the satisfaction of a guest will assuredly bring the housekeeper wealth, reputation, long life, and a place in heaven."

The householder's wife then came to serve up the food, rice and split peas, oil, and spices, all cooked in a new earthen pot with pure firewood. Part of the meal was served and the rest remained to be served, when the woman's little child began to cry aloud and to catch hold of its mother's dress. She endeavoured to release herself, but the boy would not let go, and the more she coaxed the more he cried, and was obstinate. On this the mother became angry, took up the boy and threw him upon the fire, which instantly burnt him to ashes.

Madhusadan, the Jogi, seeing this, rose up without eating. The master of the house said to him, "Why eatest thou not?" He replied, "I am ' Atithi,' that is to say, to be entertained at your house, but how can one eat under the roof of a person who has committed such a Rakshasa-like (devilish) deed? Is it not said, 'He who does not govern his passions, lives in vain'? 'A foolish king, a person puffed up with riches, and a weak child, desire that which cannot be procured'? Also, 'A king destroys his enemies, even when flying; and the touch of an elephant, as well as the breath of a serpent, are fatal; but the wicked destroy even while laughing'?"

Hearing this, the householder smiled; presently he arose and went to another part of the tenement, and brought back with him a book, treating on Sanjivnividya, or the science of restoring the dead to life. This he had taken from its hidden place, two beams almost touching one another with the ends in the opposite wall. The precious volume was in single leaves, some six inches broad by treble that length, and the paper was stained with yellow orpiment and the juice of tamarind seeds to keep away insects.

The householder opened the cloth containing the book, untied the flat boards at the top and bottom, and took out from it a charm. Having repeated this Mantra, with many ceremonies, he at once restored the child to life, saying, "Of all precious things, knowledge is the most valuable; other riches may be stolen, or diminished by expenditure, but knowledge is immortal, and the greater the expenditure the greater the increase; it can be shared with none, and it defies the power of the thief."

The Jogi, seeing this marvel, took thought in his heart, "If I could obtain that book, I would restore my beloved to life, and give up this course of uncomfortable postures and difficulty of breathing." With this resolution he sat down to his food, and remained in the house.

At length night came, and after a time,. all, having eaten supper, and gone to their sleeping-places, lay down. The Jogi also went to rest in one part of the house, but did not allow sleep to close his eyes. When he thought that a fourth part of the hours of darkness had sped, and that all were deep in slumber, then he got up very quietly, and going into the room of the master of the house, he took down the book from the beam-ends and went his ways.

Madhusadan, the Jogi, went straight to the place where the beautiful Sweet Jasmine had been burned. There he found his two rivals sitting talking together and comparing experiences. They recognized him at once, and cried aloud to him, "Brother! thou also hast been wandering over the world; tell us this—hast thou learned anything which can profit us?" He replied, "I have learned the science of restoring the dead to life"; upon which they both exclaimed, "If thou hast really learned such knowledge, restore our beloved to life."

Madhusadan proceeded to make his incantations, despite terrible sights in the air, the cries of jackals, owls, crows, cats, asses, vultures, dogs, and lizards, and the wrath of innumerable invisible beings, such as messengers of Yama (Pluto), ghosts, devils, demons, imps, fiends, devas, succubi, and others. All the three lovers drawing blood from their own bodies, offered it to the goddess Chandi, repeating the following incantation, "Hail! supreme delusion! Hail! goddess of the universe! Hail! thou who fulfillest the desires of all. May I presume to offer thee the blood of my body; and wilt thou deign to accept it, and be propitious towards me!"

They then made a burnt-offering of their flesh, and each one prayed, "Grant me, O goddess! to see the maiden alive again, in proportion to the fervency with which I present thee with mine own flesh, invoking thee to be propitious to me. Salutation to thee again and again, under the mysterious syllables any! any!"

Then they made a heap of the bones and the ashes, which had been carefully kept by Tribikram and Baman. As the Jogi Madhusadan proceeded with his incantation, a white vapour arose from the ground, and, gradually condensing, assumed a perispiritual form—the fluid envelope of the soul. The three spectators felt their blood freeze as the bones and the ashes were gradually absorbed into the before shadowy shape, and they were restored to themselves only when the maiden Madhuvati begged to be taken home to her mother.

Then Kama, God of Love, blinded them, and they began fiercely to quarrel about who should have the beautiful maid. Each wanted to be her sole master. Tribikram declared the bones to be the great fact of the incantation; Baman swore by the ashes; and Madhusadan laughed them both to scorn. No one could decide the dispute; the wisest doctors were all nonplussed; and as for the Raja—well! we do not go for wit or wisdom to kings. I wonder if the great Raja Vikram could decide which person the woman belonged to?

"To Baman, the man who kept her ashes, fellow!" exclaimed the hero, not a little offended by the free remarks of the fiend.

"Yet," rejoined the Baital impudently, "if Tribikram had not preserved her bones how could she have been restored to life? And if Madhusadan had not learned the science of restoring the dead to life how could she have been revivified? At least, so it seems to me. But perhaps your royal wisdom may explain."

"Devil!" said the king angrily, "Tribikram, who preserved her bones, by that act placed himself in the position of her son; therefore he could not marry her. Madhusadan, who, restoring her to life, gave her life, was evidently a father to her; he could not, then, become her husband. Therefore she was the wife of Baman, who had collected her ashes."

"I am happy to see, O king," exclaimed the Vampire, "that in spite of my presentiments, we are not to part company just yet. These little trips I hold to be, like lovers' quarrels, the prelude to closer union. With your leave we will still practice a little suspension."

And so saying, the Baital again ascended the tree, and was suspended there.

"Would it not be better," thought the monarch, after recapturing and shouldering the fugitive, "for me to sit down this time and listen to the fellow's story? Perhaps the double exercise of walking and thinking confuses me."

With this idea Vikram placed his bundle upon the ground, well tied up with turband and waistband; then he seated himself cross-legged before it, and bade his son do the same.

The Vampire strongly objected to this measure, as it was contrary, he asserted, to the covenant between him and the Raja. Vikram replied by citing the very words of the agreement, proving that there was no allusion to walking or sitting.

Then the Baital became sulky, and swore that he would not utter another word. But he, too, was bound by the chain of destiny. Presently he opened his lips, with the normal prelude that he was about to tell a true tale.

Seventh Story

Showing the Exceeding Folly of Many Wise Fools

The Baital resumed.

Of all the learned Brahmans in the learnedest university of Gaur (Bengal) none was so celebrated as Vishnu Swami. He could write verse as well as prose in dead languages, not very correctly, but still, better than all his fellows—which constituted him a distinguished writer. He had history, theosophy, and the four Vedas of Scriptures at his fingers' ends, he was skilled in the argute science of Nyasa or Disputation, his mind was a mine of Pauranic or cosmogonico-traditional lore, handed down from the ancient fathers to the modern fathers: and he had written bulky commentaries, exhausting all that tongue of man has to say, upon the obscure text of some old philosopher whose works upon ethics, poetry, and rhetoric were supposed by the sages of Gaur to contain the germs of everything knowable. His fame went over all the country; yea, from country to country. He was a sea of excellent qualities, the father and mother of Brahmans, cows, and women, and the horror of loose persons, cut-throats, courtiers, and courtesans. As a benefactor he was equal to Karna, most liberal of heroes. In regard to truth he was equal to the veracious king Yudhishtira.

True, he was sometimes at a loss to spell a common word in his mother tongue, and whilst he knew to a fingerbreadth how many palms and paces the sun, the moon, and all the stars are distant from the earth, he would have been puzzled to tell you where the region called Yavana lies. Whilst he could enumerate, in strict chronological succession, every important event that happened five or six million years before he was born, he was profoundly ignorant of those that occurred in his own day. And once he asked a friend seriously, if a cat let loose in the jungle would not in time become a tiger.

Yet did all the members of alma mater Kasi, Pandits as well as students, look with awe upon Vishnu Swami's livid cheeks, and lack-lustre eyes, grimed hands and soiled cottons.

Now it so happened that this wise and pious Brahmanic peer had four sons, whom he brought up in the strictest and most serious way. They were taught to repeat their prayers long before they understood a word of them, and when they reached the age of four they had read a variety of hymns and spiritual songs. Then they were set to learn by heart precepts that inculcate sacred duties, and arguments relating to theology, abstract and concrete.

Their father, who was also their tutor, sedulously cultivated, as all the best works upon education advise, their implicit obedience, humble respect, warm attachment, and the virtues and sentiments generally. He praised them secretly and reprehended them openly, to exercise their humility. He derided their looks, and dressed them coarsely, to preserve them from vanity and conceit. Whenever they anticipated a "treat," he punctually disappointed them, to teach them self-denial. Often when he had promised them a present, he would revoke, not break his word, in order that discipline might have a name and habitat in his household. And knowing by experience how much stronger than love is fear, he frequently threatened, browbeat, and overawed them with the rod and the tongue, with the terrors of this world, and with the horrors of the next, that they might be kept in the right way by dread of falling into the bottomless pits that bound it on both sides.

At the age of six they were transferred to the Chatushpati or school. Every morning the teacher and his pupils assembled in the hut where the different classes were called up by turns. They laboured till noon, and were allowed only two hours, a moiety of the usual time, for bathing, eating, sleep, and worship, which took up half the period. At 3 P.M. they resumed their labours, repeating to the tutor what they had learned by heart, and listening to the meaning of it: this lasted till twilight. They then worshipped, ate and drank for an hour: after which came a return of study, repeating the day's lessons, till 10 P.M.

In their rare days of ease—for the learned priest, mindful of the words of the wise, did not wish to dull them by everlasting work—they were enjoined to disport themselves with the gravity and the decorum that befit young Samditats, not to engage in night frolics, not to use free jests or light expressions, not to draw pictures on the walls, not to eat honey, flesh, and sweet substances turned acid, not to talk to little girls at the well-side, on no account to wear sandals, carry an umbrella, or handle a die even for love, and by no means to steal their neighbours' mangoes.

As they advanced in years their attention during work time was unremittingly directed to the Vedas. Wordly studies were almost excluded, or to speak more correctly, whenever wordly studies were brought upon the carpet, they were so evil entreated, that they well nigh lost all form and feature. History became "The Annals of India on Brahminical Principles," opposed to the Buddhistical; geography "The Lands of the Vedas," none other being deemed worthy of notice; and law, "The Institutes of Manu," then almost obsolete, despite their exceeding sanctity.

But Jatu-harini had evidently changed these children before they were born; and Shani must have been in the ninth mansion when they came to light.

Each youth as he attained the mature age of twelve was formally entered at the University of Kasi, where, without loss of time, the first became a gambler, the second a confirmed libertine, the third a thief, and the fourth a high Buddhist, or in other words an utter atheist.

Here King Vikram frowned at his son, a hint that he had better not behave himself as the children of highly moral and religious parents usually do. The young prince understood him, and briefly remarking that such things were common in distinguished Brahman families, asked the Baital what he meant by the word "Atheist."

Of a truth (answered the Vampire) it is most difficult to explain. The sages assign to it three or four several meanings: first, one who denies that the gods exist secondly, one who owns that the gods exist but denies that they busy themselves with human affairs; and thirdly, one who believes in the gods and in their providence, but also believes that they are easily to be set aside. Similarly some atheists derive all things from dead and unintelligent matter; others from matter living and energetic but without sense or will: others from matter with forms and qualities generable and conceptible; and others from a plastic and methodical nature. Thus the Vishnu Swamis of the world have invested the subject with some confusion. The simple, that is to say, the mass of mortality, have confounded that confusion by reproachfully applying the word atheist to those whose opinions differ materially from their own.

But I being at present, perhaps happily for myself, a Vampire, and having, just now, none of these human or inhuman ideas, meant simply to say that the pious priest's fourth son being great at second and small in the matter of first causes, adopted to their fullest extent the doctrines of the philosophical Buddhas. Nothing according to him exists but the five elements, earth, water, fire, air (or wind), and vacuum, and from the last proceeded the penultimate, and so forth. With the sage Patanjali, he held the universe to have the power of perpetual progression. He called that Matra (matter), which is an eternal and infinite principle, beginningless and endless. Organization, intelligence, and design, he opined, are inherent in matter as growth is in a tree. He did not believe in soul or spirit, because it could not be detected in the body, and because it was a departure from physiological analogy.

The idea "I am," according to him, was not the identification of spirit with matter, but a product of the mutation of matter in this cloud-like, error-formed world. He believed in Substance (Sat) and scoffed at Unsubstance (Asat). He asserted the subtlety and globularity of atoms which are uncreate. He made mind and intellect a mere secretion of the brain, or rather words expressing not a thing, but a state of things. Reason was to him developed instinct, and life an element of the atmosphere affecting certain organisms. He held good and evil to be merely geographical and chronological expressions, and he opined that what is called Evil is mostly an active and transitive form of Good. Law was his great Creator of all things, but he refused a creator of law, because such a creator would require another creator, and so on in a quasi-interminable series up to absurdity.

This reduced his law to a manner of haphazard. To those who, arguing against it, asked him their favourite question, How often might a man after he had jumbled a set of letters in a bag fling them out upon the ground before they would fall into an exact poem? he replied that the calculation was beyond his arithmetic, but that the man had only to jumble and fling long enough inevitably to arrive at that end. He rejected the necessity as well as the existence of revelation, and he did not credit the miracles of Krishna, because, according to him, nature never suspends her laws, and, moreover, he had never seen aught supernatural.

He ridiculed the idea of Mahapralaya, or the great destruction, for as the world had no beginning, so it will have no end. He objected to absorption, facetiously observing with the sage Jamadagni, that it was pleasant to eat sweetmeats, but that for his part he did not wish to become the sweetmeat itself. He would not believe that Vishnu had formed the universe out of the wax in his ears. He positively asserted that trees are not bodies in which the consequences of merit and demerit are received. Nor would he conclude that to men were attached rewards and punishments from all eternity.

He made light of the Sanskara, or sacrament. He admitted Satwa, Raja, and Tama, but only as properties of matter. He acknowledged gross matter (Sthulasharir), and atomic matter (Shukshma-sharir), but not Linga-sharir, or the archetype of bodies. To doubt all things was the foundation of his theory, and to scoff at all who would not doubt was the corner-stone of his practice. In debate he preferred logical and mathematical grounds, requiring a categorical "because" in answer to his "why?" He was full of morality and natural religion, which some say is no religion at all. He gained the name of atheist by declaring with Gotama that there are innumerable worlds, that the earth has nothing beneath it but the circumambient air, and that the core of the globe is incandescent.

And he was called a practical atheist—a worse form apparently—for supporting the following dogma: "that though creation may attest that a creator has been, it supplies no evidence to prove that a creator still exists." On which occasion, Shiromani, a nonplussed theologian, asked him, "By whom and for what purpose west thou sent on earth?" The youth scoffed at the word "sent," and replied, "Not being thy Supreme Intelligence, or Infinite Nihility, I am unable to explain the phenomenon." Upon which he quoted:

How sunk in darkness Gaur must be Whose guide is blind Shiromani!

At length it so happened that the four young men, having frequently been surprised in flagrant delict, were summoned to the dread presence of the university Gurus, who addressed them as follows:

"There are four different characters in the world: he who perfectly obeys the commands; he who practices the commands, but follows evil; he who does neither good nor evil; and he who does nothing but evil. The third

character, it is observed, is also an offender, for he neglects that which he ought to observe. But ye all belong to the fourth category." Then turning to the elder they said:

"In works written upon the subject of government it is advised, 'Cut off the gambler's nose and ears, hold up his name to public contempt, and drive him out of the country, that he may thus become an example to others. For they who play must more often lose than win; and losing, they must either pay or not pay. In the latter case they forfeit caste, in the former they utterly reduce themselves. And though a gambler's wife and children are in the house, do not consider them to be so, since it is not known when they will be lost. Thus he is left in a state of perfect not-twoness (solitude), and he will be reborn in hell.' O young man! thou hast set a bad example to others, therefore shalt thou immediately exchange this university for a country life."

Then they spoke to the second offender thus:

"The wise shun woman, who can fascinate a man in the twinkling of an eye; but the foolish, conceiving an affection for her, forfeit in the pursuit of pleasure their truthfulness, reputation, and good disposition, their way of life and mode of thought, their vows and their religion. And to such the advice of their spiritual teachers comes amiss, whilst they make others as bad as themselves. For it is said, 'He who has lost all sense of shame, fears not to disgrace another; 'and there is the proverb, 'A wild cat that devours its own young is not likely to let a rat escape; ' therefore must thou too, O young man! quit this seat of learning with all possible expedition."

The young man proceeded to justify himself by quotations from the Lila-shastra, his text-book, by citing such lines as—

Fortune favours folly and force,

and by advising the elderly professors to improve their skill in the peace and war of love. But they drove him out with execrations.

As sagely and as solemnly did the Pandits and the Gurus reprove the thief and the atheist, but they did not dispense the words of wisdom in equal proportions. They warned the former that petty larceny is punishable with fine, theft on a larger scale with mutilation of the hand, and robbery, when detected in the act, with loss of life; that for cutting purses, or for snatching them out of a man's waistcloth, 'the first penalty is chopping off the fingers, the second is the loss of the hand, and the third is death.

Then they call him a dishonour to the college, and they said, "Thou art as a woman, the greatest of plunderers; other robbers purloin property which is worthless, thou stealest the best; they plunder in the night, thou in the day," and so forth. They told him that he was a fellow who had read his Chauriya Vidya to more purpose then his ritual. And they drove him from the door as he in his shamelessness began to quote texts about the four approved ways of housebreaking, namely, picking out burnt bricks, cutting through unbaked bricks, throwing water on a mud wall, and boring one of wood with a centre-bit.

But they spent six mortal hours in convicting the atheist, whose abominations they refuted by every possible argumentation: by inference, by comparison, and by sounds, by Sruti and Smriti, *i.e.*, revelational and traditional, rational and evidential, physical and metaphysical, analytical and synthetical, philosophical and philological, historical, and so forth. But they found all their endeavours vain. "For," it is said, "a man who has lost all shame, who can talk without sense, and who tries to cheat his opponent, will never get tired, and will never be put down." He declared that a non-ad was far more probable than a monad (the active principle), or the duad (the passive principle or matter.)

He compared their faith with a bubble in the water, of which we can never predicate that it does exist or it does not. It is, he said, unreal, as when the thirsty mistakes the meadow mist for a pool of water. He proved the eternity of sound. He impudently recounted and justified all the villanies of the Vamachari or left-handed sects. He told them that they had taken up an ass's load of religion, and had better apply to honest industry. He fell foul of the gods; accused Yama of kicking his own mother, Indra of tempting the wife of his spiritual guide, and Shiva of associating with low women. Thus, he said, no one can respect them. Do not we say when it thunders awfully, "the rascally gods are dying!" And when it is too wet, "these villain gods are sending too much rain"? Briefly, the young Brahman replied to and harangued them all so impertinently, if not pertinently, that they, waxing angry, fell upon him with their staves, and drove him out of assembly.

Then the four thriftless youths returned home to their father, who in his just indignation had urged their disgrace upon the Pandits and Gurus, otherwise these dignitaries would never have resorted to such extreme measures with so distinguished a house. He took the opportunity of turning them out upon the world, until such time as they might be able to show substantial signs of reform. "For," he said, "those who have read science in their boyhood, and who in youth, agitated by evil passions, have remained in the insolence of ignorance, feel regret in their old age, and are consumed by the fire of avarice." In order to supply them with a motive for the task proposed, he stopped their monthly allowance But he added, if they would repair to the neighbouring university of Jayasthal, and there show themselves something better than a disgrace to their family, he would direct their maternal uncle to supply them with all the necessaries of food and raiment.

In vain the youths attempted, with sighs and tears and threats of suicide, to soften the paternal heart. He was inexorable, for two reasons. In the first place, after wondering away the wonder with which he regarded his own failure, he felt that a stigma now attached to the name of the pious and learned Vishnu Swami, whose lectures upon "Management during Teens," and whose "Brahman Young Man's Own Book," had become standard works. Secondly, from a sense of duty, he determined to omit nothing that might tend to reclaim the reprobates. As regards the monthly allowance being stopped, the reverend man had become every year a little fonder of his purse; he had hoped that his sons would have qualified themselves to take pupils, and thus achieve for themselves, as he phrased it, "A genteel independence"; whilst they openly derided the career, calling it "an admirable provision for the more indigent members of the middle classes." For which reason he referred them to their maternal uncle, a man of known and remarkable penuriousness.

The four ne'er-do-weals, foreseeing what awaited them at Jayasthal, deferred it as a last resource; determining first to see a little life, and to push their way in the world, before condemning themselves to the tribulations of reform.

They tried to live without a monthly allowance, and notably they failed; it was squeezing, as men say, oil from sand. The gambler, having no capital, and, worse still, no credit, lost two or three suvernas at play, and could not pay them; in consequence of which he was soundly beaten with iron-shod staves, and was nearly compelled by the keeper of the hell to sell himself into slavery. Thus he became disgusted; and telling his brethren that they would find him at Jayasthal, he departed, with the intention of studying wisdom.

A month afterwards came the libertine's turn to be disappointed. He could no longer afford fine new clothes; even a well-washed coat was beyond his means. He had reckoned upon his handsome face, and he had matured a plan for laying various elderly conquests under contribution. Judge, therefore, his disgust when all the women—high and low, rich and poor, old and young, ugly and beautiful—seeing the end of his waistcloth thrown empty over his shoulder, passed him in the streets without even deigning a look. The very shopkeepers' wives, who once had adored his mustachio and had never ceased talking of his "elegant" gait, despised him; and the wealthy old person who formerly supplied his small feet with the choicest slippers, left him to starve. Upon which he also in a state of repentance, followed his brother to acquire knowledge.

"Am I not," quoth the thief to himself, "a cat in climbing, a deer in running, a snake in twisting, a hawk in pouncing, a dog in scenting?—keen as a hare, tenacious as a wolf, strong as a lion?—a lamp in the night, a horse on a plain, a mule on a stony path, a boat in the water, a rock on land?" The reply to his own questions was of course affirmative. But despite all these fine qualities, and notwithstanding his scrupulous strictness in invocating the house-breaking tool and in devoting a due portion of his gains to the gods of plunder, he was caught in a store-room by the proprietor, who inexorably handed him over to justice.

As he belonged to the priestly caste, the fine imposed upon him was heavy. He could not pay it, and therefore he was thrown into a dungeon, where he remained for some time. But at last he escaped from jail, when he made his parting bow to Kartikeya, stole a blanket from one of the guards, and set out for Jayasthal, cursing his old profession.

The atheist also found himself in a position that deprived him of all his pleasures. He delighted in afterdinner controversies, and in bringing the light troops of his wit to bear upon the unwieldy masses of lore and logic opposed to him by polemical Brahmans who, out of respect for his father, did not lay an action against him for overpowering them in theological disputation. In the strange city to which he had removed no one knew the son of Vishnu Swami, and no one cared to invite him to the house.

Once he attempted his usual trick upon a knot of sages who, sitting round a tank, were recreating themselves with quoting mystical Sanskrit shlokas of abominable long-windedness. The result was his being obliged to ply his heels vigorously in flight from the justly incensed literati, to whom he had said "tush" and "pish," at least a dozen times in as many minutes. He therefore also followed the example of his brethren, and started for Jayasthal with all possible expedition.

Arrived at the house of their maternal uncle, the young men, as by one assent, began to attempt the unloosening of his purse-strings. Signally failing in this and in other notable schemes, they determined to lay in that stock of facts and useful knowledge which might reconcile them with their father, and restore them to that happy life at Gaur which they then despised, and which now brought tears into their eyes.

Then they debated with one another what they should study:

That branch of the preternatural, popularly called "white magic," found with them favour.

They chose a Guru or teacher strictly according to the orders of their faith, a wise man of honourable family and affable demeanour, who was not a glutton nor leprous, nor blind of one eye, nor blind of both eyes, nor very short, nor suffering from whitlows, asthma, or other disease, nor noisy and talkative, nor with any defect about the fingers and toes, nor subject to his wife.

A grand discovery had been lately made by a certain physiologico-philosophico-psychologico-materialist, a Jayasthalian. In investigating the vestiges of creation, the cause of causes, the effect of effects, and the original origin of that Matra (matter) which some regard as an entity, others as a non-entity, others self-existent, others merely specious and therefore unexistent, he became convinced that the fundamental form of organic being is a globule having another globule within itselsh After inhabiting a garret and diving into the depths of his self-consciousness for a few score years, he was able to produce such complex globule in triturated and roasted flint by means of—I will not say what. Happily for creation in general, the discovery died a natural death some centuries ago. An edifying spectacle, indeed, for the world to see; a cross old man sitting amongst his gallipots and crucibles, creating animalculae, providing the corpses of birds, beasts, and fishes with what is vulgarly called life, and supplying to epigenesis all the latest improvements!

In those days the invention, being a novelty, engrossed the thoughts of the universal learned, who were in a fever of excitement about it. Some believed in it so implicity that they saw in every experiment a hundred things which they did not see. Others were so sceptical and contradictory that they would not preceive what they did see. Those blended with each fact their own deductions, whilst these span round every reality the web of their own prejudices. Curious to say, the Jayasthalians, amongst whom the luminous science arose, hailed it with delight, whilst the Gaurians derided its claim to be considered an important addition to human knowledge.

Let me try to remember a few of their words.

"Unfortunate human nature," wrote the wise of Gaur against the wise of Jayasthal, "wanted no crowning indignity but this! You had already proved that the body is made of the basest element—earth. You had argued away the immovability, the ubiquity, the permanency, the eternity, and the divinity of the soul, for is not your favourite axiom, ' It is the nature of limbs which thinketh in man'? The immortal mind is, according to you, an ignoble viscus; the godlike gift of reason is the instinct of a dog somewhat highly developed. Still you left us something to hope. Still you allowed us one boast. Still life was a thread connecting us with the Giver of Life. But now, with an impious hand, in blasphemous rage ye have rent asunder that last frail tie." And so forth.

"Welcome! thrice welcome! this latest and most admirable development of human wisdom," wrote the sage Jayasthalians against the sage Gaurians, "which has assigned to man his proper state and status and station in the magnificent scale of being. We have not created the facts which we have investigated, and which we now proudly publish. We have proved materialism to be nature's own system. But our philosophy of matter cannot overturn any truth, because, if erroneous, it will necessarily sink into oblivion; if real, it will tend only to instruct and to enlighten the world. Wise are ye in your generation, O ye sages of Gaur, yet withal wondrous illogical." And much of this kind.

Concerning all which, mighty king! I, as a Vampire, have only to remark that those two learned bodies, like your Rajaship's Nine Gems of Science, were in the habit of talking most about what they least understood.

The four young men applied the whole force of their talents to mastering the difficulties of the life-giving process; and in due time, their industry obtained its reward.

Then they determined to return home. As with beating hearts they approached the old city, their birthplace, and gazed with moistened eyes upon its tall spires and grim pagodas, its verdant meads and venerable groves, they saw a Kanjar, who, having tied up in a bundle the skin and bones of a tiger which he had found dead, was about to go on his way. Then said the thief to the gambler, "Take we these remains with us, and by means of them prove the truth of our science before the people of Gaur, to the offence of their noses." Being now possessed of knowledge, they resolved to apply it to its proper purpose, namely, power over the property of others. Accordingly, the wencher, the gambler, and the atheist kept the Kanjar in conversation whilst the thief vivified a shank bone; and the bone thereupon stood upright, and hopped about in so grotesque and wonderful a way that the man, being frightened, fled as if I had been close behind him.

Vishnu Swami had lately written a very learned commentary on the mystical words of Lokakshi:

"The Scriptures are at variance—the tradition is at variance. He who gives a meaning of his own, quoting the Vedas, is no philosopher.

"True philosophy, through ignorance, is concealed as in the fissures of a rock.

"But the way of the Great One—that is to be followed."

And the success of his book had quite effaced from the Brahman mind the holy man's failure in bringing up his children. He followed up this by adding to his essay on education a twentieth tome, containing recipes for the "Reformation of Prodigals."

The learned and reverend father received his sons with open arms. He had heard from his brother-in-law that the youths were qualified to support themselves, and when informed that they wished to make a public experiment of their science, he exerted himself, despite his disbelief in it, to forward their views.

The Pandits and Gurus were long before they would consent to attend what they considered dealings with Yama (the Devil).

In consequence, however, of Vishnu Swami's name and importunity, at length, on a certain day, all the pious, learned, and reverend tutors, teachers, professors, prolocutors, pastors, spiritual fathers, poets, philosophers, mathematicians, schoolmasters, pedagogues, bear-leaders, institutors, gerund-grinders, preceptors, dominies, brushers, coryphaei, dry-nurses, coaches, mentors, monitors, lecturers, prelectors, fellows, and heads of houses at the university at Gaur, met together in a large garden, where they usually diverted themselves out of hours with ball-tossing, pigeon-tumbling, and kite-flying.

Presently the four young men, carrying their bundle of bones and the other requisites, stepped forward, walking slowly with eyes downcast, like shrinking cattle: for it is said, the Brahman must not run, even when it rains.

After pronouncing an impromptu speech, composed for them by their father, and so stuffed with erudition that even the writer hardly understood it, they announced their wish to prove, by ocular demonstration, the truth of a science upon which their short-sighted rivals of Jayasthal had cast cold water, but which, they remarked in the eloquent peroration of their discourse, the sages of Gaur had welcomed with that wise and catholic spirit of inquiry which had ever characterized their distinguished body.

Huge words, involved sentences, and the high-flown compliment, exceedingly undeserved, obscured, I suppose, the bright wits of the intellectual convocation, which really began to think that their liberality of opinion deserved all praise.

None objected to what was being prepared, except one of the heads of houses; his appeal was generally scouted, because his Sanskrit style was vulgarly intelligible, and he had the bad name of being a practical man. The metaphysician Rashik Lall sneered to Vaiswata the poet, who passed on the look to the theo-philosopher Vardhaman. Haridatt the antiquarian whispered the metaphysician Vasudeva, who burst into a loud laugh; whilst Narayan, Jagasharma, and Devaswami, all very learned in the Vedas, opened their eyes and stared at him with well-simulated astonishment. So he, being offended, said nothing more, but arose and walked home.

A great crowd gathered round the four young men and their father, as opening the bundle that contained the tiger's remains, they prepared for their task.

One of the operators spread the bones upon the ground and fixed each one into its proper socket, not forgetting even the teeth and tusks.

The second connected, by means of a marvellous unguent, the skeleton with the muscles and heart of an elephant, which he had procured for the purpose.

The third drew from his pouch the brain and eyes of a large tom-cat, which he carefully fitted into the animal's skull, and then covered the body with the hide of a young rhinoceros.

Then the fourth—the atheist—who had been directing the operation, produced a globule having another globule within itself. And as the crowd pressed on them, craning their necks, breathless with anxiety, he placed the Principle of Organic Life in the tiger's body with such effect that the monster immediately heaved its chest, breathed, agitated its limbs, opened its eyes, jumped to its feet, shook itself, glared around, and began to gnash its teeth and lick its chops, lashing the while its ribs with its tail.

The sages sprang back, and the beast sprang forward. With a roar like thunder during Elephanta-time, it flew at the nearest of the spectators, flung Vishnu Swami to the ground and clawed his four sons. Then, not even stopping to drink their blood, it hurried after the flying herd of wise men. Jostling and tumbling, stumbling and catching at one another's long robes, they rushed in hottest haste towards the garden gate. But the beast, having the muscles of an elephant as well as the bones of a tiger, made a few bounds of eighty or ninety feet each, easily distanced them, and took away all chance of escape.

To be brief: as the monster was frightfully hungry after its long fast, and as the imprudent young men had furnished it with admirable implements of destruction, it did not cease its work till one hundred and twenty-one learned and highly distinguished Pandits and Gurus lay upon the ground chawed, clawed, sucked dry, and in most cases stone-dead. Amongst them, I need hardly say, were the sage Vishnu Swami and his four sons.

Having told this story the Vampire hung silent for a time. Presently he resumed:

> *"Now, heed my words, Raja Vikram! I am about to ask thee, Which of all those learned men was the most finished fool? The answer is easily found, yet it must be distasteful to thee. Therefore mortify thy vanity, as soon as possible, or I shall be talking, and thou wilt be walking through this livelong night, to scanty purpose. Remember! science without understanding is of little use; indeed, understanding is superior to science, and those devoid of understanding perish as did the persons who revivified the tiger. Before this, I warned thee to beware of thyself, and of shine own conceit. Here, then, is an opportunity for self-discipline—which of all those learned men was the greatest fool?"*

The warrior king mistook the kind of mortification imposed upon him, and pondered over the uncomfortable nature of the reply—in the presence of his son.

Again the Baital taunted him.

"The greatest fool of all," at last said Vikram, in slow and by no means willing accents, "was the father. Is it not said, 'There is no fool like an old fool'?"

"Gramercy!" cried the Vampire, bursting out into a discordant laugh, "I now return to my tree. By this head! I never before heard a father so readily condemn a father." With these words he disappeared, slipping out of the bundle.

The Raja scolded his son a little for want of obedience, and said that he had always thought more highly of his acuteness—never could have believed that he would have been taken in by so shallow a trick. Dharma Dhwaj answered not a word to this, but promised to be wiser another time.

Then they returned to the tree, and did what they had so often done before.

And, as before, the Baital held his tongue for a time. Presently he began as follows.

Eighth Story

Of the Use and Misuse of Magic Pills

The lady Chandraprabha, daughter of the Raja Subichar, was a particularly beautiful girl, and marriageable withal. One day as Vasanta, the Spring, began to assert its reign over the world, animate and inanimate, she went accompanied by her young friends and companions to stroll about her father's pleasure-garden.

The fair troop wandered through sombre groves, where the dark tamale-tree entwined its branches with the pale green foliage of the nim, and the pippal's domes of quivering leaves contrasted with the columnar aisles of the banyan fig. They admired the old monarchs of the forest, bearded to the waist with hangings of moss, the flowing creepers delicately climbing from the lower branches to the topmost shoots, and the cordage of llianas stretching from trunk to trunk like bridges for the monkeys to pass over.

Then they issued into a clear space dotted with asokas bearing rich crimson fiowers, cliterias of azure blue, madhavis exhibiting petals virgin white as the snows on Himalaya, and jasmines raining showers of perfumed blossoms upon the grateful earth. They could not sufficiently praise the tall and graceful stem of the arrowy areca, contrasting with the solid pyramid of the cypress, and the more masculine stature of the palm. Now they lingered in the trellised walks closely covered over with vines and creepers; then they stopped to gather the golden bloom weighing down the mango boughs, and to smell the highly-scented flowers that hung from the green fretwork of the chambela.

It was spring, I have said. The air was still except when broken by the hum of the large black bramra bee, as he plied his task amidst the red and orange flowers of the dak, and by the gushings of many waters that made music as they coursed down their stuccoed channels between borders of many coloured poppies and beds of various flowers. From time to time the dulcet note of the kokila bird, and the hoarse plaint of the turtle-dove deep hid in her leafy bower, attracted every ear and thrilled every heart. The south wind—"breeze of the south, the friend of love and spring" blew with a voluptuous warmth, for rain clouds canopied the earth, and the breath of the narcissus, the rose, and the citron, teemed with a languid fragrance.

The charms of the season affected all the damsels. They amused themselves in their privacy with pelting blossoms at one another, running races down the smooth broad alleys, mounting the silken swings that hung between the orange trees, embracing one another, and at times trying to push the butt of the party into the fishpond. Perhaps the liveliest of all was the lady Chandraprabha, who on account of her rank could pelt and push all the others, without fear of being pelted and pushed in return.

It so happened, before the attendants had had time to secure privacy for the princess and her women, that Manaswi, a very handsome youth, a Brahman's son, had wandered without malicious intention into the garden. Fatigued with walking, and finding a cool shady place beneath a tree, he had lain down there, and had gone to sleep, and had not been observed by any of the king's people. He was still sleeping when the princess and her companions were playing together.

Presently Chandraprabha, weary of sport, left her friends, and singing a lively air, tripped up the stairs leading to the summerhouse. Aroused by the sound of her advancing footsteps, Manaswi sat up; and the princess, seeing a strange man, started. But their eyes had met, and both were subdued by love—love vulgarly called "love at first sight."

"Nonsense!" exclaimed the warrior king, testily, "I can never believe in that freak of Kama Deva." He spoke feelingly, for the thing had happened to himself more than once, and on no occasion had it turned out well.

"But there is such a thing, O Raja, as love at first sight," objected the Baital, speaking dogmatically.

"Then perhaps thou canst account for it, dead one," growled the monarch surlily.

"I have no reason to do so, O Vikram," retorted the Vampire, "when you men have already done it. Listen, then, to the words of the wise. In the olden time, one of your great philosophers invented a fluid pervading all matter, strongly self-repulsive like the steam of a brass pot, and widely spreading like the breath of scandal. The repulsiveness, however, according to that wise man, is greatly modified by its second property, namely, an energetic attraction or adhesion to all material bodies. Thus every substance contains a part, more or less, of this fluid, pervading it throughout, and strongly bound to each component atom. He called it 'Ambericity,' for the best of reasons, as it has no connection with amber, and he described it as an imponderable, which, meaning that it could not be weighed, gives a very accurate and satisfactory idea of its nature.

"Now, said that philosopher, whenever two bodies containing that unweighable substance in unequal proportions happen to meet, a current of imponderable passes from one to the other, producing a kind of attraction, and tending to adhere. The operation takes place instantaneously when the force is strong and much condensed. Thus the vulgar who call things after their effects and not from their causes, term the action of this imponderable love at first sight; the wise define it to be a phenomenon of ambericity. As regards my own opinion about the matter, I have long ago told it to you, O Vikram! Silliness."

"Either hold your tongue, fellow, or go on with your story," cried the Raja, wearied out by so many words that had no manner of sense.

Well! the effect of the first glance was that Manaswi, the Brahman's son, fell back in a swoon and remained senseless upon the ground where he had been sitting; and the Raja's daughter began to tremble upon her feet, and presently dropped unconscious upon the floor of the summerhouse. Shortly after this she was found by her companions and attendants, who, quickly taking her up in their arms and supporting her into a litter, conveyed her home.

Manaswi, the Brahman's son, was so completely overcome, that he lay there dead to everything. Just then the learned, deeply read, and purblind Pandits Muldev and Shashi by name, strayed into the garden, and stumbled upon the body.

"Friend," said Muldev, "how came this youth thus to fall senseless on the ground?"

"Man," replied Shashi, "doubtless some damsel has shot forth the arrows of her glances from the bow of her eyebrows, and thence he has become insensible!"

"We must lift him up then," said Muldev the benevolent.

"What need is there to raise him?" asked Shashi the misanthrope by way of reply.

Muldev, however, would not listen to these words. He ran to the pond hard by, soaked the end of his waistcloth in water, sprinkled it over the young Brahman, raised him from the ground, and placed him sitting against the wall. And perceiving, when he came to himself, that his sickness was rather of the soul than of the body, the old men asked him how he came to be in that plight.

"We should tell our griefs," answered Manaswi, "only to those who will relieve us! What is the use of communicating them to those who, when they have heard, cannot help us? What is to be gained by the empty pity or by the useless condolence of men in general?"

The Pandits, however, by friendly looks and words, presently persuaded him to break silence, when he said, "A certain princess entered this summerhouse, and from the sight of her I have fallen into this state. If I can obtain her, I shall live; if not, I must die."

"Come with me, young man!" said Muldev the benevolent: "I will use every endeavour to obtain her, and if I do not succeed I will make thee wealthy and independent of the world."

Manaswi rejoined: "The Deity in his beneficence has created many jewels in this world, but the pearl, woman, is chiefest of all; and for her sake only does man desire wealth. What are riches to one who has abandoned his wife? What are they who do not possess beautiful wives? they are but beings inferior to the beasts! wealth is the fruit of virtue; ease, of wealth; a wife, of ease. And where no wife is, how can there be happiness?" And the enamoured youth rambled on in this way, curious to us, Raja Vikram, but perhaps natural enough in a Brahman's son suffering under that endemic malady—determination to marry.

"Whatever thou mayest desire," said Muldev, "shall by the blessing of heaven be given to thee."

Manaswi implored him, saying most pathetically, "O Pandit, bestow then that damsel upon me!"

Muldev promised to do so, and having comforted the youth, led him to his own house. Then he welcomed him politely, seated him upon the carpet, and left him for a few minutes, promising him to return. When he reappeared, he held in his hand two little balls or pills, and showing them to Manaswi, he explained their virtues as follows:

> *"There is in our house an hereditary secret, by means of which I try to promote the weal of humanity. But in all cases my success depends mainly upon the purity and the hear/wholeness of those that seek my aid. If thou place this in thy mouth, thou shalt be changed into a damsel twelve years old, and when thou withdrawest it again, thou shalt again recover shine original form. Beware, however, that thou use the power for none but a good purpose; otherwise some great calamity will befall thee. Therefore, take counsel of thyself before undertaking this trial!"*

What lover, O warrior king Vikram, would have hesitated, under such circumstances, to assure the Pandit that he was the most innocent, earnest, and well-intentioned being in the Three Worlds?

The Brahman's son, at least, lost no time in so doing. Hence the simple-minded philosopher put one of the pills into the young man's mouth, warning him on no account to swallow it, and took the other into his own mouth. Upon which Manaswi became a sprightly young maid, and Muldev was changed to a reverend and decrepid senior, not fewer than eighty years old.

Thus transformed, the twain walked up to the palace of the Raja Subichar, and stood for a while to admire the gate. Then passing through seven courts, beautiful as the Paradise of Indra, they entered, unannounced, as became the priestly dignity, a hall where, surrounded by his courtiers, sat the ruler. The latter, seeing the Holy Brahman under his roof, rose up, made the customary humble salutation, and taking their right hands, led what appeared to be the father and daughter to appropriate seats. Upon which Muldev, having recited a verse, bestowed upon the Raja a blessing whose beauty has been diffused over all creation.

"May that Deity who as a mannikin deceived the great king Bali; who as a hero, with a monkey-host, bridged the Salt Sea; who as a shepherd lifted up the mountain Gobarddhan in the palm of his hand, and by it saved the cowherds and cowherdesses from the thunders of heaven—may that Deity be thy protector!"

Having heard and marvelled at this display of eloquence, the Raja inquired, "Whence hath your holiness come?"

"My country," replied Muldev, "is on the northern side of the great mother Ganges, and there too my dwelling is. I travelled to a distant land, and having found in this maiden a worthy wife for my son, I straightway returned homewards. Meanwhile a famine had laid waste our village, and my wife and my son have fled I know not where. Encumbered with this damsel, how can I wander about seeking them? Hearing the name of a pious and generous ruler, I said to myself, ' I will leave her under his charge until my return.' Be pleased to take great care of her."

For a minute the Raja sat thoughtful and silent. He was highly pleased with the Brahman's perfect compliment. But he could not hide from himself that he was placed between two difficulties: one, the charge of a beautiful young girl, with pouting lips, soft speech, and roguish eyes; the other, a priestly curse upon himself and his kingdom. He thought, however, refusal the more dangerous; so he raised his face and exclaimed, "O produce of Brahma's head, I will do what your highness has desired of me."

Upon which the Brahman, after delivering a benediction of adieu almost as beautiful and spirit-stirring as that with which he had presented himself, took the betel and went his ways.

Then the Raja sent for his daughter Chandraprabha and said to her, "This is the affianced bride of a young Brahman, and she has been trusted to my protection for a time by her father-in-law. Take her therefore into the inner rooms, treat her with the utmost regard, and never allow her to be separated from thee, day or night, asleep or awake, eating or drinking, at home or abroad."

Chandraprabha took the hand of Sita—as Manaswi had pleased to call himself—and led the way to her own apartment. Once the seat of joy and pleasure, the rooms now wore a desolate and melancholy look. The windows were darkened, the attendants moved noiselessly over the carpets, as if their footsteps would cause headache, and there was a faint scent of some drug much used in cases of deliquium. The apartments were handsome, but the only ornament in the room where they sat was a large bunch of withered flowers in an arched recess, and these, though possibly interesting to some one, were not likely to find favour as a decoration in the eyes of everybody.

The Raja's daughter paid the greatest attention and talked with unusual vivacity to the Brahman's daughter-in-law, either because she had roguish eyes, or from some presentiment of what was to occur, whichever you please, Raja Vikram, and it is no matter which. Still Sita could not help perceiving that there was a shade of sorrow upon the forehead of her fair new friend, and so when they retired to rest she asked the cause of it.

Then Chandraprabha related to her the sad tale: "One day in the spring season, as I was strolling in the garden along with my companions, I beheld a very handsome Brahman, and our eyes having met, he became unconscious, and I also was insensible. My companions seeing my condition, brought me home, and therefore I know neither his name nor his abode. His beautiful form is impressed upon my memory. I have now no desire to eat or to drink, and from this distress my colour has become pale and my body is thus emaciated." And the beautiful princess sighed a sigh that was musical and melancholy, and concluded by predicting for herself—as persons similarly placed often do—a sudden and untimely end about the beginning of the next month.

"What wilt thou give me," asked the Brahman's daughter-in-law demurely, "if I show thee thy beloved at this very moment?"

The Raja's daughter answered, "I will ever be the lowest of thy slaves, standing before thee with joined hands."

Upon which Sita removed the pill from her mouth, and instantly having become Manaswi, put it carefully away in a little bag hung round his neck. At this sight Chandraprabha felt abashed, and hung down her head in beautiful confusion. To describe:

> *"I will have no descriptions, Vampire!" cried the great Vikram, jerking the bag up and down as if he were sweating gold in it. "The fewer of thy descriptions the better for us all."*

Briefly (resumed the demon), Manaswi reflected upon the eight forms of marriage—*viz.*, Bramhalagan, when a girl is given to a Brahman, or man of superior caste, without reward; Daiva, when she is presented as a gift or fee to the officiating priest at the close of a sacrifice; Arsha, when two cows are received by the girl's father in exchange for the bride; Prajapatya, when the girl is given at the request of a Brahman, and the father says to his daughter and her to betrothed, "Go, fulfil the duties of religion"; Asura, when money is received by the father in exchange for the bride; Rakshasha, when she is captured in war, or when her bridegroom overcomes his rival; Paisacha, when the girl is taken away from her father's house by craft; and eighthly, Gandharva-lagan, or the marriage that takes place by mutual consent.

Manaswi preferred the latter, especially as by her rank and age the princess was entitled to call upon her father for the Lakshmi Swayambara wedding, in which she would have chosen her own husband. And thus it is that Rama, Arjuna, Krishna, Nala, and others, were proposed to by the princesses whom they married. For five months after these nuptials, Manaswi never stirred out of the palace, but remained there by day a woman, and a man by night. The consequence was that he—I call him "he," for whether Manaswi or Sita, his mind ever remained masculine—presently found himself in a fair way to become a father.

Now, one would imagine that a change of sex every twenty-four hours would be variety enough to satisfy even a man. Manaswi, however, was not contented. He began to pine for more liberty, and to find fault with his wife for not taking him out into the world. And you might have supposed that a young person who, from love at first sight, had fallen senseless upon the steps of a summerhouse, and who had devoted herself to a sudden and untimely end because she was separated from her lover, would have repressed her yawns and little irritable words even for a year after having converted him into a husband.

But no! Chandraprabha soon felt as tired of seeing Manaswi and nothing but Manaswi, as Manaswi was weary of seeing Chandraprabha and nothing but Chandraprabha. Often she had been on the point of proposing visits and out-of-door excursions. But when at last the idea was first suggested by her husband, she at once became an injured woman. She hinted how foolish it was for married people to imprison themselves and to quarrel all day.

When Manaswi remonstrated, saying that he wanted nothing better than to appear before the world with her as his wife, but that he really did not know what her father might do to him, she threw out a cutting sarcasm upon his effeminate appearance during the hours of light. She then told him of an unfortunate young woman in an old nursery tale who had unconsciously married a fiend that became a fine handsome man at night when no eye could see him, and utter ugliness by day when good looks show to advantage. And lastly, when inveighing against the changeableness, fickleness, and infidelity of mankind, she quoted the words of the poet:

Out upon change! it tires the heart And weighs the noble spirit down; A vain, vain world indeed thou art That can such vile condition own The veil hath fallen from my eyes, I cannot love where I despise....

You can easily, O King Vikram, continue for yourself and conclude this lecture, which I leave unfinished on account of its length.

Chandraprabha and Sita, who called each other the Zodiacal Twins and Laughter Light, and All-consenters, easily persuaded the old Raja that their health would be further improved by air, exercise, and distractions. Subichar, being delighted with the change that had taken place in a daughter whom he loved, and whom he had feared to lose, told them to do as they pleased. They began a new life, in which short trips and visits, baths and dances, music parties, drives in bullock chariots, and water excursions succeeded one another.

It so happened that one day the Raja went with his whole family to a wedding feast in the house of his grand treasurer, where the latter's son saw Manaswi in the beautiful shape of Sita. This was a third case of love at first sight, for the young man immediately said to a particular friend, "If I obtain that girl, I shall live; if not, I shall abandon life."

In the meantime the king having enjoyed the feast, came back to his palace with his whole family. The condition of the treasurer's son, however, became very distressing; and through separation from his beloved, he gave up eating and drinking. The particular friend had kept the secret for some days, though burning to tell it. At length he found an excuse for himself in the sad state of his friend, and he immediately went and divulged all that he knew to the treasurer. After this he felt relieved.

The minister repaired to the court, and laid his case before the king, saying, "Great Raja! through the love of that Brahman's daughter-in-law, my son's state is very bad; he has given up eating and drinking; in fact he is consumed by the fire of separation. If now your majesty could show compassion, and bestow the girl upon him, his life would be saved. If not—"

"Fool!" cried the Raja, who, hearing these words, had waxed very wroth; "it is not right for kings to do injustice. Listen!

when a person puts any one in charge of a protector, how can the latter give away his trust without consulting the person that trusted him? And yet this is what you wish me to do."

The treasurer knew that the Raja could not govern his realm without him, and he was well acquainted with his master's character. He said to himself, "This will not last long;" but he remained dumb, simulating hopelessness, and hanging down his head, whilst Subichar alternately scolded and coaxed, abused and flattered him, in order to open his lips. Then, with tears in his eyes, he muttered a request to take leave; and as he passed through the palace gates, he said aloud, with a resolute air, "It will cost me but ten days of fasting!"

The treasurer, having returned home, collected all his attendants, and went straightway to his son's room. Seeing the youth still stretched upon his sleeping-mat, and very yellow for the want of food he took his hand, and said in a whisper, meant to be audible, "Alas! poor son, I can do nothing but perish with thee."

The servants, hearing this threat, slipped one by one out of the room, and each went to tell his friend that the grand treasurer had resolved to live no longer. After which, they went back to the house to see if their master intended to keep his word, and curious to know, if he did intend to die, how, where, and when it was to be. And they were not disappointed: I do not mean that the wished their lord to die, as he was a good master to them but still there was an excitement in the thing—

(Raja Vikram could not refrain from showing his anger at the insult thus cast by the Baital upon human nature; the wretch, however, pretending not to notice it, went on without interrupting himself)

—which somehow or other pleased them.

When the treasurer had spent three days without touching bread or water, all the cabinet council met and determined to retire from business unless the Raja yielded to their solicitations. The treasurer was their working man. "Besides which," said the cabinet council, "if a certain person gets into the habit of refusing us, what is to be the end of it, and what is the use of being cabinet councillors any longer?"

Early on the next morning, the ministers went in a body before the Raja, and humbly represented that "the treasurer's son is at the point of death, the effect of a full heart and an empty stomach. Should he die, the father, who has not eaten or drunk during the last three days" (the Raja trembled to hear the intelligence, though he knew it), "his father, we say, cannot be saved. If the father dies the affairs of the kingdom come to ruin,—is he not the grand treasurer? It is already said that half the accounts have been gnawed by white ants, and that some pernicious substance in the ink has eaten jagged holes through the paper, so that the other half of the accounts is illegible. It were best, sire, that you agree to what we represent."

The white ants and corrosive ink were too strong for the Raja's determination. Still, wishing to save appearances, he replied, with much firmness, that he knew the value of the treasurer and his son, that he would do much to save them, but that he had passed his royal word, and had undertaken a trust. That he would rather die a dozen deaths than break his promise, or not discharge his duty faithfully. That man's condition in this world is to depart from it, none remaining in it; that one comes and that one goes, none knowing when or where; but that eternity is eternity for happiness or misery. And much of the same nature, not very novel, and not perhaps quite to the purpose, but edifying to those who knew what lay behind the speaker's words.

The ministers did not know their lord's character so well as the grand treasurer, and they were more impressed by his firm demeanour and the number of his words than he wished them to be. After allowing his speech to settle in their minds, he did away with a great part of its effect by declaring that such were the sentiments and the principles—when a man talks of his principles, O Vikram! ask thyself the reason why—instilled into his youthful mind by the most honourable of fathers and the most virtuous of mothers. At the same time that he was by no means obstinate or proof against conviction. In token whereof he graciously permitted the councillors to convince him that it was his royal duty to break his word and betray his trust, and to give away another man's wife.

Pray do not lose your temper, O warrior king! Subichar, although a Raja, was a weak man; and you know, or you ought to know, that the wicked may be wise in their generation, but the weak never can.

Well, the ministers hearing their lord's last words, took courage, and proceeded to work upon his mind by the figure of speech popularly called "rigmarole." They said: "Great king! that old Brahman has been gone many days, and has not returned; he is probably dead and burnt. It is therefore right that by giving to the grand treasurer's son his daughter-in-law, who is only affianced, not fairly married, you should establish your government firmly. And even if he should return, bestow villages and wealth upon him; and if he be not then content, provide another and a more beautiful wife for his son, and dismiss him. A person should be sacrificed for the sake of a family, a family for a city, a city for a country, and a country for a king!"

Subichar having heard them, dismissed them with the remark that as so much was to be said on both sides, he must employ the night in thinking over the matter, and that he would on the next day favour them with his decision. The cabinet councillors knew by this that he meant that he would go and consult his wives. They retired contented, convinced that every voice would be in favour of a wedding, and that the young girl, with so good an offer, would not sacrifice the present to the future.

That evening the treasurer and his son supped together.

The first words uttered by Raja Subichar, when he entered his daughter's apartment, were an order addressed to Sita: "Go thou at once to the house of my treasurer's son."

Now, as Chandraprabha and Manaswi were generally scolding each other, Chandraprabha and Sita were hardly on speaking terms. When they heard the Raja's order for their separation they were:

"Delighted?" cried Dharma Dhwaj, who for some reason took the greatest interest in the narrative.

"Overwhelmed with grief, thou most guileless Yuva Raja (young prince)!" ejaculated the Vampire.

Raja Vikram reproved his son for talking about thing of which he knew nothing, and the Baital resumed.

They turned pale and wept, and they wrung their hands, and they begged and argued and refused obedience. In fact they did everything to make the king revoke his order.

"The virtue of a woman," quoth Sita, "is destroyed through too much beauty; the religion of a Brahman is impaired by serving kings; a cow is spoiled by distant pasturage, wealth is lost by committing injustice, and prosperity departs from the house where promises are not kept."

The Raja highly applauded the sentiment, but was firm as a rock upon the subject of Sita marrying the treasurer's son.

Chandraprabha observed that her royal father, usually so conscientious, must now be acting from interested motives, and that when selfishness sways a man, right becomes left and left becomes right, as in the reflection of a mirror.

Subichar approved of the comparison; he was not quite so resolved, but he showed no symptoms of changing his mind.

Then the Brahman's daughter-in-law, with the view of gaining time—a famous stratagem amongst feminines—said to the Raja: "Great king, if you are determined upon giving me to the grand treasurer's son, exact from him the promise that he will do what I bid him. Only on this condition will I ever enter his house!"

"Speak, then," asked the king; "what will he have to do?"

She replied, "I am of the Brahman or priestly caste, he is the son of a Kshatriya or warrior: the law directs that before we twain can wed, he should perform Yatra (pilgrimage) to all the holy places."

"Thou hast spoken Veda-truth, girl," answered the Raja, not sorry to have found so good a pretext for temporizing, and at the same time to preserve his character for firmness, resolution, determination. That night Manaswi and Chandraprabha, instead of scolding each other, congratulated themselves upon having escaped an imminent danger—which they did not escape.

In the morning Subichar sent for his ministers, including his grand treasurer and his love-sick son, and told them how well and wisely the Brahman's daughter-in-law had spoken upon the subject of the marriage. All of them approved of the condition; but the young man ventured to suggest, that while he was a-pilgrimaging the maiden should reside under his father's roof.

As he and his father showed a disposition to continue their fasts in case of the small favour not being granted, the Raja, though very loath to separate his beloved daughter and her dear friend, was driven to do it. And Sita was carried off, weeping bitterly, to the treasurer's palace. That dignitary solemnly committed her to the charge of his third and youngest wife, the lady Subhagya-Sundari, who was about her own age, and said, "You must both live together, without any kind of wrangling or contention, and do not go into other people's houses." And the grand treasurer's son went off to perform his pilgrimages.

It is no less sad than true, Raja Vikram, that in less than six days the disconsolate Sita waxed weary of being Sita, took the ball out of her mouth, and became Manaswi. Alas for the infidelity of mankind! But it is gratifying to reflect that he met with the punishment with which the Pandit Muldev had threatened him. One night the magic pill slipped down his throat. When morning dawned, being unable to change himself into Sita, Manaswi was obliged to escape through a window from the lady Subhagya-Sundari's room. He sprained his ankle with the leap, and he lay for a time upon the ground—where I leave him whilst convenient to me.

When Muldev quitted the presence of Subichar, he resumed his old shape, and returning to his brother Pandit Shashi, told him what he had done. Whereupon Shashi, the misanthrope, looked black, and used hard words and told his friend that good nature and soft-heartedness had caused him to commit a very bad action—a grievous sin. Incensed at this charge, the philanthropic Muldev became angry, and said, "I have warned the youth about his purity; what harm can come of it?"

"Thou hast," retorted Shashi, with irritating coolness, "placed a sharp weapon in a fool's hand."

"I have not," cried Muldev, indignantly.

"Therefore," drawled the malevolent, "you are answerable for all the mischief he does with it, and mischief assuredly he will do."

"He will not, by Brahma!" exclaimed Muldev.

"He will, by Vishnu!" said Shashi, with an amiability produced by having completely upset his friend's temper; "and if within the coming six months he does not disgrace himself, thou shalt have the whole of my bookcase; but if he does, the philanthropic Muldev will use all his skill and ingenuity in procuring the daughter of Raja Subichar as a wife for his faithful friend Shashi."

Having made this covenant, they both agreed not to speak of the matter till the autumn.

The appointed time drawing near, the Pandits began to make inquiries about the effect of the magic pills. Presently they found out that Sita, alias Manaswi, had one night mysteriously disappeared from the grand treasurer's house, and had not been heard of since that time. This, together with certain other things that transpired presently, convinced Muldev, who had cooled down in six months, that his friend had won the wager. He prepared to make honourable payment by handing a pill to old Shashi, who at once became a stout, handsome young Brahman, some twenty years old. Next putting a pill into his own mouth, he resumed the shape and form under which he had first appeared before Raja Subichar; and, leaning upon his staff, he led the way to the palace.

The king, in great confusion, at once recognized the old priest, and guessed the errand upon which he and the youth were come. However, he saluted them, and offered them seats, and receiving their blessings, he began to make inquiries about their health and welfare. At last he mustered courage to ask the old Brahman where he had been living for so long a time.

"Great king," replied the priest, "I went to seek after my son, and having found him, I bring him to your majesty. Give him his wife, and I will take them both home with me."

Raja Subichar prevaricated not a little; but presently, being hard pushed, he related everything that had happened.

"What is this that you have done?" cried Muldev, simulating excessive anger and astonishment. "Why have you given my son's wife in marriage to another man? You have done what you wished, and now, therefore, receive my Shrap (curse)!"

The poor Raja, in great trepidation, said, "O Vivinity! be not thus angry! I will do whatever you bid me."

Said Muldev, "If through dread of my excommunication you will freely give whatever I demand of you, then marry your daughter, Chandraprabha, to this my son. On this condition I forgive you. To me, now a necklace of pearls and a venomous krishna (cobra capella); the most powerful enemy and the kindest friend, the most precious gem and a clod of earth; the softest bed and the hardest stone; a blade of grass and the loveliest woman—are precisely the same. All I desire is that in some holy place, repeating the name of God, I may soon end my days."

Subichar, terrified by this additional show of sanctity, at once summoned an astrologer, and fixed upon the auspicious moment and lunar influence. He did not consult the princess, and had he done so she would not have resisted his wishes. Chandraprabha had heard of Sita's escape from the treasurer's house, and she had on the subject her own suspicions. Besides which she looked forward to a certain event, and she was by no means sure that her royal father approved of the Gandharba form of marriage—at least for his daughter. Thus the Brahman's son receiving in due time the princess and her dowry, took leave of the king and returned to his own village.

Hardly, however, had Chandraprabha been married to Shashi the Pandit, when Manaswi went to him, and began to wrangle, and said, "Give me my wife!" He had recovered from the effects of his fall, and having lost her he therefore loved her—very dearly.

But Shashi proved by reference to the astrologers, priests, and ten persons as witnesses, that he had duly wedded her, and brought her to his home; "therefore," said he, "she is my spouse."

Manaswi swore by all holy things that he had been legally married to her, and that he was the father of her child that was about to be. "How·then," continued he, "can she be thy spouse?" He would have summoned Muldev as a witness, but that worthy, after remonstrating with him, disappeared. He called upon Chandraprabha to confirm his statement, but she put on an innocent face, and indignantly denied ever having seen the man.

Still, continued the Baital, many people believed Manaswi's story, as it was marvellous and incredible. Even to the present day, there are many who decidedly think him legally married to the daughter of Raja Subichar.

"Then they are pestilent fellows!" cried the warrior king Vikram, who hated nothing more than clandestine and runaway matches. "No one knew that the villain, Manaswi, was the father of her child; whereas, the Pandit Shashi married her lawfully, before witnesses, and with all the ceremonies. She therefore remains his wife, and the child will perform the funeral obsequies for him, and offer water to the manes of his pitris (ancestors). At least, so say law and justice."

"Which justice is often unjust enough!" cried the Vampire; "and ply thy legs, mighty Raja; let me see if thou canst reach the sires-tree before I do."

Ninth Story

Showing that a Man's Wife belongs not to His Body but to His Head

Far and wide through the lovely land overrun by the Arya from the Western Highlands spread the fame of Unmadini, the beautiful daughter of Haridas the Brahman. In the numberless odes, sonnets, and acrostics addressed to her by a hundred Pandits and poets her charms were sung with prodigious triteness.

Her presence was compared to light shining in a dark house; her face to the full moon; her complexion to the yellow champaka flower; her curls to female snakes; her eyes to those of the deer; her eyebrows to bent bows; her teeth to strings of little opals; her feet to rubies and red gems, and her gait to that of the wild goose. And none forgot to say that her voice affected the author like the song of the kokila bird, sounding from the shadowy brake, when the breeze blows coolly, or that the fairy beings of Indra's heaven would have shrunk away abashed at her loveliness.

But, Raja Vikram! all the poets failed to win the fair Unmadini's love. To praise the beauty of a beauty is not to praise her. Extol her wit and talents, which has the zest of novelty, then you may succeed. For the same reason, read inversely, the plainer and cleverer is the bosom you would fire, the more personal you must be upon the subject of its grace and loveliness. Flattery you know, is ever the match which kindles the Flame of love. True it is that some by roughness of demeanour and bluntness in speech, contrasting with those whom they call the "herd," have the art to succeed in the service of the bodyless god. But even they must—

The young prince Dharma Dhwaj could not help laughing at the thought of how this must sound in his father's ear. And the Raja hearing the ill-timed merriment, sternly ordered the Baital to cease his immoralities and to continue his story.

Thus the lovely Unmadini, conceiving an extreme contempt for poets and literati, one day told her father who greatly loved her, that her husband must be a fine young man who never wrote verses. Withal she insisted strongly on mental qualities and science, being a person of moderate mind and an adorer of talent—when not perverted to poetry.

As you may imagine, Raja Vikram, all the beauty's bosom friends, seeing her refuse so many good offers, confidently predicted that she would pass through the jungle and content herself with a bad stick, or that she would lead ring-tailed apes in Patala.

At length when some time had elapsed, four suitors appeared from four different countries, all of them claiming equal excellence in youth and beauty, strength and understanding. And after paying their respects to Haridas, and telling him their wishes, they were directed to come early on the next morning and to enter upon the first ordeal—an intellectual conversation.

This they did.

"Foolish the man," quoth the young Mahasani, "that seeks permanence in this world—frail as the stem of the plantain-tree, transient as the ocean foam.

"All that is high shall presently fall; all that is low must finally perish.

"Unwillingly do the manes of the dead taste the tears shed by their kinsmen: then wail not, but perform the funeral obsequies with diligence."

"What ill-omened fellow is this?" quoth the fair Unmadini, who was sitting behind her curtain;" besides, he has dared to quote poetry! "There was little chance of success for that suitor.

"She is called a good woman, and a woman of pure descent," quoth the second suitor, "who serves him to whom her father and mother have given her; and it is written in the scriptures that a woman who in the lifetime of her husband, becoming a devotee, engages in fasting, and in austere devotion, shortens his days, and hereafter falls into the fire. For it is said—

"A woman's bliss is found not in the smile Of father, mother, friend, nor in herself; Her husband is her only portion here, Her heaven hereafter."

The word "serve," which might mean "obey," was peculiarly disagreeable to the fair one's ears, and she did not admire the check so soon placed upon her devotion, or the decided language and manner of the youth. She therefore mentally resolved never again to see that person, whom she determined to be stupid as an elephant.

"A mother," said Gunakar, the third candidate, "protects her son in babyhood, and a father when his offspring is growing up. But the man of warrior descent defends his brethren at all times. Such is the custom of the world, and such is my state. I dwell on the heads of the strong!"

Therefore those assembled together looked with great respect upon the man of velour.

Devasharma, the fourth suitor, contented himself with listening to the others, who fancied that he was overawed by their cleverness. And when it came to his turn he simply remarked, "Silence is better than speech." Being further pressed, he said, "A wise man will not proclaim his age, nor a deception practised upon himself, nor his riches, nor the loss of riches, nor family faults, nor incantations, nor conjugal love, nor medicinal prescriptions, nor religious duties, nor gifts, nor reproach, nor the infidelity of his wife."

Thus ended the first trial. The master of the house dismissed the two former speakers, with many polite expressions and some trifling presents. Then having given betel to them, scented their garments with attar, and sprinkled rose-water over their heads, he accompanied them to the door, showing much regret. The two latter speakers he begged to come on the next day.

Gunakar and Devasharma did not fail. When they entered the assembly-room and took the seats pointed out to them, the father said, "Be ye pleased to explain and make manifest the effects of your mental qualities. So shall I judge of them."

"I have made," said Gunakar, "a four-wheeled carriage, in which the power resides to carry you in a moment wherever you may purpose to go."

"I have such power over the angel of death," said Devasharma, "that I can at all times raise a corpse, and enable my friends to do the same."

Now tell me by thy brains, O warrior King Vikram, which of these two youths was the fitter husband for the maid?

Either the Raja could not answer the question, or perhaps he would not, being determined to break the spell which had already kept him walking to and fro for so many hours. Then the Baital, who had paused to let his royal carrier commit himself, seeing that the attempt had failed, proceeded without making any further comment.

The beautiful Unmadini was brought out, but she hung down her head and made no reply. Yet she took care to move both her eyes in the direction of Devasharma. Whereupon Haridas, quoting the proverb that "pearls string with pearls," formally betrothed to him his daughter. The soldier suitor twisted the ends of his mustachios into his eyes, which were red with wrath, and fumbled with his fingers about the hilt of his sword. But he was a man of noble birth, and presently his anger passed away.

Mahasani the poet, however, being a shameless person—and when can we be safe from such?—forced himself into the assembly and began to rage and to storm, and to quote proverbs in a loud tone of voice. He remarked that in this world women are a mine of grief, a poisonous root, the abode of solicitude, the destroyers of resolution, the occasioners of fascination, and the plunderers of all virtuous qualities. From the daughter he passed to the father, and after saying hard things of him as a "Maha-Brahman," who took cows and gold and worshipped a monkey, he fell with a sweeping censure upon all priests and sons of priests, more especially Devasharma. As the bystanders remonstrated with him, he became more violent, and when Haridas, who was a weak man, appeared terrified by his voice, look, and gesture, he swore a solemn oath that despite all the betrothals in the world, unless Unmadini became his wife he would commit suicide, and as a demon haunt the house and injure the inmates.

Gunakar the soldier exhorted this shameless poet to slay himself at once, and to go where he pleased. But as Haridas reproved the warrior for inhumanity, Mahasani nerved by spite, love, rage, and perversity to an heroic death, drew a noose from his bosom, rushed out of the house, and suspended himself to the nearest tree.

And, true enough, as the midnight gong struck, he appeared in the form of a gigantic and malignant Rakshasa (fiend), dreadfully frightened the household of Haridas, and carried off the lovely Unmadini, leaving word that she was to he found on the topmost peak of Himalaya.

The unhappy father hastened to the house where Devasharma lived. There, weeping bitterly and wringing his hands in despair, he told the terrible tale, and besought his intended son-in-law to be up and doing.

The young Brahman at once sought his late rival, and asked his aid. This the soldier granted at once, although he had been nettled at being conquered in love by a priestling.

The carriage was at once made ready, and the suitors set out, bidding the father be of good cheer, and that before sunset he should embrace his daughter. They then entered the vehicle; Gunakar with cabalistic words caused it to rise high in the air, and Devasharma put to flight the demon by reciting the sacred verse, "Let us meditate on the supreme splendour (or adorable light) of that Divine Ruler (the sun) who may illuminate our understandings. Venerable men, guided by the intelligence, salute the divine sun (Sarvitri) with oblations and praise. Om!"

Then they returned with the girl to the house, and Haridas blessed them, praising the sun aloud in the joy of his heart. Lest other accidents might happen, he chose an auspicious planetary conjunction, and at a fortunate moment rubbed turmeric upon his daughter's hands.

The wedding was splendid, and broke the hearts of twenty-four rivals. In due time Devasharma asked leave from his father-in-law to revisit his home, and to carry with him his bride. This request being granted, he set out accompanied by Gunakar the soldier, who swore not to leave the couple before seeing them safe under their own roof-tree.

It so happened that their road lay over the summits of the wild Vindhya hills, where dangers of all kinds are as thick as shells upon the shore of the deep. Here were rocks and jagged precipices making the traveller's brain whirl when he looked into them. There impetuous torrents roared and flashed down their beds of black stone, threatening destruction to those who would cross them. Now the path was lost in the matted thorny underwood and the pitchy shades of the jungle, deep and dark as the valley of death. Then the thunder-cloud licked the earth with its fiery tongue, and its voice shook the crags and filled their hollow caves. At times, the sun was so hot, that wild birds fell dead from the air. And at every moment the wayfarers heard the trumpeting of giant elephants, the fierce howling of the tiger, the grisly laugh of the foul hyaena, and the whimpering of the wild dogs as they coursed by on the tracks of their prey.

Yet, sustained by the five-armed god the little party passed safely through all these dangers. They had almost emerged from the damp glooms of the forest into the open plains which skirt the southern base of the hills, when one night the fair Unmadini saw a terrible vision.

She beheld herself wading through a sluggish pool of muddy water, which rippled, curdling as she stepped into it, and which, as she advanced, darkened with the slime raised by her feet. She was bearing in her arms the semblance of a sick child, which struggled convulsively and filled the air with dismal wails. These cries seemed to be answered by a multitude of other children, some bloated like toads, others mere skeletons lying upon the bank, or floating upon the thick brown waters of the pond. And all seemed to address their cries to her, as if she were the cause of their weeping; nor could all her efforts quiet or console them for a moment.

When the bride awoke, she related all the particulars of her ill-omened vision to her husband; and the latter, after a short pause, informed her and his friend that a terrible calamity was about to befall them. He then drew from his travelling wallet a skein of thread. This he divided into three parts, one for each, and told his companions that in case of grievous bodily injury, the bit of thread wound round the wounded part would instantly make it whole.

After which he taught them the Mantra, or mystical word by which the lives of men are restored to their bodies, even when they have taken their allotted places amongst the stars, and which for evident reasons I do not want to repeat. It concluded, however, with the three Vyahritis, or sacred syllables—Bhuh, Bhuvah, Svar!

Raja Vikram was perhaps a little disappointed by this declaration. He made no remark, however, and the Baital thus pursued:

As Devasharma foretold, an accident of a terrible nature did occur. On the evening of that day, as they emerged upon the plain, they were attacked by the Kiratas, or savage tribes of the mountain. A small, black, wiry figure, armed with a bow and little cane arrows, stood in their way, signifying by gestures that they must halt and lay down their arms. As they continued to advance, he began to speak with a shrill chattering, like the note of an affrighted bird, his restless red eyes glared with rage, and he waved his weapon furiously round his head. Then from the rocks and thickets on both sides of the path poured a shower of shafts upon the three strangers.

The unequal combat did not last long. Gunakar, the soldier, wielded his strong right arm with fatal effect and struck down some threescore of the foes. But new swarms came on like angry hornets buzzing round the destroyer of their nests. And when he fell, Devasharma, who had left him for a moment to hide his beautiful wife in the hollow of a tree, returned, and stood fighting over the body of his friend till he also, overpowered by numbers, was thrown to the ground. Then the wild men, drawing their knives, cut off the heads of their helpless enemies, stripped their bodies of all their ornaments, and departed, leaving the woman unharmed for good luck.

When Unmadini, who had been more dead than alive during the affray, found silence succeed to the horrid din of shrieks and shouts, she ventured to creep out of her refuge in the hollow tree. And what does she behold? her husband and his friend are lying upon the ground, with their heads at a short distance from their bodies. She sat down and wept bitterly.

Presently, remembering the lesson which she had learned that very morning, she drew forth from her bosom the bit of thread and proceeded to use it. She approached the heads to the bodies, and tied some of the magic string round each neck. But the shades of evening were fast deepening, and in her agitation, confusion and terror, she made a curious mistake by applying the heads to the wrong trunks. After which, she again sat down, and having recited her prayers, she pronounced, as her husband had taught her, the life-giving incantation.

In a moment the dead men were made alive. They opened their eyes, shook themselves, sat up and handled their limbs as if to feel that all was right. But something or other appeared to them all wrong. They placed their palms upon their foreheads, and looked downwards, and started to their feet and began to stare at their hands and legs. Upon which they scrutinized the very scanty articles of dress which the wild men had left upon them, and lastly one began to eye the other with curious puzzled looks.

The wife, attributing their gestures to the confusion which one might expect to find in the brains of men who have just undergone so great a trial as amputation of the head must be, stood before them for a moment or two. She then with a cry of gladness flew to the bosom of the individual who was, as she supposed, her husband.

He repulsed her, telling her that she was mistaken. Then, blushing deeply in spite of her other emotions, she threw both her beautiful arms round the neck of the person who must be, she naturally concluded, the right man. To her utter confusion, he also shrank back from her embrace.

Then a horrid thought flashed across her mind: she perceived her fatal mistake, and her heart almost ceased to beat.

"This is thy wife!" cried the Brahman's head that had been fastened to the soldier's body.

"No; she is thy wife!" replied the soldier's head which had been placed upon the Brahman's body.

"Then she is my wife!" rejoined the first compound creature.

"By no means! she is my wife," cried the second.

"What then am I?" asked Devasharma-Gunakar.

"What do you think I am?" answered GunakarDevasharma, with another question.

"Unmadini shall be mine," quoth the head.

"You lie, she shall be mine," shouted the body.

"Holy Yama, hear the villain," exclaimed both of them at the same moment.

In short, having thus begun, they continued to quarrel violently, each one declaring that the beautiful Unmadini belonged to him, and to him only. How to settle their dispute Brahma the Lord of creatures only knows. I do not, except by cutting off their heads once more, and by putting them in their proper places. And I am quite sure, O Raja Vikram! that thy wits are quite unfit to answer the question, To which of these two is the beautiful Unmadini wife? It is even said—amongst us Baitals—that when this pair of half-husbands appeared in the presence of the Just King, a terrible confusion arose, each head declaiming all the sins and peccadilloes which its body had committed, and that Yama the holy ruler himself hit his forefinger with vexation.

Here the young prince Dharma Dhwaj burst out laughing at the ridiculous idea of the wrong heads. And the warrior king, who, like single-minded fathers in general, was ever in the idea that his son had a velleity for deriding and otherwise vexing him, began a severe course of reproof. He reminded the prince of the common saying that merriment without cause degrades a man in the opinion of his fellows, and indulged him with a quotation extensively used by grave fathers, namely, that the loud laugh bespeaks a vacant mind. After which he proceeded with much pompousness to pronounce the following opinion:

"*It is said in the Shastras*——"

"Your majesty need hardly display so much erudition! Doubtless it comes from the lips of Jayudeva or some other one of your Nine Gems of Science, who know much more about their songs and their stanzas than they do about their scriptures," insolently interrupted the Baital, who never lost an opportunity of carping at those reverend men.

"It is said in the Shastras," continued Raja Vikram sternly, after hesitating whether he should or should not administer a corporeal correction to the Vampire, "that Mother Ganga is the queen amongst rivers, and the mountain Sumeru is the monarch among mountains, and the tree Kalpavriksha is the king of all trees, and the head of man is the best and most excellent of limbs. And thus, according to this reason, the wife belonged to him whose noblest position claimed her."

"The next thing your majesty will do, I suppose," continued the Baital, with a sneer, "is to support the opinions of the Digambara, who maintains that the soul is exceedingly rarefied, confined to one place, and of equal dimensions with the body, or the fancies of that worthy philosopher Jaimani, who, conceiving soul and mind and matter to be things purely synonymous, asserts outwardly and writes in his books that the brain is the organ of the mind which is acted upon by the immortal soul, but who inwardly and verily believes that the brain is the mind, and consequently that the brain is the soul or spirit or whatever you please to call it; in fact, that soul is a natural faculty of the body. A pretty doctrine, indeed, for a Brahman to hold. You might as well agree with me at once that the soul of man resides, when at home, either in a vein in the breast, or in the pit of his stomach, or that half of it is in a man's brain and the other or reasoning half is in his heart, an organ of his body."

"What has all this string of words to do with the matter, Vampire?" asked Raja Vikram angrily.

"Only," said the demon laughing, "that in my opinion, as opposed to the Shastras and to Raja Vikram, that the beautiful Unmadini belonged, not to the head part but to the body part. Because the latter has an immortal soul in the pit of its stomach, whereas the former is a box of bone, more or less thick, and contains brains which are of much the same consistence as those of a calf."

"Villain!" exclaimed the Raja, "does not the soul or conscious life enter the body through the sagittal suture and lodge in the brain, thence to contemplate, through the same opening, the divine perfections?"

"I must, however, bid you farewell for the moment, O warrior king, Sakadhipati-Vikramadityal! I feel a sudden and ardent desire to change this cramped position for one more natural to me."

The warrior monarch had so far committed himself that he could not prevent the Vampire from flitting. But he lost no more time in following him than a grain of mustard, in its fall, stays on a cow's horn. And when he had thrown him over his shoulder, the king desired him of his own accord to begin a new tale.

"O my left eyelid flutters," exclaimed the Baital in despair, "my heart throbs, my sight is dim: surely now beginneth the end. It is as Vidhata hath written on my forehead—how can it be otherwise? Still listen, O mighty Raja, whilst I recount to you a true story, and Saraswati sit on my tongue."

Tenth Story

Of the Marvellous Delicacy of Three Queens

The Baital said, O king, in the Gaur country, Vardhman by name, there is a city, and one called Gunshekhar was the Raja of that land. His minister was one Abhaichand, a Jain, by whose teachings the king also came into the Jain faith.

The worship of Shiva and of Vishnu, gifts of cows, gifts of lands, gifts of rice balls, gaming and spirit-drinking, all these he prohibited. In the city no man could get leave to do them, and as for bones, into the Ganges no man was allowed to throw them, and in these matters the minister, having taken orders from the king, caused a proclamation to be made about the city, saying, "Whoever these acts shall do, the Raja having confiscated, will punish him and banish him from the city."

Now one day the Diwan began to say to the Raja, "O great king, to the decisions of the Faith be pleased to give ear. Whosoever takes the life of another, his life also in the future birth is taken: this very sin causes him to be born again and again upon earth and to die And thus he ever continues to be born again and to die. Hence for one who has found entrance into this world to cultivate religion is right and proper. Be pleased to behold! By love, by wrath, by pain, by desire, and by fascination overpowered, the gods Brahma, Vishnu, and

Mahadeva (Shiva) in various ways upon the earth are ever becoming incarnate. Far better than they is the Cow, who is free from passion, enmity, drunkenness, anger, covetousness, and inordinate affection, who supports mankind, and whose progeny in many ways give ease and solace to the creatures of the world These deities and sages (munis) believe in the Cow.

"For such reason to believe in the gods is not good. Upon this earth be pleased to believe in the Cow. It is our duty to protect the life of everyone, beginning from the elephant, through ants, beasts, and birds, up to man. In the world righteousness equal to that there is none. Those who, eating the flesh of other creatures, increase their own flesh, shall in the fulness of time assuredly obtain the fruition of Narak; hence for a man it is proper to attend to the conversation of life. They who understand not the pain of other creatures, and who continue to slay and to devour them, last but few days in the land, and return to mundane existence, maimed, limping, one-eyed, blind, dwarfed, hunchbacked, and imperfect in such wise. Just as they consume the bodies of beasts and of birds, even so they end by spoiling their own bodies. From drinking spirits also the great sin arises, hence the consuming of spirits and flesh is not advisable."

The minister having in this manner explained to the king the sentiments of his own mind, so brought him over to the Jain faith, that whatever he said, so the king did. Thus in Brahmans, in Jogis, in Janganis, in Sevras, in Sannyasis, and in religious mendicants, no man believed, and according to this creed the rule was carried on.

Now one day, being in the power of Death, Raja Gunshekhar died. Then his son Dharmadhwaj sat upon the carpet (throne), and began to rule. Presently he caused the minister Abhaichand to be seized, had his head shaved all but seven locks of hair, ordered his face to be blackened, and mounting him on an ass, with drums beaten, had him led all about the city, and drove him from the kingdom. From that time he carried on his rule free from all anxiety.

It so happened that in the season of spring, the king Dharmadhwaj, taking his queens with him, went for a stroll in the garden, where there was a large. tank with lotuses blooming within it. The Raja admiring its beauty, took off his clothes and went down to bathe.

After plucking a flower and coming to the bank, he was going to give it into the hands of one of his queens, when it slipped from his fingers, fell upon her foot, and broke it with the blow. Then the Raja being alarmed, at once came out of the tank, and began to apply remedies to her.

Hereupon night came on, and the moon shone brightly: the falling of its rays on the body of the second queen formed blisters And suddenly from a distance the sound of a wooden pestle came out of a householder's dwelling, when the third queen fainted away with a severe pain in the head

Having spoken thus much the Baital said "O my king! of these three which is the most delicate?" The Raja answered, "She indeed is the most delicate who fainted in consequence of the headache." The Baital hearing this speech, went and hung himself from the very same tree, and the Raja, having gone there and taken him down and fastened him in the bundle and placed him on his shoulder, carried him away.

Eleventh Story

Which Puzzles Raja Vikram

There is a queer time coming, O Raja Vikram!—a queer time coming (said the Vampire), a queer time coming. Elderly people like you talk abundantly about the good old days that were, and about the degeneracy of the days that are. I wonder what you would say if you could but look forward a few hundred years.

Brahmans shall disgrace themselves by becoming soldiers and being killed, and Serviles (Shudras) shall dishonour themselves by wearing the thread of the twiceborn, and by refusing to be slaves; in fact, society shall be all "mouth" and mixed castes. The courts of justice shall be disused; the great works of peace shall no longer be undertaken; wars shall last six weeks, and their causes shall be clean forgotten; the useful arts and great sciences shall die starved; there shall be no

Gems of Science; there shall be a hospital for destitute kings, those, at least, who do not lose their heads, and no Vikrama—

A severe shaking stayed for a moment the Vampire's tongue.

He presently resumed. Briefly, building tanks feeding Brahmans; lying when one ought to lie; suicide, the burning of widows, and the burying of live children, shall become utterly unfashionable.

The consequence of this singular degeneracy, O mighty Vikram, will be that strangers shall dwell beneath the roof tree in Bharat Khanda (India), and impure barbarians shall call the land their own. They come from a wonderful country, and I am most surprised that they bear it. The sky which ought to be gold and blue is there grey, a kind of dark white; the sun looks deadly pale, and the moon as if he were dead. The sea, when not dirty green, glistens with yellowish foam, and as you approach the shore, tall ghastly cliffs, like the skeletons of giants, stand up to receive or ready to repel. During the greater pert of the sun's Dakhshanayan (southern declination) the country is covered with a sort of cold white stuff which dazzles the eyes; and at such times the air is obscured with what appears to be a shower of white feathers or flocks of cotton. At other seasons there is a pale glare produced by the mist clouds which spread themselves over the lower firmament. Even the faces of the people are white; the men are white when not painted blue; the women are whiter, and the children are whitest: these indeed often have white hair.

"Truly," exclaimed Dharma Dhwaj, "says the proverb, 'Whoso seeth the world telleth many a lie.'"

At present (resumed the Vampire, not heeding the interruption), they run about naked in the woods, being merely Hindu outcastes. Presently they will change—the wonderful white Pariahs! They will eat all food indifferently, domestic fowls, onions, hogs fed in the street, donkeys, horses, hares, and (most horrible!) the flesh of the sacred cow. They will imbibe what resembles meat of colocynth, mixed with water, producing a curious frothy liquid, and a fiery stuff which burns the mouth, for their milk will be mostly chalk and pulp of brains; they will ignore the sweet juices of fruits and sugar-cane, and as for the pure element they will drink it, but only as medicine, They will shave their beards instead of their heads, and stand upright when they should sit down, and squat upon a wooden frame instead of a carpet, and appear in red and black like the children of Yama.

They will never offer sacrifices to the manes of ancestors, leaving them after their death to fry in the hottest of places. Yet will they perpetually quarrel and fight about their faith; for their tempers are fierce, and they would burst if they could not harm one another. Even now the children, who amuse themselves with making puddings on the shore, that is to say, heaping up the sand, always end their little games with "punching," which means shutting the hand and striking one another's heads, and it is soon found that the children are the fathers of the men.

These wonderful white outcastes will often be ruled by female chiefs, and it is likely that the habit of prostrating themselves before a woman who has not the power of cutting off a single head, may account for their unusual degeneracy and uncleanness. They will consider no occupation so noble as running after a jackal; they will dance for themselves, holding on to strange women, and they will take a pride in playing upon instruments, like young music girls.

The women, of course, relying upon the aid of the female chieftains, will soon emancipate themselves from the rules of modesty. They will eat with their husbands and with other men, and yawn and sit carelessly before them showing the backs of their heads. They will impudently quote the words, "By confinement at home, even under affectionate and observant guardians, women are not secure, but those are really safe who are guarded by their own inclinations "; as the poet sang:

Woman obeys one only word, her heart.

They will not allow their husbands to have more than one wife, and even the single wife will not be his slave when he needs her services, busying herself in the collection of wealth, in ceremonial purification, and feminine duty; in the preparation of daily food and in the superintendence of household utensils. What said Rama of Sita his wife?" If I chanced to be angry, she bore my impatience like the patient earth without a murmur; in the hour of necessity she cherished me as a mother does her child; in the moments of repose she was a lover to me; in times of gladness she was to me as a friend."

And it is said, "a religious wife assists her husband in his worship with a spirit as devout as his own. She gives her whole mind to make him happy; she is as faithful to him as a shadow to the body, and she esteems him, whether poor or rich, good or bad, handsome or deformed. In his absence or his sickness she renounces every gratification; at his death she dies with him, and he enjoys heaven as the fruit of her virtuous deeds. Whereas if she be guilty of many wicked actions and he should die first, he must suffer much for the demerits of his wife."

But these women will talk aloud, and scold as the braying ass, and make the house a scene of variance, like the snake with the ichneumon, the owl with the crow, for they have no fear of losing their noses or parting with their ears. They will (O my mother!) converse with strange men and take their hands; they will receive presents from them, and, worst of all, they will show their white faces openly without the least sense of shame; they will ride publicly in chariots and mount horses, whose points they pride themselves upon knowing, and eat and drink in crowded places—their husbands looking on the while, and perhaps even leading them through the streets.

And she will be deemed the pinnacle of the pagoda of perfection, that most excels in wit and shamelessness, and who can turn to water the livers of most men. They will dance and sing instead of minding their children, and when these grow up they will send them out of the house to shift for themselves, and care little if they never see them again. But the greatest sin of all will be this: when widowed they will ever be on the lookout for a second husband, and instances will be known of women fearlessly marrying three, four, and five times. You would think that all this licence satisfies them. But no! The more they have the more their weak minds covet. The men have admitted them to an equality, they will aim at an absolute superiority, and claim respect and homage; they will eternally raise tempests about their rights, and if anyone should venture to chastise them as they deserve, they would call him a coward and run off to the judge.

The men will, I say, be as wonderful about their women as about all other matters. The sage of Bharat Khanda guards the frail sex strictly, knowing its frailty, and avoids teaching it to read and write, which it will assuredly use for a bad purpose. For women are ever subject to the god with the sugar-cane bow and string of bees, and arrows tipped with heating blossoms, and to him they will ever surrender man, dhan, tan—mind, wealth, and body. When, by exceeding cunning, all human precautions have been made vain, the wise man bows to Fate, and he forgets, or he tries to forget, the past. Whereas this race of white Pariahs will purposely lead their women into every kind of temptation, and, when an accident occurs, they will rage at and accuse them, killing ten thousand with a word, and cause an uproar, and talk scandal and be scandalized, and go before the magistrate, and make all the evil as public as possible. One would think they had in every way done their duty to their women!

And when all this change shall have come over them, they will feel restless and take flight, and fall like locusts upon the Aryavartta (land of India). Starving in their own country, they will find enough to eat here, and to carry away also. They will be mischievous as the saw with which ornament-makers trim their shells, and cut ascending as well as descending. To cultivate their friendship will be like making a gap in the water, and their partisans will ever fare worse than their foes. They will be selfish as crows, which, though they eat every kind of flesh, will not permit other birds to devour that of the crow.

In the beginning they will hire a shop near the mouth of mother Ganges, and they will sell lead and bullion, fine and coarse woollen cloths, and all the materials for intoxication. Then they will begin to send for soldiers beyond the sea, and to enlist warriors in Zambudwipa (India). They will from shopkeepers become soldiers: they will beat and be beaten; they will win and lose; but the power of their star and the enchantments of their Queen Kompani, a daina or witch who can draw the blood out of a man and slay him with a look, will turn everything to their good. Presently the noise of their armies shall be as the roaring of the sea; the dazzling of their arms shall blind the eyes like lightning; their battle-fields shall be as the dissolution of the world; and the slaughter-ground shall resemble a garden of plantain trees after a storm.

At length they shall spread like the march of a host of ants over the land They will swear, "Dehar Ganga!" and they hate nothing so much as being compelled to destroy an army, to take and loot a city, or to add a rich slip of territory to their rule. And yet they will go on killing and capturing and adding region to region, till the Abode of Snow (Himalaya) confines them to the north, the Sindhu-naddi (Incus) to the west, and elsewhere the sea. Even in this, too, they will demean themselves as lords and masters, scarcely allowing poor Samudradevta to rule his own waves.

Raja Vikram was in a silent mood, otherwise he would not have allowed such ill-omened discourse to pass uninterrupted. Then the Baital, who in vain had often paused to give the royal carrier a chance of asking him a curious question, continued his recital in a dissonant and dissatisfied tone of voice.

By my feet and your head, O warrior king! it will fare badly in those days for the Rajas of Hindustan, when the red-coated men of Shaka shall come amongst them. Listen to my words.

In the Vindhya Mountain there will be a city named Dharmapur, whose king will be called Mahabul. He will be a mighty warrior, well-skilled in the dhanur-veda (art of war), and will always lead his own armies to the field. He will duly regard all the omens, such as a storm at the beginning of the march, an earthquake, the implements of war dropping from the hands of the soldiery, screaming vultures passing over or walking near the army, the clouds and the sun's rays waxing red, thunder in a clear sky, the moon appearing small as a star, the dropping of blood from the clouds, the falling of lightning bolts, darkness filling the four quarters of the heavens, a corpse or a pan of water being carried to the right of the army, the sight of a female beggar with dishevelled hair, dressed in red, and preceding the vanguard, the starting of the flesh over the left ribs of the commander-in-chief, and the weeping or turning back of the horses when urged forward.

He will encourage his men to single combats, and will carefully train them to gymnastics. Many of the wrestlers and boxers will be so strong that they will often beat all the extremities of the antagonist into his body, or break his back, or rend him into two pieces. He will promise heaven to those who shall die in the front of battle and he will have them taught certain dreadful expressions of abuse to be interchanged with the enemy when commencing the contest. Honours will be conferred on those who never turn their backs in an engagement, who manifest a contempt of death, who despise fatigue, as well as the most formidable enemies, who shall be found invincible in every combat, and who display a courage which increases before danger, like the glory of the sun advancing to his meridian splendour.

But King Mahabul will be attacked by the white Pariahs, who, as usual, will employ against him gold, fire, and steel. With gold they will win over his best men, and persuade them openly to desert when the army is drawn out for battle. They will use the terrible "fire weapon," large and small tubes, which discharge flame and smoke, and bullets as big as those hurled by the bow of Bharata. And instead of using swords and shields, they will fix daggers to the end of their tubes, and thrust with them like lances.

Mahabul, distinguished by valour and military skill, will march out of his city to meet the white foe. In front will be the ensigns, bells, cows'-tails, and flags, the latter painted with the bird Garura, the bull of Shiva, the Bauhinia tree, the monkey-god Hanuman, the lion and the tiger, the fish, an alms-dish, and seven palm-trees. Then will come the footmen armed with fire-tubes, swords and shields, spears and daggers, clubs, and bludgeons. They will be followed by fighting men on horses and oxen, on camels and elephants. The musicians, the water-carriers, and lastly the stores on carriages, will bring up the rear.

The white outcastes will come forward in a long thin red thread, and vomiting fire like the Jwalamukhi. King Mahabul will receive them with his troops formed in a circle; another division will be in the shape of a halfmoon; a third like a cloud, whilst others shall represent a lion, a tiger, a carriage, a lily, a giant, and a bull. But as the elephants will all turn round when they feel the fire, and trample upon their own men, and as the cavalry defiling in front of the host will openly gallop away; Mahabul, being thus without resource, will enter his palanquin, and accompanied by his queen and their only daughter, will escape at night-time into the forest.

The unfortunate three will be deserted by their small party, and live for a time on jungle food, fruits and roots; they will even be compelled to eat game. After some days they will come in sight of a village, which Mahabul will enter to obtain victuals. There the wild Bhils, famous for long years, will come up, and surrounding the party, will bid the Raja throw down his arms. Thereupon Mahabul, skilful in aiming, twanging and wielding the bow on all sides, so as to keep off the bolts of the enemy, will discharge his bolts so rapidly, that one will drive forward another, and none of the barbarians will be able to approach. But he will have failed to bring his quiver containing an inexhaustible store of arms, some of which, pointed with diamonds, shall have the faculty of returning again to their case after they have done their duty. The conflict will continue three hours, and many of the Bhils will be slain: at length a shaft will cleave the king's skull, he will fall dead, and one of the wild men will come up and cut off his head.

When the queen and the princess shall have seen that Mahabul fell dead, they will return to the forest weeping and beating their bosoms. They will thus escape the Bhils, and after journeying on for four miles, at length they will sit down wearied, and revolve many thoughts ir; their minds.

They are very lovely (continued the Vampire), as I see them with the eye of clear-seeing. What beautiful hair! it hangs down like the tail of the cow of Tartary, or like the thatch of a house; it is shining as oil, dark as the clouds, black as blackness itself. What charming faces! likest to water-lilies, with eyes as the stones in unripe mangos, noses resembling the beaks of parrots, teeth like pearls set in corals, ears like those of the redthroated vulture, and mouths like the water of life. What excellent forms! breasts like boxes containing essences, the unopened fruit of plantains or a couple of crabs; loins the width of a span, like the middle of the viol; legs like the trunk of an elephant, and feet like the yellow lotus.

And a fearful place is that jungle, a dense dark mass of thorny shrubs, and ropy creepers, and tall canes, and tangled brake, and gigantic gnarled trees, which groan wildly in the night wind's embrace. But a wilder horror urges the unhappy women on; they fear the polluting touch of the Bhils; once more they rise and plunge deeper into its gloomy depths.

The day dawns. The white Pariahs have done their usual work, They have cut off the hands of some, the feet and heads of others, whilst many they have crushed into shapeless masses, or scattered in pieces upon the ground. The field is strewed with corpses, the river runs red, so that the dogs and jackals swim in blood; the birds of prey sitting on the branches, drink man's life from the stream, and enjoy the sickening smell of burnt flesh.

Such will be the scenes acted in the fair land of Bharat.

Perchance two white outcastes, father and son, who with a party of men are scouring the forest and slaying everything, fall upon the path which the women have taken shortly before. Their attention is attracted by footprints leading towards a place full of tigers, leopards, bears, wolves, and wild dogs. And they are utterly confounded when, after inspection, they discover the sex of the wanderers.

"How is it," shall say the father, "that the footprints of mortals are seen in this part of the forest?"

The son shall reply, "Sir, these are the marks of women's feet: a man's foot would not be so small."

"It is passing strange," shall rejoin the elder white Pariah, "but thou speakest truth. Certainly such a soft and delicate foot cannot belong to anyone but a woman."

"They have only just left the track," shall continue the son, "and look! this is the step of a married woman. See how she treads on the inside of her sole, because of the bending of her ankles." And the younger white outcaste shall point to the queen's footprints.

"Come, let us search the forest for them," shall cry the father, "what an opportunity of finding wives fortune has thrown in our hands. But no! thou art in error," he shall continue, after examining the track pointed out by his son, "in supposing this to be the sign of a matron. Look at the other, it is much longer; the toes have scarcely touched the ground, whereas the marks of the heels are deep. Of a truth this must be the married woman." And the elder white outcaste shall point to the footprints of the princess.

"Then," shall reply the son, who admires the shorter foot, "let us first seek them, and when we find them, give to me her who has the short feet, and take the other to wife thyself."

Having made this agreement they shall proceed on their way, and presently they shall find the women lying on the earth, half dead with fatigue and fear. Their legs and feet are scratched and torn by brambles, their ornaments have fallen off, and their garments are in strips. The two white outcastes find little difficulty, the first surprise over, in persuading the unhappy women to follow them home, and with great delight, conformably to their arrangement, each takes up his prize on his horse and rides back to the tents. The son takes the queen, and the father the princess.

In due time two marriages come to pass; the father, according to agreement, espouses the long foot, and the son takes to wife the short foot. And after the usual interval, the elder white outcaste, who had married the daughter, rejoices at the birth of a boy, and the younger white outcaste, who had married the mother, is gladdened by the sight of a girl.

Now then, by my feet and your head, O warrior king Vikram, answer me one question. What relationship will there be between the children of the two white Pariahs?

Vikram's brow waxed black as a charcoal-burner's, when he again heard the most irreverent oath ever proposed to mortal king. The question presently attracted his attention, and he turned over the Baital's words in his head, confusing the ties of filiality, brotherhood, and relationship, and connection in general.

"Hem!" said the warrior king, at last perplexed, and remembering, in his perplexity, that he had better hold his tongue—"ahem!"

"I think your majesty spoke? " asked the Vampire, in an inquisitive and insinuating tone of voice.

"Hem!" ejaculated the monarch.

The Baital held his peace for a few minutes, coughing once or twice impatiently. He suspected that the extraordinary nature of this last tale, combined with the use of the future tense, had given rise to a taciturnity so unexpected in the warrior king. He therefore asked if Vikram the Brave would not like to hear another little anecdote.

"This time the king did not even say "hem!" Having walked at an unusually rapid pace, he distinguished at a distance the fire kindled by the devotee, and he hurried towards it with an effort which left him no breath wherewith to speak, even had he been so inclined.

"Since your majesty is so completely dumbfoundered by it, perhaps this acute young prince may be able to answer my question?" insinuated the Baital, after a few minutes of anxious suspense.

But Dharma Dhwaj answered not a syllable.

Conclusion

At Raja Vikram's silence the Baital was greatly surprised, and he praised the royal courage and resolution to the skies. Still he did not give up the contest at once.

"Allow me, great king," pursued the Demon, in a dry tone of voice, "to wish you joy. After so many failures you have at length succeeded in repressing your loquacity. I will not stop to enquire whether it was humility and self-restraint which prevented your answering my last question, or whether Rajait was mere ignorance and inability. Of course I suspect the latter, but to say the truth your condescension in at last taking a Vampire's advice, flatters me so much, that I will not look too narrowly into cause or motive."

Raja Vikram winced, but maintained a stubborn silence, squeezing his lips lest they should open involuntarily.

"Now, however, your majesty has mortified, we will suppose, a somewhat exacting vanity, I also will in my turn forego the pleasure which I had anticipated in seeing you a corpse and in entering your royal body for a short time, just to know how queer it must feel to be a king. And what is more, I will now perform my original promise, and you shall derive from me a benefit which none but myself can bestow. First, however, allow me to ask you, will you let me have a little more air?"

Dharma Dhwaj pulled his father's sleeve, but this time Raja Vikram required no reminder: wild horses or the executioner's saw, beginning at the shoulder, would not have drawn a word from him. Observing his obstinate silence, the Baital, with an ominous smile, continued:

> *"Now give ear, O warrior king, to what I am about to tell thee, and bear in mind the giant's saying, 'A man is justified in killing one who has a design to kill him.' The young merchant Mal Deo, who placed such magnificent presents at your royal feet, and Shanta-Shil the devotee saint, who works his spells, incantations, and magical rites in a cemetery on the banks of the Godaveri river, are, as thou knowest, one person—the terrible Jogi, whose wrath your father aroused in his folly, and whose revenge your blood alone can satisfy. With regard to myself, the oilman's son, the same Jogi, fearing lest I might interfere with his projects of universal dominion, slew me by the power of his penance, and has kept me suspended, a trap for you, head downwards from the sires-tree.*

"That Jogi it was, you now know, who sent you to fetch me back to him on your back. And when you cast me at his feet he will return thanks to you and praise your velour, perseverance and resolution to the skies. I warn you to beware. He will lead you to the shrine of Durga, and when he has finished his adoration he will say to you, 'O great king, salute my deity with the eightlimbed reverence.' "

Here the Vampire whispered for a time and in a low tone, lest some listening goblin might carry his words if spoken out loud to the ears of the devotee Shanta-Shil.

At the end of the monologue a rustling sound was heard. It proceeded from the Baital, who was disengaging himself from the dead body in the bundle, and the burden became sensibly lighter upon the monarch's back.

The departing Baital, however, did not forget to bid farewell to the warrior king and to his son. He complimented the former for the last time, in his own way, upon the royal humility and the prodigious self-mortification which he had displayed—qualities, he remarked, which never failed to ensure the proprietor's success in all the worlds.

Raja Vikram stepped out joyfully, and soon reached the burning ground. There he found the Jogi, dressed in his usual habit, a deerskin thrown over his back, and twisted reeds instead of a garment hanging round his loins. The hair had fallen from his limbs and his skin was bleached ghastly white by exposure to the elements. A fire seemed to proceed from his mouth, and the matted locks dropping from his head to the ground were changed by the rays of the sun to the colour of gold or saffron. He had the beard of a goat and the ornaments of a king; his shoulders were high and his arms long, reaching to his knees: his nails grew to such a length as to curl round the ends of his fingers, and his feet resembled those of a tiger. He was drumming upon a skull, and incessantly exclaiming, "Ho, Kali! ho, Durga! ho, Devi!"

As before, strange beings were holding their carnival in the Jogi's presence. Monstrous Asuras, giant goblins, stood grimly gazing upon the scene with fixed eyes and motionless features. Rakshasas and messengers of Yama, fierce and hideous, assumed at pleasure the shapes of foul and ferocious beasts.

Nagas and Bhutas, partly human and partly bestial, disported themselves in throngs about the upper air, and were dimly seen in the faint light of the dawn. Mighty Daityas, Bramba-daityas, and Pretas, the size of a man's thumb, or dried up like leaves, and Pisachas of terrible power guarded the place.

There were enormous goats, vivified by the spirits of those who had slain Brahmans; things with the bodies of men and the faces of horses, camels and monkeys; hideous worms containing the souls of those priests who had drunk spirituous liquors; men with one leg and one ear, and mischievous blood-sucking demons, who in life had stolen church property. There were vultures, wretches that had violated the beds of their spiritual fathers, restless ghosts that had loved low-caste women, shades for whom funeral rites had not been performed, and who could not cross the dread Vaitarani stream, and vital souls fresh from the horrors of Tamisra, or utter darkness, and the Usipatra Vana, or the sword-leaved forest. Pale spirits, Alayas, Gumas, Baitals, and Yakshas, beings of a base and vulgar order, glided over the ground, amongst corpses and skeletons animated by female fiends, Dakinis, Yoginis, Hakinis, and Shankinis, which were dancing in frightful revelry.

The air was filled with supernatural sights and sounds, cries of owls and jackals, cats and crows, dogs, asses, and vultures, high above which rose the clashing of the bones with which the Jogi sat drumming upon the skull before him, and tending a huge cauldron of oil whose smoke was of blue fire. But as he raised his long lank arm, silver-white with ashes, the demons fled, and a momentary silence succeeded to their uproar. The tigers ceased to roar and the elephants to scream; the bears raised their snouts from their foul banquets, and the wolves dropped from their jaws the remnants of human flesh. And when they disappeared, the hooting of the owl, and ghastly "ha! ha!" of the curlew, and the howling of the jackal died away in the far distance, leaving a silence still more oppressive.

As Raja Vikram entered the burning-ground, the hollow sound of solitude alone met his ear. Sadly wailed the wet autumnal blast. The tall gaunt trees groaned aloud, and bowed and trembled like slaves bending before their masters. Huge purple clouds and patches and lines of glaring white mist coursed furiously across the black expanse of firmament, discharging threads and chains and lozenges and balls of white and blue, purple and pink lightning, followed by the deafening crash and roll of thunder, the dreadful roaring of the mighty wind, and the torrents of plashing rain.

At times was heard in the distance the dull gurgling of the swollen river, interrupted by explosions, as slips of earth-bank fell headlong into the stream. But once more the Jogi raised his arm and all was still: nature lay breathless, as if awaiting the effect of his tremendous spells.

The warrior king drew near the terrible man, unstrung his bundle from his back, untwisted the portion which he held, threw open the cloth, and exposed to Shanta-Shil's glittering eyes the corpse, which had now recovered its proper form—that of a young child. Seeing it, the devotee was highly pleased, and thanked Vikram the Brave, extolling his courage and daring above any monarch that had yet lived. After which he repeated certain charms facing towards the south, awakened the dead body, and placed it in a sitting position. He then in its presence sacrificed to his goddess, the White One, all that he had ready by his side—betel leaf and flowers, sandal wood and unbroken rice, fruits, perfumes, and the flesh of man untouched by steel. Lastly, he half filled his skull with burning embers, blew upon them till they shot forth tongues of crimson light, serving as a lamp, and motioning the Raja and his son to follow him, led the way to a little fane of the Destroying Deity erected in a dark clump of wood, outside and close to the burning ground.

They passed through the quadrangular outer court of the temple whose piazza was hung with deep shade. In silence they circumambulated the small central shrine, and whenever Shanta-Shil directed, Raja Vikram entered the Sabha, or vestibule, and struck three times upon the gong, which gave forth a loud and warning sound.

They then passed over the threshold, and looked into the gloomy inner depths. There stood Smashana-Kali, the goddess, in her most horrid form. She was a naked and very black woman, with half-severed head, partly cut and partly painted, resting on her shoulder; and her tongue lolled out from her wide yawning mouth; her eyes were red like those of a drunkard; and her eyebrows were of the same colour: her thick coarse hair hung like a mantle to her heels. She was robed in an elephant's hide, dried and withered, confined at the waist with a belt composed of the hands of the giants whom she had slain in war: two dead bodies formed her earrings, and her necklace was of bleached skulls. Her four arms supported a scimitar, a noose, a trident, and a ponderous mace. She stood with one leg on the breast of her husband, Shiva, and she rested the other on his thigh. Before the idol lay the utensils of worship, namely, dishes for the offerings, lamps, jugs, incense, copper cups, conches and gongs; and all of them smelt of blood.

As Raja Vikram and his son stood gazing upon the hideous spectacle, the devotee stooped down to place his skull-lamp upon the ground, and drew from out his ochre-coloured cloth a sharp sword which he hid behind his back.

"Prosperity to shine and thy son's for ever and ever, O mighty Vikram!" exclaimed Shanta-Shil, after he had muttered a prayer before the image. "Verily thou hast right royally redeemed thy pledge, and by the virtue of thy presence all my wishes shall presently be accomplished. Behold! the Sun is about to drive his car over the eastern hills, and our task now ends. Do thou reverence before this my deity, worshipping the earth through thy nose, and so prostrating thyself that thy eight limbs may touch the ground. Thus shall thy glory and splendour be great; the Eight Powers and the Nine Treasures shall be thine, and prosperity shall ever remain under thy roof-tree."

Raja Vikram, hearing these words, recalled suddenly to mind all that the Vampire had whispered to him. He brought his joined hands open up to his forehead, caused his two thumbs to touch his brow several times, and replied with the greatest humility,

"O pious person! I am a king ignorant of the way to do such obeisance. Thou art a spiritual preceptor: be pleased to teach me and I will do even as thou desirest."

Then the Jogi, being a cunning man, fell into his own net. As he bent him down to salute the goddess, Vikram, drawing his sword, struck him upon the neck so violent a blow, that his head rolled from his body upon the ground. At the same moment Dharma Dhwaj, seizing his father's arm, pulled him out of the way in time to escape being crushed by the image, which fell with the sound of thunder upon the floor of the temple.

A small thin voice in the upper air was heard to cry, "A man is justified in killing one who has the desire to kill him." Then glad shouts of triumph and victory were heard in all directions.

They proceeded from the celestial choristers, the heavenly dancers, the mistresses of the gods, and the nymphs of Indra's Paradise, who left their beds of gold and precious stones, their seats glorious as the meridian sun, their canals of crystal water, their perfumed groves, and their gardens where the wind ever blows in softest breezes, to applaud the velour and good fortune of the warrior king. At last the brilliant god, Indra himself, with the thousand eyes, rising from the shade of the Parigat tree, the fragrance of whose flowers fills the heavens, appeared in his car drawn by yellow steeds and cleaving the thick vapours which surround the earth—whilst his attendants sounded the heavenly drums and rained a shower of blossoms and perfumes—bade the Vikramajit the Brave ask a boon.

The Raja joined his hands and respectfully replied,

"O mighty ruler of the lower firmament, let this my history become famous throughout the world!"

"It is well," rejoined the god. "As long as the sun and moon endure, and the sky looks down upon the ground, so long shall this thy adventure be remembered over all the earth. Meanwhile rule thou mankind."

Thus saying, Indra retired to the delicious Amrawati Vikram took up the corpses and threw them into the cauldron which Shanta-Shil had been tending. At once two heroes started into life, and Vikram said to them, "When I call you, come!"

With these mysterious words the king, followed by his son, returned to the palace unmolested. As the Vampire had predicted, everything was prosperous to him, and he presently obtained the remarkable titles, Sakaro, or foe of the Sakas, and Sakadhipati-Vikramaditya.

And when, after a long and happy life spent in bringing the world under the shadow of one umbrella, and in ruling it free from care, the warrior king Vikram entered the gloomy realms of Yama, from whom for mortals there is no escape, he left behind him a name that endured amongst men like the odour of the flower whose memory remains long after its form has mingled with the dust.

stopped her. "Aunty," he said, " I will give you food." He put his hand into his bag, saying, "Bag, I want some dinner," and the. bag gave him instantly a delicious dinner, served up on two gold plates. The old woman and the Raja's son then dined together.

When they had finished eating, 'the old woman said, "Now I will fetch some water."

"Don't go," said the prince. "You shall have plenty of water directly." So he took his bowl and said to it, "Bowl, I want some water," and then it filled with water. When it was full, the prince cried out, "Stop, bowl!" and the bowl stopped filling. "See, aunty," he said, "with this bowl I can always get as much water as I want."

By this time night had come. "Aunty," said the Raja's son, "why don't you light a lamp?"

"There is no need," she said. "Our king has forbidden the people in his country to light any lamps; for, as soon as it is dark, his daughter, the Princess Labam, comes and sits on her roof, and she shines so that she lights up all the country and our houses, and we can see to do our work as if it were day."

When it was quite black night the princess got up. She dressed herself in her rich clothes and jewels, and rolled up her hair, and across her head she put a band of diamonds and pearls. Then she shone like the moon and her beauty made night day. She came out of her room and sat on the roof of her palace. In the daytime she never came out of her house; she only came out at night. All the people in her father's country then went about their work and finished it.

The Raja's son watched the princess quietly, and was very happy. He said to himself, " How lovely she is!"

At midnight, when everybody had gone to bed, the princess came down from her roof and went to her room; and when she was in bed and asleep, the Raja's son got up softly and sat on his bed. "Bed," he said to it, "I want to go to the Princess Labam's bedroom." So the little bed carried him to the room where she lay fast asleep.

The young Raja took his bag and said, "I want a great deal of betel-leaf," and it at once gave him quantities of betel-leaf. This he laid near the princess's bed, and then his little bed carried him back to the old woman's house.

Next morning all the princess's servants found the betel-leaf, and began to eat it.

"Where did you get all that betel-leaf?" asked the princess.

"We found it near your bed," answered the servants. Nobody knew the prince had come in the night and put it all there.

In the morning the old woman came to the Raja's son. "Now it is morning," she said, "and you must go; for if the king finds out all I have done for you, he will seize me."

"I am ill today, dear aunty," said the prince; "do let me stay till tomorrow morning."

"Good," said the old woman. So he stayed, and they took their dinner out of the bag, and the bowl gave them water.

When night came the princess got up and sat on her roof, and at twelve o'clock, when every one was in bed, she went to her bedroom, and was soon fast asleep. Then the Raja's son sat on his bed, and it carried him to the princess. He took his bag and said, "Bag, I want a most lovely shawl;" It gave him a splendid shawl, and he spread it over the princess as she lay asleep. Then he went back to the old woman's house and slept till morning.

In the morning, when the princess saw the shawl she was delighted. "See, mother," she said; "Khuda must have given me this shawl, it is so beautiful." Her mother was very glad too. "Yes, my child," she said; "Khuda must have given you this splendid shawl."

When it was morning the old woman said to the Raja's son, "Now you must really go."

"Aunty," he answered, "I am not well enough yet. Let me stay a few days longer. I will remain hidden in your house, so that no one may see me." So the old woman let him stay.

When it was black night, the princess put on her lovely clothes and jewels and sat on her roof. At midnight she went to her room and went to sleep. Then the Raja's son sat on his bed and flew to her bedroom. There he said to his bag, "Bag, I want a very, very beautiful ring." The bag gave him a glorious ring. Then he took the Princess Labam's hand gently to put on the ring, and she started up very much frightened.

"Who are you?" she said to the prince. "Where do you come from? Why do you come to my room?"

"Do not be afraid, princess," he said; "I am no thief. I am a great Raja's son. Hiraman parrot, who lives in the jungle where I went to hunt, told me your name, and then I left my father and mother and came to see you."

"Well," said the princess, "as you are the son of such a great kaja, I will not have you killed, and I will tell my father and mother that I wish to marry you."

The prince then returned to the old woman's house; and when morning came the princess said to her mother, "The son of a great Raja has come to this country, and I wish to marry him." Her mother told this to the king.

"Good," said the king; "but if this Raja's son wishes to marry my daughter, he must first do whatever I bid him. If he fails I will kill him. I will give him eighty pounds weight of mustard seed, and out of this he must crush the oil in one day. If he cannot do this he shall die."

In the morning the Raja's son told the old woman that he intended to marry the princess. "Oh," said the old woman, "go away from this country, and do not think of marrying her. A great many Rajas and Rajas' sons have come here to marry her, and her father has had them all killed. He says whoever wishes to marry his daughter must first do whatever he bids him. If he can, then he shall marry the princess; if he cannot, the king will have him killed. But no one can do the things the king tells him to do; so all the Rajas and Rajas' sons who have tried have been put to death. You will be killed too, if you try. Do go away." But the prince would not listen to anything she said.

The king sent for the prince to the old woman's house, and his servants brought the Raja's son to the king's courthouse to the king. There the king gave him eighty pounds of mustard seed, and told him to crush all the oil out of it that day, and bring it next morning to him to the courthouse. "Whoever wishes to marry my daughter" he said to the prince, "must first do all I tell him. If he cannot, then I have him killed. So if you cannot crush all the oil out of this mustard seed you will die."

The prince was very sorry when he heard this. "How can I crush the oil out of all this mustard seed in one thy?" he said to himself; "and if I do not, the king will kill me." He took the mustard seed to the old woman's house, and did not know what to do. At last he remembered the Ant-Raja, and the moment he did so, the Ant-Raja and his ants came to him. "Why do you look so sad?" said the Ant-Raja.

The prince showed him the mustard seed, and said to him, "How can I crush the oil out of all this mustard seed in one day? And if I do not take the oil to the king tomorrow morning, he will kill me."

"Be happy," said the Ant-Raja; "lie down and sleep; we will crush all the oil out for you during the day, and tomorrow morning you shall take it to the king." The Raja's son lay down and slept, and the ants crushed out the oil for him. The prince was very glad when he saw the oil.

The next morning he took it to the court-house to the king. But the king said," You cannot yet marry my daughter. If you wish to do so, you must first fight with my two demons, and kill them." The king a long time ago had caught two demons, and then, as he did not know what to do with them, he had shut them up in a cage. He was afraid to let them loose for fear they would eat up all the people in his country; and he did not know how to kill them. So all the kings and kings' sons who wanted to marry the Princess Labam had to fight with these demons; "for," said the king to himself, "perhaps the demons may be killed, and then I shall be rid of them."

When he heard of the demons the Raja's son was very sad. "What can I do?" he said to himself. "How can I fight with these two demons?" Then he thought of his tiger: and the tiger and his wife came to him and said, "Why are you so sad?" The Raja's son answered, "The king has ordered me to fight with his two demons and kill them. How can I do this? " "Do not be frightened," said the tiger. "Be happy. I and my wife will fight with them for you."

Then the Raja's son took out of his bag two splendid coats. They were all gold and silver, and covered with pearls and diamonds. These he put on the tigers to make them beautiful, and he took them to the king, and said to him,. "May these tigers fight your demons for me?"

"Yes," said' the king, who did not care in the least who killed his demons, provided they were killed. "Then call your demons," said the Raja's son, "and these tigers will fight them." The king did so, and the tigers and the demons fought and fought until the tigers had killed the demons.

"That is good," said the king. "But you must do something else before I give you my daughter. Up in the sky I have a kettledrum. You must go and beat it. If you cannot do this, I will kill you."

The Raja's son thought of his little bed; so he went to the old woman's house and sat on his bed. "Little bed!' he said, "up in the sky is the king's kettledrum. I want to go to it." The bed flew up with him, and the Raja's son beat the drum, and the king heard him. Still, when he came down, the king would not give him his daughter. "You have," he said to the prince, "done the three things I told you to do; but you must do one thing more."

"If I can, I will," said the Raja's son.

Then the king showed him the trunk of a tree that was lying near his court-house. It was a very, very, thick trunk. He gave the prince a wax hatchet, and said, "Tomorrow morning you must cut this trunk in two with this wax hatchet."

The Raja's son went back to the old woman's house. He was very sad, and thought that now the Raja would certainly kill him. "I had his oil crushed out by the ants," he said to himself. "I had his demons killed by the tigers. My bed helped me to beat his kettledrum. But now what can I do? How can I cut that thick tree-trunk in two with a wax hatchet?"

At night he went on his bed to see the princess. "To morrow," he said to her, "your father will kill me." "Why?" asked the princess.

"He has told me to cut a thick tree-trunk in two with a wax hatchet. How can I ever do that?" said the Raja's son. "Do not be afraid," said the princess; "do as I bid you, and you will cut it in two quite easily."

Then she pulled out a hair from her head and gave it to the prince. "Tomorrow," she said, "when no one is near you, you must say to the tree-trunk, 'The Princess Labam commands you to let yourself be cut in two by this hair. Then stretch the hair down the edge of the wax hatchet's blade."

The prince next day did exactly as the princess had told him; and the minute the hair that was stretched down the edge of the hatchet-blade touched the tree-trunk it split into two pieces.

The king said, "Now you can marry my daughter." Then the wedding took place. All the Rajas and kings of the countries round were asked to come to it, and there were great rejoicings. After a few days the prince's son said to his wife, "Let us go to my father's country." The Princess Labam's father gave them a quantity of camels and horses and rupees and servants; and they travelled in great state to the prince's country, where they lived happily.

The prince always kept his bag, bowl, bed, and stick; only, as no one ever came to make war on him, he never needed to use the stick.

The Lambikin

Once upon a time there was a wee wee Lambikin, who frolicked about on his little tottery legs, and enjoyed himself amazingly.

Now one day he set off to visit his Granny, and was jumping with joy to think of all the good things he should get from her, when who should he meet but a Jackal, who looked at the tender young morsel and said: "Lambikin! Lambikin! I'll EAT YOU!"

But Lambikin only gave a little frisk, and said:

"To Granny's house I go,
Where I shall fatter grow,
Then you can eat me so."

The Jackal thought this reasonable, and let Lambikin pass.

By-and-by he met a Vulture, and the Vulture, looking hungrily at the tender morsel before him, said: "Lambikin! Lambikin! I'll EAT YOU!"

But Lambikin only gave a little frisk, and said:

"To Granny's house I go,
Where I shall fatter grow
Then you can eat me so."

The Vulture thought this reasonable, and let Lambikin pass.

And by-and-by he met a Tiger, and then a Wolf, and a Dog, and an Eagle; and all these, when they saw the tender little morsel, said: "Lambikin! Lambikin! I'll EAT YOU!"

But to all of them Lambikin replied, with a little frisk:

"To Granny's house I go,
Where I shall fatter grow,
Then you can eat me so."

At last he reached his Granny's house, and said, all in a great hurry, "Granny dear, I've promised to get very fat; so, as people ought to keep their promises, please put me into the corn-bin at once."

So his Granny said he was a good boy, and put him into the corn-bin, and there the greedy little Lambikin stayed for seven days, and ate, and ate, and ate, until he could scarcely waddle, and his Granny said he was fat enough for anything, and must go home. But cunning little Lambikin said that would never do, for some animal would be sure to eat him on the way back, he was so plump and tender.

"I'll tell you what you must do," said Master Lambikin; "you must make a little drumikin out of the skin of my little brother who died, and then I can sit inside and trundle along nicely, for I'm as tight as a drum myself.'

So his Granny made a nice little drumikin out of his brother's skin, with the wool inside, and Lambikin curled himself up snug and warm in the middle, and trundled away gaily. Soon he met with the Eagle, who called out:

"Drumikin! Drumikin!
Have you seen Lambikin?"

And Mr. Lambikin, curled up in his soft warm nest, replied:

"Fallen into the fire, and so will you
On little Drumikin. Tum-pa, tum-too!"

"How very annoying!" sighed the Eagle, thinking regretfully of the tender morsel he had let slip.

Meanwhile Lambikin trundled along, laughing to himself, and singing:

"Tum-pa, tum-too;
Tum-pa, tum-too!"

Every animal and bird he met asked him the same question:

"Drumikin! Drumikin!
Have you seen Lambikin?"

And to each of them the little slyboots replied:

"Fallen into the fire, and so will you
On little Drumikin. Tum-pa, tum-too;
Tum-pa, tum-too; Tum-pa, tum-too!"

Then they all sighed to think of the tender little morsel they had let slip.

At last the Jackal came limping along, for all his sorry looks as sharp as a needle, and he too called out:

"Drumikin! Drumikin!
Have you seen Lambikin?"

And Lambikin, curled up in his snug little nest, replied gaily:

"Fallen into the fire, and so will you
On little Drumikin! Tum-pa—"

But he never got any further, for the Jackal recognised his voice at once, and cried: "Hullo! you've turned yourself inside out, have you? Just you come out of that!"

Whereupon he tore open Drumikin and gobbled up Lambikin.

Punchkin

Once upon a time there was a Raja who had seven beautiful daughters. They were all good girls; but the youngest, named Balna, was more clever than the rest. The Raja's wife died when they were quite little children, so these seven poor Princesses were left with no mother to take care of them.

The Raja's daughters took it by turns to cook their father's dinner every day, whilst he was absent deliberating with his Ministers on the affairs of the nation.

About this time the Prudhan died, leaving a widow and one daughter; and every day, every day, when the seven Princesses were preparing their father's dinner, the Prudhan's widow and daughter would come and beg for a little fire from the hearth. Then Balna used to say to her sisters, "Send that woman away; send her away. Let her get the fire at her own house. What does she want with ours? If we allow her to come here, we shall suffer for it some day."

But the other sisters would answer, "Be quiet, Balna; why must you always be quarrelling with this poor woman? Let her take some fire if she likes." Then the Prudhan's widow used to go to the hearth and take a few sticks from it; and whilst no one was looking, she would quickly throw some mud into the midst of the dishes which were being prepared for the Raja's dinner.

Now the Raja was very fond of his daughters. Ever since their mother's death they had cooked his dinner with their own hands, in order to avoid the danger of his being poisoned by his enemies. So, when he found the mud mixed up with his dinner, he thought it must arise from their carelessness, as it did not seem likely that any one should have put mud there on purpose; but being very kind he did not like to reprove them for it, although this spoiling of the curry was repeated many successive days.

At last, one day, he determined to hide, and watch his daughters cooking, and see how it all happened; so he went into the next room, and watched them through a hole in the wall.

There he saw his seven daughters carefully washing the rice and preparing the curry, and as each dish was completed, they put it by the fire ready to be cooked. Next he noticed the Prudhan's widow come to the door and beg for a few sticks from the fire to cook her dinner with Balna turned to her angrily and said, "Why don't you keep fuel in your own house, and not come here every day and take ours? Sisters, don't give this woman any more wood; let her buy it for herself."

Then the eldest sister answered, "Balna, let the poor woman take the wood and the fire; she does us no harm." But Balna replied, "If you let her come here so often, maybe she will do us some harm, and make us sorry for it some day."

The Raja then saw the Prudhan's widow go to the place where all his dinner was nicely prepared, and, as she took the wood, she threw a little mud into each of the dishes.

At this he was very angry, and sent to have the woman seized and brought before him. But when the widow came, she told him that she had played this trick because she wanted to gain an audience with him; and she spoke so cleverly, and pleased him so well with her cunning words, that, instead of punishing her, the Raja married her, and made her his Ranee, and she and her daughter came to live in the palace.

Now the new Ranee hated the seven poor Princesses, and wanted to get them, if possible, out of the way, in order that her daughter might have all their riches, and live in the palace as Princess in their place; and instead of being grateful to them for their kindness to her, she did all she could to make them miserable. She gave them nothing but bread to eat, and very little of that, and very little water to drink; so these seven poor little Princesses, who had been accustomed to have everything comfortable about them, and good food and good clothes all their lives long, were very miserable and unhappy; and they used to go out every day and sit by their dead mother's tomb and cry—and say:

"Oh mother, mother, cannot you see your poor children, how unhappy we are, and how we are starved by our cruel stepmother?"

One day, whilst they were thus sobbing and crying, lo and behold! a beautiful pomelo-tree grew up out of the grave, covered with fresh ripe pomeloes, and the children satisfied their hunger by eating some of the fruit; and every day after this, instead of trying to eat the bad dinner their stepmother provided for them, they used to go out to their mother's grave and eat the pomeloes which grew there on the beautiful tree.

Then the Ranee said to her daughter, "I cannot tell how it is, every day those seven girls say they don't want any dinner, and won't eat any; and yet they never grow thin nor look ill; they look better than you do. I cannot tell how it is." And she bade her watch the seven Princesses, and see if any one gave them anything to eat.

So next day, when the Princesses went to their mother's grave, and were eating the beautiful pomeloes, the Prudhan's daughter followed them and saw them gathering the fruit.

Then Balna said to her sisters, "Do you not see that girl watching us? Let us drive her away, or hide the pomeloes, else she will go and tell her mother all about it, and that will be very bad for us."

But the other sisters said, "Oh no, do not be unkind, Balna. The girl would never be so cruel as to tell her mother. Let us rather invite her to come and have some of the fruit."

And calling her to them, they gave her one of the pomeloes.

No sooner had she eaten it, however, than the Prudhan's daughter went home and said to her mother, "I do not wonder the seven Princesses will not eat the dinner you prepare for them, for by their mother's grave there grows a beautiful pomelo-tree, and they go there every day and eat the pomeloes. I ate one, and it was the nicest I have ever tasted."

The cruel Ranee was much vexed at hearing this, and all next day she stayed in her room, and told the Raja that she had a very bad headache. The Raja was deeply grieved, and said to his wife, "What can I do for you?" She answered, "There is only one thing that will make my headache well.

By your dead wife's tomb there grows a fine pomelo-tree; you must bring that here and boil it, root and branch, and put a little of the water in which it has been boiled on my forehead, and that will cure my headache." So the Raja sent his servants, and had the beautiful pomelo-tree pulled up by the roots, and did as the Ranee desired; and when some of the water in which it had been boiled was put on her forehead, she said her headache was gone and she felt quite well.

Next day, when the seven Princesses went as usual to the grave of their mother, the pomelo-tree had disappeared. Then they all began to cry very bitterly.

Now there was by the Ranee's tomb a small tank, and as they were crying they saw that the tank was filled with a rich cream-like substance, which quickly hardened into a thick white cake. At seeing this all the Princesses were very glad, and they ate some of the cake and liked it; and next day the same thing happened, and so it went on for many days.

Every morning the Princesses went to their mother's grave, and found the little tank filled with the nourishing cream-like cake. Then the cruel stepmother said to her daughter: "I cannot tell how it is, I have had the pomelo-tree which used to grow by the Ranee's grave destroyed, and yet the Princesses grow no thinner, nor look more sad, though they never eat the dinner I give them. I cannot tell how it is! "

And her daughter said, "I will watch."

Next day, while the Princesses were eating the cream-cake, who should come by but their stepmothers daughter. Balna saw her first, and said, "See, sisters, there comes that girl again. Let us sit round the edge of the tank and not allow her to see it, for if we give her some of our cake, she will go and tell her mother, and that will be very unfortunate for us.

The other sisters, however, thought Balna unnecessarily suspicious, and, instead of following her advice, they gave the Prudhan's daughter, some of the cake, and she went home and

er mother all about it. The Ranee, on hearing how well
rincesses fared, was exceedingly angry, and sent her servants to pull down the dead Ranee's tomb and fill the little tank with the ruins. And not content with this, she next day pretended to be very, very ill—in fact, at the point of death—and when the Raja was much grieved, and asked her whether it was in his power to procure her any remedy, she said to him:

"Only one thing can save my life, but I know you will not 'do it." He replied, "Yes, whatever it is, I will do it." She then said, "To save my life, you must kill the seven daughters of your first wife, and put some of their blood on my forehead and on the palms of my hands, and their death will be my life." At these words the Raja was very sorrowful; but because he feared to break his word, he went out with a heavy heart to find his daughters.

He found them crying by the ruins of their mother's grave.

Then, feeling he could not kill them, the Raja spoke kindly to them, and told them to come out into the jungle with him; and there he made a fire and cooked some rice, and gave it to them. But in the afternoon, it being very hot, the seven Princesses all fell asleep, and when he saw they were fast asleep, the Raja, their father, stole away and left them (for he feared, his wife), saying to himself: "It is better my poor daughters should die here than be killed by their stepmother."

He then shot a deer, and returning home, put some of its blood on the forehead and hands of the Ranee, and she thought then that he had really killed the Princesses, and said she felt quite well. Meantime the seven Princesses awoke, and when they found themselves all alone in the thick jungle they were much frightened, and began to call out as loud as they could, in hopes of making their father hear; but he was by that time far away, and would not have been able to hear them even had their voices been as loud as thunder.

It so happened that this very day the seven young sons of a neighbouring Raja chanced to be hunting in that same jungle, and as they were returning home, after the day's sport was over, the youngest Prince said to his brothers:

"Stop, I think I hear some one crying and calling out. Do you not hear voices? Let us go in the direction of the sound, and find out what it is."

So the seven Princes rode through the wood until they came to the place where the seven Princesses sat crying and wringing their hands. At the sight of them the young Princes were very much astonished, and still more so on learning their story; and they settled that each should take one of these poor forlorn ladies home with him and marry her.

So the first and eldest Prince took the eldest Princess home with him and married her.

And the second took the second;

And the third took the third;

And the fourth took the fourth;

And the fifth took the fifth;

And the sixth took the sixth;

And the seventh, and the handsomest of all, took the beautiful Balna.

And when they got to their own land there was great rejoicing throughout the kingdom at the marriage of the seven young Princes to seven such beautiful Princesses.

About a year after this Balna had a little son, and his uncles and aunts were so fond of the boy that it was as if he had seven fathers and seven mothers. None of the other Princes and Princesses had any children, so the son of the seventh Prince and Balna was acknowledged their heir by all the rest.

They had thus lived very happily for some time, when one fine day the seventh Prince (Balna's husband) said he would go out hunting, and away he went; and they waited long for him, but he never came back.

Then his six brothers said they would go and see what had become of him; and they went away, but they also did not return.

And the seven Princesses grieved very much, for they feared that their kind husbands must have been killed.

One day, not long after this had happened, as Balna was rocking her baby's cradle, and whilst her sisters were working in the room below, there came to the palace door a man in a long black dress, who said that he was a Fakir, and came to beg. The servants said to him, "You cannot go into the palace—the Raja's sons have all gone away; we think they must be dead, and their widows cannot be interrupted by your begging." But he said, "I am a holy man, you must let me in." Then the stupid servants let him walk through the palace, but they did not know that this was no Fakir, but a wicked Magician named Punchkin.

Punchkin Fakir wandered through the palace, and saw many beautiful things there, till at last he reached the room where Balna sat singing beside her little boy's cradle. The Magician thought her more beautiful than all the other beautiful things he had seen, insomuch that he asked her to go home with him and to marry him. But she said, "My husband, I fear, is dead, but my little boy is still quite young; I will stay here and teach him to grow up a clever man, and when he is grown up he shall go out into the world, and try and learn tidings of his father. Heaven forbid that I should ever leave him, or marry you." At these words the Magician was very angry, and turned her into a little black dog, and led her away, saying, "Since you will not come with me of your own free will, I will make you." So the poor Princess was dragged away, without any power of effecting an escape or of letting her sisters know what had become of her. As Punchkin passed through the palace gate the servants said to him, "Where did you get that pretty little dog?" And he answered, "One of the Princesses gave it to me as a present." At hearing which they let him go without further questioning.

Soon after this, the six elder Princesses heard the little baby, their nephew, begin to cry, and when they went upstairs they were much surprised to find him all alone, and Balna nowhere to be seen. Then they questioned the servants, and when they heard of the Fakir and the little black dog, they guessed what had happened, and sent in every direction seeking them, but neither the Fakir nor the dog were to be found. What could six poor women do? They gave up all hopes of ever seeing their kind husbands, and their sister, and her husband, again, and devoted themselves thenceforward to teaching and taking care of their little nephew.

Thus time went on, till Balna's son was fourteen years old, Then, one day, his aunts told him the history of the family; and no sooner did he hear it than he was seized with great desire to go in search of his father and mother and uncles, and if he could find them alive to bring them home again. His aunts, on learning his determination, were much alarmed, and tried to dissuade him, saying, "We have lost our husbands and our sister and her husband, and you are now our sole hope; if you go away, what shall we do?" But he replied, " I pray you not to be discouraged; I will return soon, and if it is possible bring my father and mother and uncles with me." So he set out on his travels; but for some months he could learn nothing to help him in his search.

At last, after he had journeyed many hundreds of weary miles, and become almost hopeless of ever hearing anything further of his parents, he one day came to a country that seemed full of stones, and rocks, and trees, and there he saw a large palace with a high tower; hard by which was a Maee's little house.

As he was looking about, the Malee's wife saw him, and ran out of the house and said, "My dear boy, who are you that dare venture to this dangerous place?" He answered, "I am a Raja's son, and I come in search of my father, and my uncles, and my mother, whom a wicked enchanter bewitched."

Then the Malee's wife said, "This country and this palace belong to a great enchanter; he is all-powerful, and if any one displeases him he can turn them into stones and trees. All the rocks and trees you see here were living people once, and the Magician turned them to what they now are. Some time ago a Raja's son came here, and shortly afterwards came his six brothers, and they were all turned into stones and trees; and these are not the only unfortunate ones, for up in that tower lives a beautiful Princess, whom the Magician has kept prisoner there for twelve years, because she hates him and will not marry him."

Then the little Prince thought, "These must be my parents and my uncles. I have found what I seek at last." So he told his story to the Malee's wife, and begged her to help him to remain in that place awhile and inquire further concerning the unhappy people she mentioned; and she promised to befriend him, and advised his disguising himself lest the Magician should see him, and turn him likewise into stone. To this the Prince agreed. So the Malee's wife dressed him up in a saree, and pretended that he was her daughter.

One day, not long after this, as the Magician was walking in his garden he saw the little girl (as he thought) playing about, and asked her who she was. She told him she was the Malee's daughter, and the Magician said, "You are a pretty little girl, and tomorrow you shall take a present of flowers from me to the beautiful lady who lives in the tower.

The young Prince was much delighted at hearing this, and went immediately to inform the Malee's wife; after consultation with whom he determined that it would be more safe for him to retain his disguise and trust to the chance of a favourable opportunity for establishing some communication with his mother, if it were indeed she.

Now it happened that at Balna's marriage her husband had given her a small gold ring on which her name was engraved, and she had put it on her little son's finger when he was a baby, and afterwards when be was older his aunt had had it enlarged for him, so that he was still able to wear it.

The Melee's wife advised him to fasten the well-known treasure to one of the bouquets he presented to his mother, and trust to her recognising it. This was not to be done without difficulty, as such a strict watch was kept over the poor Princess (for fear of her ever establishing communication with her friends) that, though the supposed Malee's daughter was permitted to take her flowers every day, the Magician or one of his slaves was always in the room at the time. At last one day, however, opportunity favoured him, and when no one was looking, the boy tied the ring to a nosegay and threw it at Balna's feet. It fell with a clang on the floor, and Balna, looking to see what made the strange sound, found the little ring tied to the flowers. On recognising it, she at once believed the story her son told her of his long search, and begged him to advise her as to what she had better do; at the same time entreating him on no account to endanger his life by trying to rescue her. She told him that for twelve long years the Magician had kept her shut up in the tower because she refused to marry him, and she was so closely guarded that she saw no hope of release.

Now Balna's son was a bright, clever boy, so he said, "Do not fear, dear mother; the first thing to do is to discover how far the Magician's power extends, in order that we may be able to liberate my father and uncles, whom he has imprisoned in the form of rocks and trees. You have spoken to him angrily for twelve long years; now rather speak kindly. Tell him you have given up all hopes of again seeing the husband you have so long mourned, and say you are willing to marry him. Then endeavour to find out what his power consists in, and whether he is immortal, or can be put to death."

Balna determined to take her son's advice; and the next day sent for Punchkin, and spoke to him as had been suggested.

The Magician, greatly delighted, begged her to allow the wedding to take place as soon as possible.

But she told him that before she married him he must allow her a little more time in which she might make his acquaintance, and that, after being enemies so long, their friendship could but strengthen by degrees. "And do tell me," she said, "are you quite immortal? Can death never touch you? And are you too great an enchanter ever to feel human suffering?"

"Why do you ask?" said he.

"Because," she replied, "if I am to be your wife, I would fain know all about you, in order, if any calamity threatens you, to overcome, or if possible to avert it."

"It is true," he added, "that I am not as others. Far, far away, hundreds of thousands of miles from this, there lies a desolate country covered with thick jungle. In the midst of the jungle grows a circle of palm trees, and in the centre of the circle stand six chattees full of water, piled one above another: below the sixth chattee is a small cage which contains a little green parrot; on the life of the parrot depends my life; and if the parrot is killed I must die. It is, however," he added, "impossible that the parrot should sustain any injury, both on account of the inaccessibility of the country, and because, by my appointment, many thousand genii surround the palm-trees, and kill all who approach the place."

Balna told her son what Punchkin had said; but at the same time implored him to give up all idea of getting the parrot.

The Prince, however, replied, "Mother, unless I can get hold of that parrot, you, and my father, and uncles, cannot be liberated: be not afraid, I will shortly return. Do you meantime, keep the Magician in good humour—still putting off your marriage with him on various pretexts; and before he finds out the cause of delay, I will be here." So saying, he went away.

Many, many weary miles did he travel, till at last he came to a thick jungle; and, being very tired, sat down under a tree and fell asleep. He was awakened by a soft rustling sound, and looking about him, saw a large serpent which was making its way to an eagle's nest built in the tree under which he lay, and in the nest were two young eagles. The Prince seeing the danger of the young birds, drew his sword and killed the serpent; at the same moment a rushing sound was heard in the air, and the two old eagles, who had been out hunting for food for their young ones, returned.

They quickly saw the dead serpent and the young Prince standing over it; and the old mother eagle said to him, "Dear boy, for many years all our young ones have been devoured by that cruel serpent; you have now saved the lives of our children; whenever you are in need 'therefore, send to, us and we will help you; and as for these little eagles, take them, and let them be your servants."

At this the Prince was very glad, and the two eaglets crossed their wings, on which he mounted; and they carried him far, far away over the thick jungles, until be came to the place where grew the circle of palm-trees, in the midst of which stood the six chattees full of water. It was the middle of the day, and the heat was very great.

All round the trees were the genii fast asleep; nevertheless, there were such countless thousands of them, that it would have been quite impossible for anyone to walk through their ranks to the place; down swooped the strong-winged eaglets—down jumped the Prince; in an instant he had overthrown the six chattees full of water, and seized the little green parrot, which he rolled up in his cloak; while, as he mounted again into the air, all the genii below awoke, and finding their treasure gone, set up a wild and melancholy howl.

Away, away flew the little eagles, till they came to their home in the great tree; then the Prince said to the old eagles, "Take back your little ones; they have done me good service; if ever again I stand in need of help, I will not fail to come to you." He then continued his journey on foot till he arrived once more at the Magician's palace, where he sat down at the door and began playing with the parrot. Punchkin saw him, and came to him quickly, and said, "My boy, where did you get that parrot? Give it to me, I pray you."

But the Prince answered, "Oh no, I cannot give away my parrot, it is a great pet of mine; I have bad it many· years."

Then the Magician said, "If it is an old favourite, I can understand you not caring to give it away; but come, what will you sell it for?"

"Sir," replied the Prince, "I will not sell my parrot."

Then Punchkin got frightened, and said, "Anything, anything; name what price you will, and it shall be yours." The Prince answered, "Let the seven Raja's sons whom you turned into rocks and trees be instantly liberated."

"It is done as you desire," said the Magician, "only give me my parrot." And with that, by a stroke of his wand, Balna's husband and his brothers resumed their natural shapes. "Now, give me my parrot," repeated Punchkin.

"Not so fast, my master," rejoined the Prince; "I must first beg that you will restore to life all whom you have thus imprisoned." The Magician immediately waved his Wand again; and, whilst he cried, in an imploring voice, "Give me my parrot!" the whole garden became suddenly alive: where rocks, and stones, and trees had been before, stood Rajas, and Punts, and Sirdars, and mighty men on prancing horses, and jewelled pages, and troops of armed attendants.

"Give me my parrot!" cried Punchkin; Then the boy took bold of the parrot, and tore off one of its wings; and as he did so the Magician's right arm fell off.

Punchkin then stretched out his left arm, crying, "Give me my parrot!" The Prince pulled off the parrot's second wing, and the Magician's left arm tumbled off.

"Give me my parrot!" cried he, and be fell on his knees. The Prince pulled off the parrot's right leg, the Magician's right leg fell off: the Prince pulled off the parrot's left leg, down fell the Magician's left.

Nothing remained of him save the limbless body and the head; but still be rolled his eyes, and cried, "Give me my parrot!" "Take your parrot, then," cried the boy, and with that he wrung the bird's neck and threw it at the Magician; and, as he did so, Punchkin's head twisted round, and, with a fearful groan, be died!

Then they let Balna out of the tower; and she, her son, and the seven Princes went to their own country, and lived very happily ever afterwards. And as to the rest of the world, every one went to his own house.

The Broken Pot

There lived in a certain place a Brahman, whose name was Svabhavakripana, which means "a born miser." He had collected a quantity of rice by begging, and after having dined off it, he filled a pot with what was left over. He hung the pot on a peg on the wall, placed his couch beneath, and looking intently at it all the night, he thought, "Ah, that pot is indeed brimful of rice. Now, if there should be a famine, I should certainly make a hundred rupees by it. With this I shall buy a couple of goats. They will have young ones every six months, and thus I shall have a whole herd of goats. Then, with the goats, I shall buy cows. As soon as they have calved, I shall sell the calves. Then, with the calves, I shall buy buffaloes; with the buffaloes, mares. When the mares have foaled, I shall have plenty of horses; and when I sell them, plenty of gold. With that gold I shall get a house with four wings.

And then a Brahman will come to my house, and will give me his beautiful daughter, with a large dowry. She will have a son, and I shall call him Somasarman. When he is old enough to be danced on his father's knee, I shall sit with a book at the back of the stable, and while I am reading, the boy will see me, jump from his mother's lap, and run towards me to be danced on my knee. He will come too near the horse's hoof, and, full of anger, I shall call to my wife, 'Take the baby; take him!' But she, distracted by some domestic work, does not hear me. Then I get up, and give her such a kick with my foot." While he thought this, he gave a kick with his foot, and broke the pot. All the rice fell over him, and made him quite white. Therefore, I say, "He who makes foolish plans for the future will be white all over, like the father of Somasarman."

The Magic Fiddle

Once upon a time there lived seven brothers and a sister. The brothers were married, but their wives did not do the cooking for the family. It was done by their sister, who stopped at home to cook. The wives for this reason bore their sister-in-law much ill-will, and at length they combined together to oust her from the office of cook and general provider, so that one of themselves might obtain it. They said, "She does not go out to the fields to work, but remains quietly at home, and yet she has not the meals ready at the proper time." They then called upon their Bonga, and vowing vows unto them they secured his goodwill and assistance; then they said to the Bonga, "At midday, when our sister-in-law goes to bring, water, cause it thus to happen, that on seeing her pitcher, the water shall vanish, and again slowly reappear. In this way she will be delayed. Let the water not flow into her pitcher, and you may keep the maiden as your own."

At noon, when she went to bring water, it suddenly dried up before her, and she began to weep. Then after a while the water began slowly to rise. When it reached her ankles she tried to fill her pitcher, but it would not go under the water. Being frightened, she began to wail and cry to her brother:

"Oh! my brother, the water reaches to my ankles,
Still, Oh! my brother, the pitcher will not dip."

The water continued to rise until it reached her knee, when she began to wail again:

"Oh! my brother, the water reaches to my knee,
Still, Oh! my brother, the pitcher will not dip."

The water continued to rise, and when it reached her waist, she cried again:

"Oh! my brother, the water reaches to my waist,
Still, Oh! my brother, the pitcher will not dip."

The water still rose, and when it reached her neck she kept on crying:

"Oh! my brother, the water reaches to my neck,
Still, Oh! my brother, the pitcher will not dip."

At length the water became so deep that she felt herself drowning, then she cried aloud:

"Oh! my brother, the water measures a man's height,
Oh! my brother, the pitcher begins to fill."

The pitcher filled with water, and along with it she sank and was drowned. The Bonga then transformed her into a Bonga like himself, and carried her off.

After a time she reappeared as a bamboo growing on the embankment of the tank in which she had been drowned. When the bamboo had grown to an immense size, a Jogi, who was in the habit of passing that way, seeing it, said to himself, "This will make a splendid fiddle." So one day he brought an axe to cut it down; but when he was about to begin, the bamboo called out, "Do not cut at the root, cut higher up." When he lifted his axe to cut high up the stem, the bamboo cried out, "Do not cut near the top, cut at the root." When the Jogi again prepared himself to cut at the root as requested, the bamboo said, "Do not cut at the root, cut higher up;" and when he was about to cut higher up, it again called out to him, "Do not cut high up, cut at the root." The Jogi by this time felt sure that a Bonga was frying to frighten him, so becoming angry he cut down the bamboo at the root, and taking it away made a fiddle out of it. The instrument had a superior tone and delighted all who heard it. The Jogi carried it with him when he went a-begging, and through the influence of its sweet music he returned home every evening with a full wallet.

He now and then visited, when on his rounds, the house of the Bonga girl's brothers, and the strains of the fiddle affected them greatly. Some of them were moved even to tears, for the fiddle seemed to wail as one in bitter anguish. The elder brother wished to purchase it, and offered to support the Jogi for a whole year if he would consent to part with his wonderful instrument. The Jogi, however, knew its value, and refused to sell it. It so happened that the Jogi some time after went to the house of a village chief, and after playing a tune or two on his fiddle asked for something to eat. They offered to buy his fiddle and promised a high price for it, but he refused to sell it, as his fiddle brought to him his means of livelihood.

When they saw that he was not to be prevailed upon, they gave him food and a plentiful supply of liquor. Of the latter he drunk so freely that he presently became intoxicated. While he was in this condition, they took away his fiddle, and substituted their own old one for it. When the Jogi recovered, he missed his instrument, and suspecting that it had been stolen asked them to return it to him. They denied having taken it, so he had to depart leaving his fiddle behind him. The chief's son, being a musician, used to play on the Jogi's fiddle, and in his hands the music it gave forth delighted the ears of all who heard it.

When all the household were absent at their labours in the fields, the Bonga girl used to come out of the bamboo fiddle, and prepared the family meal. Having eaten her own share, she placed that of the chief's son under his bed, and covering it up to keep off the dust, re-entered the fiddle. This happening every day, the other members of the house-hold thought that some girl friend of theirs was in this manner showing her interest in the young man, so they did not trouble themselves to find out how it came about. The young chief, however, was determined to watch, and see which of his girl friends was so attentive to his comfort. He said in his own mind, "I will catch her today, and give her a sound beating; she is causing me to be ashamed before the others." So saying, he hid himself in a corner in a pile of firewood.

In a short time the girl came out of the bamboo fiddle and began to dress her hair. Having completed her toilet, she cooked the meal of rice as usual, and having eaten some herself, she placed the young man's portion under his bed, as before, and was about to enter the fiddle again, when he, running out from his hiding-place, caught her in his arms. The Bonga girl exclaimed, "Fie! Fie! you may be a Don, or you maybe a Hadi of some other caste with whom I cannot marry." He said, "No. But from today, you and I are one." So they began lovingly to hold converse with each other. When the others returned home in the evening, they saw that she was both a human being and a Bonga, and they rejoiced exceedingly. Now in course of time the Bonga girl's family became very poor, and her brothers on one occasion came to the chiefs house on a visit.

The Bonga girl recognised them at once, but they did not know who she was. She brought them water on their arrival, and afterwards set cooked rice before 'them. Then sitting down near them, she began in wailing tones to upbraid them on account of the treatment she had been subjected to by their wives. She related all that had befallen her, and wound up by saying," You must have known it all, and yet you did not interfere to save me." And that was all the revenge she took.

The Cruel Crane Outwitted

Long ago the Bodisat was born to a forest life as the genius of a tree standing near a certain lotus pond. Now at that time the water used to run short at the dry season in a certain pond, not over large, in which there were a good many fish. And a crane thought on seeing the fish:

"I must outwit these fish somehow or other and make a prey of them."

And he went and sat down at the edge of the water, thinking hew he should do it.

When the fish saw him, they asked him, "What are you sitting there for, lost in thought?"

"I am sitting thinking about you," said he.

"Oh, sir what are you thinking about us?" said they.

"Why," he replied, "there is very little water in this pond, and but little for you to eat; and the heat is so great! So I was thinking, 'What in the world will these fish do now?' "

"Yes, indeed, sir! what are we to do?" said they.

"If you will only do as I bid you, I will take you in my beak to a fine large pond, covered with all the kinds of lotuses, and, put you into it," answered the crane.

"That a crane should take thought for the fishes is a thing unheard of, sir, since the world began. It's eating us, one after the other, that you're aiming at."

"Not I! So long as you trust me, I won't eat you. But if you don't believe me that there is such a pond, send one of you with me to go and see it."

Then they trusted him, and handed over to him one of their number—a big fellow, blind of one eye, whom they thought sharp enough in any emergency, afloat or ashore.

Him the crane took with him, let him go in the pond, showed him the whole of it, brought him back, and let him go again close to the other fish. And he told them all the glories of the pond.

And when they heard what he said, they exclaimed, "All right, sir! You may take us with you."

Then the crane took the old purblind fish first to the bank of the other pond, and alighted in a Varana-tree growing on the bank there. But he threw it into a fork of the tree, struck it with his beak, and killed it; and then ate its flesh, and threw its bones away at the foot of the tree. Then he went back and called out:

"I've thrown that fish in; let another one come."

And in that manner he took all the fish, one by one, and ate them, till he came back and found no more!

But there was still a crab left behind there; and the crane thought he would eat him too, and called him out:

"I say, good crab, I've taken all, the fish away, and put them into a fine large pond. Come along. I'll take you too!"

"But how will you take hold of me to carry me along?"

"I'll bite hold of you with my beak."

"You'll let me fall if you carry me like that. I won't go with you!"

"Don't be afraid! I'll hold you quite tight all the way."

Then said the crab to himself, "If this fellow once got hold of fish, he would never let them go in a pond! Now if he should really put me into the pond, it would be capital; but if he doesn't—then I'll cut his throat, and kill him!" So he said to him:

"Look here, friend, you won't be able to hold me tight enough; but we crabs have a famous grip. If you let me catch hold of you round the neck with my claws, I shall be glad to go with you."

And the other did not see that he was trying to outwit him, and agreed. So the crab caught hold of his neck with his claws as securely as with a pair of blacksmith's pincers and called out, "Off with you, now!"

And the crane took him and showed him the pond, and then turned off towards the Varana-tree.

"Uncle! " cried the crab, "the pond lies that way, but you are taking me this way!"

"Oh, that's it, is it?" answered the crane. "Your dear little uncle, your very sweet nephew, you call me! You mean me to understand, I suppose, that I am your slave, who has to lift you up and carry you about with him! Now cast your eye upon the heap of fish-bones lying at the root of yonder Varana-tree. Just as I have eaten those fish, every one of them, just so I will devour you as well!"

"Ah! those fishes got eaten through their own stupidity," answered the crab; "but I'm not going to let you eat me. On the contrary, it is you that I am going to destroy. For you in your folly have not seen that I was outwitting you. If we die we die both together; for I will cut off this head of yours, and cast it to the ground!" And so saying, he gave the crane's neck a grip with his claws, as with a vice.

Then gasping, and with tears trickling from his eyes, and trembling with the fear of death, the crane beseeched him, saying, "O my lord! Indeed I did not intend to eat you. Grant me my life!"

"Well, well! step down into the pond, and put me in there."

And he turned round and stepped down into the pond, and placed the crab on the mud at its edge. But the crab cut through its neck as clean as one would cut a lotus-stalk with a hunting-knife, and then only entered the water!

When the Genius who lived in the Varana-tree saw this strange affair, he made the wood resound with his plaudits, uttering in a pleasant voice the verse:

"The villain, though exceeding clever,
Shall prosper not by his villainy.
He may win indeed, sharp-witted in deceit,
But only as the Crane here from the Crab!"

Loving Laili

Once there was a king called King Dantal, who had a great many rupees and soldiers and horses. He had also an only son called Prince Majnun, who was a handsome boy with white teeth, red lips, blue eyes, red cheeks, red hair, and a white skin. This boy was very fond of playing with the Wazir's son, Husain Mahamat, in King Dantal's garden, which was very large and full of delicious fruits and flowers and frees. They used to take their little knives there and cut the fruits and eat them. King Dantal had a teacher for them to teach them to read and write.

One day, when they were grown two fine young men, Prince Majnun said to his father, "Husain Mahamat and I should like to go and hunt." His father said they might go, so they got ready their horses and all else they wanted for their hunting, and went to the Phalana country, hunting all the way, but they only found jackals and birds.

The Raja of the Phalana country was called Munsuk Raja, and he had a daughter named Laili, who was very beautiful; she had brown eyes and black hair.

One night, some time before Prince Majnun came to her father's kingdom, as she slept, Khuda sent to her an angel in the form of a man who told her that she should marry Prince Majnun and no one else, and that this was Khuda's command to her. When Laili woke she told her father of the angel's visit to her as she slept; but her father paid no attention to her story. From that time she began repeating, "Majnun, Majnun; I want Majnun," and would say nothing else. Even as she sat and ate her food she kept saying, "Majnun, Majnun; I want Majnun." Her father used to get quite vexed with her. "Who is this Majnun? who ever heard of this Majnun?" he would say.

"He is the man I am to marry," said Laili. "Khuda has ordered me to marry no one but Majnun." And she was half mad.

Meanwhile, Majnun and Husain Mahamat came to hunt in the Phalana country; and as they were riding about, Laili came out on her horse to eat the air, and rode behind them. All the time she kept saying, "Majnun, Majnun; I want Majnun." The prince heard her, and turned round. "Who is calling me?" he asked. At this Laili looked at him, and the moment she saw him she fell deeply in love with him, and she said to herself, "I am sure that is the Prince Majnun that Khuda says I am to marry." And she went home to her father and said, "Father, I wish to marry the prince who has come to your kingdom; for I know he is the Prince Majnun I am to marry."

"Very well, you shall have him for your husband," said Munsuk Raja. "We will ask him tomorrow." Laili consented to wait, although she was very impatient. As it happened, the prince left the Phalana kingdom that night, and when Laili heard he was gone, she went quite mad. She would not listen to a word her father, or her mother, or her servants said to her, but went off into the jungle, and wandered from jungle to jungle, till she got farther and farther away from her own country. All the time she kept saying, "Majnun, Majnun; I want Majnun;" and so she wandered about for twelve years.

At the end of the twelve years she met a fakir—he was really an angel, but she did not know this—who asked her, "Why do you always say, 'Majnun, Majnun; I want Majnun?" She answered, "I am the daughter of the king of the Phalana country, and I want to find Prince Majnun; tell me where his kingdom is."

"I think you will never get there," said the fakir, "for, it is very far from hence, and you have to cross many rivers to reach it." But Laili said she did not care; she must see Prince Majnun. "Well," said the fakir, "when you come to the Bhagirathi river you will see a big fish, a Rohu; and you must get him to carry you to Prince Majnun's country, or you will never reach it."

She went on and on, and at last she came to the Bhagirathi river. There was a great big fish called the Rohu fish. It was yawning just as she got up to it, and she instantly jumped down its throat into its stomach. All the time she kept saying, "Majnun, Majnun!" At this the Rohu fish was greatly alarmed and swam down the river as fast as he could. By degrees he got tired and went slower, and a crow came and perched on his back, and said " Caw, caw." "Oh, Mr. Crow," said the poor fish, "do see what is in my stomach that makes such a noise."

"Very well," said the crow, "open your mouth wide, and I'll fly down and see." So the Rohu opened his jaws and the crow flew down, but he came up again very quickly. "You have a Rakshas in your stomach," said the crow, and he flew away. This news did not comfort the poor Rohu, and he swam on and on till he came to Prince Majnun's country. There he stopped. And a jackal came down to the river to drink. "Oh, jackal," said the Rohu, "do tell me what I have inside me."

"How can I tell?" said the jackal. "I cannot see unless I go inside you." So the Rohu opened his mouth wide; and the jackal jumped down his throat; but he came up very quickly, looking much frightened and saying, "You have a Rakshas in your stomach, and if I don't run away quickly, I am afraid it will eat me." So off he ran. After the jackal came an enormous snake. "Oh," says the fish, "do tell me what I have in my stomach, for it rattles about so, and keeps saying, "Majnun, Majnun; I want Majnun."

The snake said, "Open your mouth wide, and I'll go down and see what it is." The snake went down: when he returned he said, "You have a Rakshas in your stomach, but if you will let me cut you open, it will come out of you." "If you do that, I shall die," said the Rohu. "Oh no," said the snake, "you will not, for I will give you a medicine that will make you quite well again." So the fish agreed, and the snake got a, knife and cut him open, and out jumped Laili.

She was now very old. Twelve years she had wandered about the jungle, and for twelve years she had lived inside her Rohu; and she was no longer beautiful, and had lost her teeth. The snake took her on his back and carried her into the country, and there he put her down, and she wandered on and on till she got to Majnun's court-house, where King Majnun was sitting. There some men heard her crying, "Majnun, Majnun; I want Majnun," and they asked her what she wanted. "I want King Majnun," she said.

So they went in and said to Prince Majnun, "An old woman outside says she wants you." "I cannot leave this place," said he; "send her in here." They brought her in and the prince asked what she wanted. "I want to marry you," she answered. "Twenty-four years ago you came to my father the Phalana Raja's country, and I wanted to marry you then; but you went away without marrying me. Then I went mad, and I have wandered about all these years looking for you." Prince Majnun said, "Very good."

"Pray to Khuda," said Laili, "to make us both young again, and then we shall be married." So the prince prayed to Khuda, and Khuda said to him, "Touch Laili's clothes and they will catch fire, and when they are on fire she and you will become young again." When he touched Laili's clothes they caught fire, and she and he became young again. And there were great feasts, and they were married, and travelled to the Phalana country to see her father and mother.

Now Laili's father and mother had wept so much for their daughter that they had become quite blind, and her father kept always repeating, "Laili, Laili, Laili." When Laili saw their blindness, she prayed to Khuda to restore their sight to them, which he did. As soon as the father and mother saw Laili, they hugged her and kissed her, and then they had the wedding all over again amid great rejoicings. Prince Majnun and Laili stayed with Munsuk Raja and his wife for three years, and then they returned to King Dantal, and lived happily for some time with him.

They used to go out hunting, and they often went from country to country to eat the air and amuse themselves.

One day Prince Majnun said to Laili, "Let us go through this jungle." "No, no," said Laili; "if we go through this jungle, some harm will happen to me." But Prince Majnun laughed, and went into the jungle. And as they were going through it, Khuda thought, "I should like to know how much Prince Majnun loves his wife. Would he be very sorry if she died? And would he many another wife? I will see." So he sent one of his angels in the form of a fakir into the jungle; and the angel went up to Laili, and threw some powder in her face, and instantly she fell to the ground a heap of ashes.

Prince Majnun was in great sorrow and grief when he saw his dear Laili turned into a little heap of ashes; and he went straight home to his father, and for a long, long time he would not be comforted. After a great many years he grew more cheerful and happy, and began to go again into his father's beautiful garden with Husain Mahamat. King Dantal wished his son to marry again. "I will only have Laili for my wife; I will not marry any other woman," said Prince Majnun.

" How can you marry Laili? Laili is dead. She will never come back to you," said the father.

"Then I'll not have any wife at all?' said Prince Majnun.

Meanwhile Laili was living in the jungle where her husband had left her a little heap of ashes. As soon as Majnun had gone, the fakir had taken her ashes and made them quite clean, and then he had mixed clay and water with the ashes, and made the figure of a woman with 'them, and so Laili regained her human form, and Khuda sent life into it. But Laili had become once more a hideous old woman, with a long, long nose, and teeth like tusks; just such an old woman, excepting her teeth, as she had been when she came out of the Rohu fish; and she lived in the jungle, and neither ate nor drank, and she kept on saying, "Majnun, Majnun; I want Majnun."

At last the angel who had, come as a fakir and thrown the powder at her, said to Khuda, "Of what use is it that this woman should sit in the jungle crying; crying for ever, 'Majnun, Majnun; I want Majnun,' and eating and drinking nothing? Let me take her to Prince Majnun." "Well," said Khuda, "you may do so; but tell her that she must not speak to Majnun if he is afraid of her when he sees her; and that if he is afraid when he sees her, she will become a little white dog the next day. Then she must go to the palace, and she will only regain her human shape when Prince Majnun loves her, feeds her with his own food, and lets her sleep in his bed."

So the angel came to Laili again as a fakir and carried her to King Dantal's garden. "Now," he said, "it is Khuda's command that you stay here till Prince Majnun comes to walk in the garden, and then you may show yourself to him. But you must not speak to him, if he is afraid of you; and should he be afraid of you, you will the next day become a little white dog." He then told her what she must do as a little dog to regain her human form.

Laili stayed in the garden, hidden in the tall grass, till Prince Majnun and Husain Mahamat came to walk in the garden. King Dantal was now a very old man, and Husain Mahamat, though he was really only as old as Prince Majnun, looked a great deal older than the prince, who had been made quite young again when he married Laili.

As Prince Majnun and the Wazir's son walked in the garden, they gathered the fruit as they had done as little children, only they bit the fruit with their teeth; they did not cut it. While Majnun was busy eating a fruit in this way, and was talking to Husain Mahamat, he turned towards him and saw Laili walking behind the Wazir's son.

"Oh, look, look!" he cried, "see what is following you; it is a Rakshas or a demon, and I am sure it is going to eat us." Laili looked at him beseechingly with all her eyes, and trembling with age and eagerness; but this only frightened Majnun the more. "It is a Rakshas, a Rakshas!" he cried, and he ran quickly to the palace with the Wazir's son; and as they ran away, Laili disappeared into the jungle. They ran to King Dantal, and Majnun told him there was a Rakshas or a demon in the garden that had come to eat them.

"What nonsense!" said his father. "Fancy two grown men being so frightened by an old ayah or a fakir! And if it had been a Rakshas, it would not have eaten you." Indeed King Dantal did not believe Majnun had seen anything at all, till Husain Mahamat said the prince was speaking the exact truth. They had the garden searched for the terrible old woman, but found nothing, and King Dantal told his son be was very silly to be so much frightened. However, Prince Majnun would not walk in the garden any more.

The next day Laili turned into a pretty little dog; and in this shape she came into the palace, where Prince Majnun soon became very fond of her. She followed him everywhere, went with him when he was out hunting, and helped him to catch his game, and Prince Majnun fed her with milk, or bread, or anything else be was eating, and at night the little dog slept in his bed.

But one night the little dog disappeared, and in its stead there lay the little old woman who had frightened him so much in the garden; and now Prince Majnun was quite sure she was a Rakshas, or a demon, or some such horrible thing come to eat him; and in his terror be cried out, "What do you want? Oh, do not eat me; do not eat me!" Poor Laili answered, "Don't you know me? I am your wife Laili, and I want to marry you. Don't you remember how you would go through that jungle, though

I begged and begged you not to go, for I told you that harm would happen to me, and then a fakir came and threw powder in my face, and I became a heap of ashes. But Khuda gave me my life again, and brought me here, after I had stayed a long, long while in the jungle crying for you, and now I am obliged to be a little dog; but if you will marry me, I shall not be a little, dog any more." Majnun, however, said, "How can I marry an old woman like you? how can you be Laili? I am sure you are a Rakshas or a demon come to eat me," and he was in great terror.

In the morning the old woman had turned into the little dog, and the prince went to his father and told him all that had happened. "An old woman! an old woman! always an old woman!" said his father. "You do nothing but think of old women. How can a strong man like you be so easily frightened?" However, when he saw that his son was really in great terror, and that he really believed the old woman would come back at night, he advised him to say to her, "I will marry you if you can make yourself a young girl again. How can I marry such an old woman as you are?"

That night as he lay trembling in bed the little old woman lay there in place of the dog, crying; " Majnun, Majnun, I want to marry you. I have loved you all these long, long years. When I·was in my father's kingdom a young girl, I knew of you, though you knew nothing of me, and we should have been married then if you had not gone away so suddenly, and for long, long years I followed you." "Well," said Majnun, "if you can make yourself a young girl again, I will marry you."

Laili said, "Oh, that is quite easy. Khuda will make me a young girl again. In two days' time you must go into the garden, and there you will, see a beautiful fruit. You must gather it and bring it into your room and cut it open yourself very gently, and you must not open it when your father or anybody else is with you, but when you are quite alone; for I shall be in the fruit quite naked, without any clothes at all on." In the morning Laili took her little dog's form and disappeared in the garden.

Prince Majnun told all this to his father, who told him to do all the old woman had bidden him. In two days' time he and the Wazir's son walked in the garden, and there they saw a large, lovely red fruit. "Oh!" said the prince, "I wonder shall I find my wife in that fruit."

Husain Mahamat wanted him to gather it and sėe, but he would not till he had told his father, who said, "That must be the fruit; go and gather it." So Majnun went back and broke the fruit off its stalk; and he said to his father, "Come with me to my room while I open it; I am afraid to open it alone, for perhaps I shall find a Rakshas in it that will eat me."

"No," said King Dantal; "remember, Laili will be naked; you must go alone and do not be afraid if, after all, a Rakshas is in the fruit, for I will stay outside the door, and you have only to call me with a loud voice, and I will come to you, so the Raksbas will not be able to eat you."

Then Majnun took the fruit and began to cut it open tremblingly, for he shook with fear; and when he had cut it, out stepped Laili, young and far more beautiful than she had ever been. At the sight of her extreme beauty, Majnun fell backwards fainting on the floor.

Laili took off his turban and wound it all round herself like a sari (for she had no clothes at all on), and then she called King Dantal, and said to him sadly, "Why has Majnun fallen down like this? Why will he not speak to me? He never used to be afraid of me; and he has seen me so many, many times."

King Dantal answered, "It is because you are so beautiful. You are far, far more beautiful than you ever were. But he will be very happy directly." Then the King got some water, and they bathed Majnun's face and gave him some to drink, and he sat up again.

Then Laili said, "Why did you faint? Did you not see I am Laili?"

"Oh!" said Prince Majnun, "I see you are Laili come back to me, but your eyes have grown so wonderfully beautiful that I fainted when I saw them." Then they were all very happy, and King Dantal had all the drums in the place beaten, and had all the musical instruments played on, and they made a grand wedding feast, and gave presents to the servants, and rice and quantities of rupees to the fakirs.

After some time had passed very happily, Prince Majnun and his wife went out to eat the air. They rode on the same horse, and had only a groom with them. They came to another kingdom, to a beautiful garden. "We must go into that garden and see it," said Majnun.

"No, no," said Laili; "it belongs to a bad Raja, Chumman Basa, a very wicked man." But Majnun insisted on going in, and in spite of all Laili could say, he got off the horse to look at the flowers. Now, as he was looking at the flowers, Laili saw Chumman Basa coming towards them, and she read in his eyes that he meant to kill her husband and seize her. So she said to Majnun, "Come, come, let us go; do not go near that bad man. I see in his eyes, and I feel in my heart, that he will kill you to seize me."

"What nonsense!" said Majnun. "I believe be is a very good Raja. Anyhow, I am so near to him that I could not get away."

"Well," said Laili, "it is better that you should be killed than I, for if I were to be killed a second time, Khuda would not give me my life again; but I can bring you to life if you are killed." Now Chumman Basa had come quite near, and seemed very pleasant, so thought Prince Majnun; but when he was speaking to Majnun, he drew his scimitar and cut off the prince's head at one blow.

Laili sat quite still on her horse, and as the Raja came towards her she said, "Why did you kill my husband?"

"Because I want to take you," he answered.

"You cannot," said Laili.

"Yes, I can," said the Raja.

"Take me then," said Laili to Chumman Basa; so he came quite close and put out his hand to take hers to lift her off her horse. But she put her hand in her pocket and pulled out a tiny knife, only as long as her hand was broad, and this knife unfolded itself in one instant till it was such a length! and then Laili made a great sweep with her arm and her long, long knife, and off came Chumman Basa's head at one touch. Then Laili slipped down off her horse, and she went to Majnun's dead body, and she cut her little finger inside her hand straight down from the top of her nail to her palm, and out of this gushed blood like healing medicine.

Then she put Majnun's head on his shoulders, and smeared her healing blood all over the wound, and Majnun woke up and said, What a delightful sleep I have had! Why, I feel as if I had slept for years!" Then he got up and saw the Raja's dead body by Laili's horse.

"What's that?" said Majnun.

"That is the wicked Raja who killed you to seize me, just as I said he would."

"Who killed him?" asked Majnun.

"I did," answered Laili, "and it was I who brought you to life."

"Do bring the poor man to life if you know how to do so," said Majnun.

"No," said Laili, "for. he is a wicked man, and will try to do you harm." But Majnun asked her for such a long time, and so earnestly, to bring the wicked Raja to life, that at last she said, "Jump up on the horse, then, and go far away with the groom."

"What will you do," said Majnun, "if I leave you? I cannot leave you."

"I will take care of myself," said Laili; "but this man is so wicked, he may kill you again if you are near him." So Majnun got up on the horse, and he and the groom went a long way off and waited for Laili. Then she set the wicked Raja's head straight on his shoulders, and she squeezed the wound in her finger till a little blood-medicine came out of it.

Then she smeared this over the place where her knife had passed, and just as she saw the Raja opening his eyes, she began to run, and she ran, and ran so fast, that she outran the Raja, who tried to catch her; and she sprang up on the horse behind her husband, and they rode so fast, so fast, till they reached King Dantal's palace.

There Prince Majnun told everything to his father, who was horrified and angry. "How lucky for you that you have such a wife," he said. "Why did you not do what she told you? But for her, you would be now dead." Then he made a great feast out of gratitude for his son's safety, and gave many, many rupees to the fakirs. And he made so much of Laili. He loved her dearly; he could not do enough for her. Then he built a splendid palace for her and his son, with a great deal of ground about it, and lovely gardens, and gave them great wealth, and heaps of servants to wait on them. But he would not allow any but their servants to enter their gardens and palace, and he would not allow Majnun to go out of them, nor Laili; "for," said King Dantal, "Laili is so beautiful, that perhaps some one may kill my son to take her away."

The Tiger, the Brahmin and the Jackal

Once upon a time, a tiger was caught in a trap. He tried in vain to get out through the bars, and rolled and bit with rage and grief when he failed.

By chance a poor Brahman came by.

"Let me out of this cage, oh pious one!" cried the tiger.

"Nay, my friend," replied the Brahman mildly, "you would probably eat me if I did."

"Not at all!" swore the tiger with many oaths; "on the contrary, I should be for ever grateful, and serve you as a slave!"

Now when the tiger sobbed and sighed and wept and swore, the pious Brahman's heart softened, and at last he consented to open the door of the cage. Out popped the tiger, and, seizing the poor man, cried, "What a fool you are! What is to prevent my eating you now, for after being cooped up so long I am just terribly hungry!"

In vain the Brahman pleaded for his life; the most he could gain was a promise to abide by the decision of the first three things he chose to question as to the justice of the tiger's action.

So the Brahman first asked a papal-tree what it thought of the matter, but the papal-tree replied coldly, "What have you to complain about? Don't I give shade and shelter to every one who passes by, and don't they in return tear down my branches to feed their cattle? Don't whimper—be a man!"

Then the Brahman, sad at heart, went further afield till he saw a buffalo turning a well-wheel; but he fared no better from it, for it answered, "You are a fool to expect gratitude! Look at me! Whilst I gave milk they fed me on cotton-seed and oil-cake, but now I am dry they yoke me here, and give me refuse as fodder!"

The Brahman, still more sad, asked the road to give him its opinion.

"My dear sir," said the road, "how foolish you are to expect anything else! Here am I, useful to everybody, yet all, rich and poor, great and small, trample on me as they go past, giving me nothing but the ashes of their pipes and the husks of their grain!"

On this the Brahman turned back sorrowfully, and on the way he met a jackal, who called out, "Why, what's the matter, Mr. Brahman? You look as miserable as a fish out of water!"

The Brahman told him all that had occurred. "How very confusing!" said the jackal, when the recital was ended; "would you mind telling me over again, for everything has got so mixed up?"

The Brahman told it all over again, but the jackal shook his head in a distracted sort of way, and still could not understand.

"It's very odd," said he, sadly, "but it all seems to go in at one ear and out at the other! I will go to the place where it all happened, and then perhaps I shall be able to give a judgment."

So they returned to the cage, by which the tiger was waiting for the Brahman, and sharpening his teeth and claws;

"You've been away a long time!" growled the savage beast, "but now let us begin our dinner."

"Our dinner!" thought the wretched Brahman, as his knees knocked together with fright; "what a remarkably delicate way of putting it!"

"Give me five minutes, my lord!" he pleaded, "in order that I may explain matters to the jackal here, who is somewhat slow in his wits."

The tiger consented, and the Brahman began the whole story over again, not missing a single detail, and spinning as long a yarn as possible.

"Oh, my poor brain! oh, my poor brain!" cried the jackal, wringing its paws. "Let me see! how did it all begin? You were in the cage, and the tiger came walking by—"

"Pooh!" interrupted the tiger, "what a fool you are! I was in the cage."

"Of course! " cried the jackal, pretending to tremble with fright; "yes! I was in the cage—no I wasn't—dear! dear! where are my wits? Let me see—the tiger was in the Brahman, and the cage came walking by—no, that's not it, either! Well, don't mind me, but begin your dinner, for I shall never understand!"

"Yes, you shall!" returned the tiger, in a rage at the jackal's stupidity; "I'll make you understand! Look here—I am the tiger—"

"Yes, my lord! "

"And that is the Brahman—"

"Yes, my lord!"

"And that is the cage—"

"Yes, my lord!"

"And I was in the cage—do you understand?"

"Yes—no-Please, my lord—"

"Well? " cried the tiger impatiently.

"Please, my lord!—how did you get in?"

"How!—why in the usual way, of course!"

"Oh, dear me!—my head is beginning to whirl again! Please don't be angry, my lord, but what is the usual way?"

At this the tiger lost patience, and, jumping into the cage, cried, "This way! Now do you understand how it was?"

"Perfectly! " grinned the jackal, as he dexterously shut the door, "and if you will permit me to say so, I think matters will remain as they were!"

The Soothsayer's Son

Soothsayer when on his deathbed wrote out the horoscope of his second son, whose name was Gangazara, and bequeathed it to him as his only property, leaving the whole of his estate to his eldest son. The second son thought over the horoscope, and said to himself:

"Alas! am I born to this only in the world? The sayings of my father never failed. I have seen them prove true to the last word while he was living; and how has he fixed my horoscope! 'From my birth, poverty!' Nor is that my only fate. 'For ten years, imprisonment '—a fate harder than poverty; and what comes next? 'Death on the seashore'; which means that I must die away from home, far from friends and relatives on a sea-coast. Now comes the most curious part of the horoscope, that I am to 'have some happiness afterwards!' What this happiness is, is an enigma to me."

Thus thought he, and after all the funeral obsequies of his father were over, took leave of his elder brother, and started for Benares. He went by the middle of the Deccan avoiding both the coasts, and went on journeying and journeying for weeks and months, till at last be reached the Vindhya mountains. While passing that desert he had to journey for a couple of days through a sandy plain, with no signs of life or vegetation. The little store of provision with which he was provided for a couple of days, at last was exhausted.

The chombu, which he carried always full, filling it with the sweet water from the flowing rivulet or plenteous tank, he had exhausted in the heat of the desert. There was not a morsel in his hand to eat; nor a drop of water to think. Turn his eyes wherever he might he found a vast desert, out of which he saw no means of escape. Still he thought within himself, "Surely my father's prophecy never proved untrue. I must survive this calamity to find my death on some sea-coast." So thought be, and this thought gave him strength of mind to walk fast and try to find a drop of water somewhere to slake his dry throat.

At last he succeeded; heaven threw in his way a ruined well. He thought he could collect some water if he let down his chombu with the string that he always carried noosed to the neck of it. Accordingly he let it down; it went some way and stopped, and the following words came from the well: "Oh, relieve me! I am the king of tigers, dying here of hunger. For the last three days I have had nothing. Fortune has sent you here. If you assist me now you will find a sure help in me throughout your life.

Do not think that I am a beast of prey. When you have become my deliverer I will never touch you. Pray, kindly lift me up." Gangazara thought: "Shall I take him out or not? If I take him out he may make me the first morsel of his hungry mouth. No; that be will not do. For my father's prophecy never came untrue. I must die on a sea-coast, and not by a tiger." Thus thinking, he asked the tiger-king to hold tight to the vessel, which he accordingly did, and he lifted him up slowly. The tiger reached the top of the well and felt himself on safe ground. True to his word, he did no harm to Gangazara. On the other hand, he walked round his patron three times, and standing before him, humbly spoke the following words:

> *"My life-giver, my benefactor! I shall never forget this day, when I regained my life through your kind hands. In return for this kind assistance I pledge my oath to stand by you in all calamities. Whenever you are in any difficulty just think of me. I am there with you ready to oblige you by all the means that I can. To tell you briefly how I came in here: Three days ago I was roaming in yonder forest, when I saw a goldsmith passing through it. I chased him. He, finding it impossible to escape my claws, jumped into this well, and is living to this moment in the very bottom of it. I also jumped in, but found myself on the first ledge of the well; he is on the last and fourth ledge. In the second lives a serpent half-*

famished with hunger. On the third lies a rat, also half-famished, and when you again begin to draw water these may request you first to release them. In the same way the goldsmith also may ask you. I beg you, as your bosom friend, never assist that wretched man, though he is your relation as a human being. Goldsmiths are never to be trusted. You can place more faith in me, a tiger, though I feast sometimes upon men, in a serpent, whose sting makes your blood cold the very next moment, or in a rat, which does a thousand pieces of mischief in your house. But never trust a goldsmith. Do not release him; and if you do, you shall surely repent of it one day or other." Thus advising, the hungry tiger went away without waiting for an answer.

Gangazara thought several times of the eloquent way in which the tiger spoke, and admired his fluency of speech. But still his thirst was not quenched. So he let down his vessel again, which was now caught hold of by the serpent, who addressed him thus: "Oh, my protector! Lift me up. I am the king of serpents, and the son of Adisesha, who is now pining away in agony for my disappearance. 'Release me now. I shall ever remain your servant, remember your assistance, and help you throughout life in all possible ways. Oblige me: I am dying." Gangazara, calling again to mind the "death on the sea-shore" of the prophecy lifted him up. He, like the tiger-king, walked round him thrice, and prostrating himself before him spoke thus: "Oh, my life-giver, my father, for so I must call you, as you have given me another birth. I was three days ago basking myself in the morning sun, when I saw a rat running before me. I chased him. He fell into this well. I followed him, but instead of falling on the third storey where he is now lying, I fell into the second. I am going away now to see my father. Whenever you are in any difficulty just think of me. I will be there by your side to assist you by all possible means." So saying, the Nagaraja glided away in zigzag movements, and was out of sight in a moment.

The poor son of the Soothsayer, who was now almost dying of thirst, let down his vessel for a third time. The rat caught hold of it, and without discussing he lifted up the poor animal at once. But it would not go away without showing its gratitude: "Oh, life of my life! My benefactor! I am the king of rats. Whenever you are in any calamity just think of me. I will come to you, and assist you. My keen ears overheard all that the tiger-king told you about the goldsmith, who is in the fourth storey.

It is nothing but a sad truth that goldsmiths ought never to be trusted. Therefore, never assist him as you have done to us all. And if you do, you will suffer for it. I am hungry; let me go for the present." Thus taking leave of his benefactor, the rat, too, ran away.

Gangazara for a while thought upon the repeated advice given by the three animals about releasing the goldsmith: "What wrong would there be in my assisting him? Why should I not release him also?" So thinking to himself, Gangazara let down the vessel again. The goldsmith caught hold of it, and demanded help. 'the Soothsayer's son had no time to lose; he was himself dying of thirst. Therefore he lifted the goldsmith up, who now began his story. "Stop for a while," said Gangazara, and after quenching his thirst by letting down his vessel for the fifth time, still fearing that some one might remain in the well and demand his assistance, he listened to the goldsmith, who began as follows: "My dear friend, my protector, what a deal of nonsense these brutes have been talking to you about me; I am glad you have not followed their advice. I am just now dying of hunger.

Permit me to go away. My name is Manikkasari. I live in the East main street of Ujjaini, which is twenty kas to the south of this place, and so lies on your way when you return from Benares. Do not forget to come to me and receive my kind remembrances of your assistance, on your way back to your country." So saying, the goldsmith took his leave, and Gangazara also pursued his way north after the above adventures.

He reached Benares, and lived there for more than ten years, and quite forgot the tiger, serpent, rat, and goldsmith. After ten years of religious life, thoughts of home and of his brother rushed into his mind. "I have secured enough merit now by my religious observances. Let me return home." Thus thought Gangazara within himself, and very soon he was on his way back to his country. Remembering the prophecy of his father he returned by the same way by which he went to Benares ten years before. While thus retracing his steps he reached the ruined well where he had released the three brute kings and the goldsmith.

At once the old recollections rushed into his mind, and he thought of the tiger to test his fidelity. Only a moment passed, and the tiger-king came running before him carrying a large crown in his mouth, the glitter of the diamonds of which for a time outshone even the bright rays of the sun. He dropped the crown at his life-giver's feet, and, putting aside all his pride, humbled himself like a pet cat to the strokes of his protector, and began in the following words: "My life-giver! How is it that you have forgotten me, your poor servant, for such a long time? I am glad to find that I still occupy a corner in your mind. I can never forget the day when I owed my life to your lotus hands. I have several jewels with me of little value.

This crown, being the best of all, I have brought here as a single ornament of great value, which you can carry with you and dispose of in your own country." Gangazara looked at the crown, examined it over and over, counted and recounted the gems, and thought within himself that he would become the richest of men by separating the diamonds and gold, and selling them in his own country. He took leave of the tiger-king, and after his disappearance thought of the kings of serpents and rats, who came in their turn with their presents, and after the usual greetings and exchange of words took their leave. Gangazara was extremely delighted at the faithfulness with which the brute beasts behaved, and went on his way to the south.

While going along he spoke to himself thus: "These beasts have been very faithful in their assistance. Much more, therefore, must Manikkasari be faithful. I do not want anything from him now. If I take this crown with me as it is, it occupies much space in my bundle. It may also excite the curiosity of some robbers on the way. I will go now to Ujjaini on my way. Manikkasari requested me to see him without failure on my return journey. I shall do so, and request him to have the crown melted, the diamonds and gold separated. He must do that kindness at least for me. I shall then roll up these diamonds and gold ball in my rags, and wend my way homewards."

Thus thinking and thinking, he reached UJjjaini. At once he inquired for the house of his goldsmith friend, and found him without difficulty. Manikkasari was extremely delighted to find on his threshold him who ten years before, notwithstanding the advice repeatedly given him by the sage-looking tiger, serpent, and rat, had relieved him from the pit of death. Gangazara at once showed him the crown that he received from the tiger-king; told him how he got it, and requested his kind assistance to separate the gold and diamonds. Manikkasari agreed to do so, and meanwhile asked his friend to rest himself for a while to have his bath and meals; and Gangazara, who was very observant of his religious ceremonies, went direct to the river to bathe.

How came the crown in the jaws of the tiger? The king of Ujjaini had a week before gone with all his hunters on a hunting expedition. All of a sudden the tiger-king started from the wood, seized the king, and vanished.

When the king's attendants informed the prince about the death of his father he wept and wailed, and gave notice that he would give half of his kingdom to any one who should bring him news about the murderer of his father. The goldsmith knew full well that it was a tiger that killed the king, and not any hunter's hands, since he had heard from Gangazara how he obtained the crown.

Still, he resolved to denounce Gangazara as the king's murderer, so, hiding the crown under his garments, he flew to the palace. He went before the prince and informed him that the assassin was caught, and placed the crown before him. The prince took it into his hands, examined it, and at once gave half the kingdom to Manikkasari, and then inquired about the murderer. "He is bathing in the river, and is of such and such appearance," was the reply. At once four armed soldiers flew to the river, and bound the poor Brahman hand and foot, while he, sitting in meditation, was without any knowledge of the fate that hung over him. They brought Gangazara to the presence of the prince, who turned his face away, from the supposed murderer, and asked his soldiers to throw him into a dungeon. In a minute, without knowing the cause, the poor Brahman found himself in the dark dungeon.

It was a dark cellar underground, built with strong stone walls, into which any criminal guilty of a capital offence was ushered to breathe his last there without food and drink. Such was the cellar into which Gangazara was thrust. What were his thoughts when he reached that plate? "It is of, no use to accuse either the goldsmith or the prince now, We are all the children of fate. We must obey her commands. This is but the first day of my father's prophecy, So far his statement is true. But how am I going to pass ten years here? Perhaps without anything to sustain life I may drag on my existence for a day or two. But how pass ten years? That cannot be, and I must die. Before death comes let me think of my faithful brute friends."

So pondered Gangazara in the dark cell underground, and at that moment thought of his three friends. The tiger-king, serpent-king, and rat-king assembled at once with their armies at a garden near the dungeon, and for a while did not know what to do. They held their council, and decided to make an underground passage from the inside of a ruined well to the dungeon. The rat raja issued an order at once to that effect to his army. They, with their teeth, bored the ground a long way to the walls of the prison. After reaching it they found that their teeth could not work on the hard stones. The bandicoots were then specially ordered 'for the business; they, with their hard teeth, made a small slit in the wall for a rat to pass and repass without difficulty. Thus a passage was effected.

The rat raja entered first to condole with his protector on his misfortune, and undertook to supply his protector with provisions. "Whatever sweetmeats or bread are prepared in any house, one and all of you must try to bring whatever you can to our benefactor. Whatever clothes you find hanging in a house, cut down, dip the pieces in water, and bring the wet bits to our benefactor. He will squeeze them and gather water for drink! and the bread and sweetmeats shall form his food." Having issued these orders, the king of the rats took leave of Gangazara. They, in obedience to their king's order, continued to supply him with provisions and water.

The snake-king said: "I sincerely condole with you in your calamity; the tiger-king also fully sympathises with you, and wants me to tell you so, as he cannot drag his huge body here as we have done with our small ones. The king of the rats has promised to do his best to provide you with food. We would now do what we can for your release. From this day we shall issue orders to our armies to oppress all the subjects of this kingdom. The deaths by snake-bite and tigers shall increase a hundredfold from this day, and day by day it shall continue to increase till your release. Whenever you hear people near you, you had better bawl out so as to be heard by them: 'The wretched prince imprisoned me on the false charge of having killed his father, while it was a tiger that killed him.

From that day these calamities have broken out in his dominions. If I were released I would save all by my powers of healing poisonous wounds and by incantations.' Some one may report this to the king, and if he knows it, you will obtain your liberty." Thus comforting his protector in trouble, he advised him to pluck up courage, and took leave of him. From that day tigers and serpents, acting under the orders of their kings, united in killing as many persons and cattle as possible. Every day people were carried away by tigers or bitten by serpents. Thus passed months and years. Gangazara sat in the dark cellar, without the sun's light falling upon him, and feasted upon the breadcrumbs and sweetmeats that the rats so kindly supplied him with. These delicacies had completely changed his body into a red, stout, huge, unwieldy mass of flesh. Thus passed full ten years, as prophesied in the horoscope.

Ten complete years rolled away in close imprisonment. On the last evening of the tenth year one of the serpents got into the bed-chamber of the princess and sucked her life. She breathed her last. She was the only daughter of the king. The king at once sent for all the snake-bite curers. He promised half his kingdom and his daughter's hand to him who would restore her to life. Now a servant of the king who had several times overheard Gangazara's cries, reported the matter to him, The king at once ordered the cell to be examined. There was the man sitting in it. How had he managed to live so long in the cell? Some whispered that he must be a divine being. Thus they discussed, while they brought Gangazara to the king.

The king no sooner saw Gangazara than he fell on the ground. He was struck by the majesty and grandeur of his person. His ten years' imprisonment in the deep cell underground had given a sort of lustre to his body. His hair had first to be cut before his face could be seen. The king begged forgiveness for his former fault, and requested him to revive his daughter.

"Bring me within an hour all the corpses of men and cattle, dying and dead, that remain unburnt or unburied within the range of your dominions; I shall revive them all," were the only words that Gangazara spoke.

Cartloads of corpses of men and cattle began to come in every minute. Even graves, it is said, were broken open, and corpses buried a day or two before were taken out and sent for their revival. As soon as all were ready, Gangazara took a vessel full of water and sprinkled it over them all, thinking only of his snake-king and tiger-king. All rose up as if from deep slumber, and went to their respective homes. The princess, too, was restored to life. The joy of the king knew no bounds. He cursed the day on which he imprisoned him, blamed himself for having believed the 'word of a goldsmith, and offered him the hand of his daughter and the whole kingdom, instead of half, as he promised. Gangazara would not accept anything, but asked the king to assemble all his subjects in a wood near the town, "I shall there call in all the tigers And serpents, and give them a general order."

When the whole town was assembled, just at the dusk of evening, Gangazara sat dumb for a moment, and thought upon the Tiger King and the Serpent King, who came with all their armies. People began to take to their heels at the sight of tigers. Gangazara assured them of safety, and stopped them.

The grey light of the evening, the pumpkin colour of Gangazara, the holy ashes scattered lavishly over his body, the tigers and, snakes humbling themselves at his feet, gave him the true majesty of the god Gangazara. For who else by a single word could thus command vast armies of tigers and serpents, said some among the people. "Care not for it; it may be by magic. That is not a great thing: That he revived cartloads of corpses shows him to be surely Gangazara," said others.

"Why should you, my children, thus trouble these poor subjects of Ujjaini? Reply to me, and henceforth desist from your ravages." Thus said the Soothsayer's son, and, the following reply came from the king of the tigers: "Why should this base king imprison your honour, believing the mere word of a goldsmith that your honour killed his father? All the hunters told him that his father was carried away by a tiger. I was the messenger of death sent to deal the blow on his neck. I did it, and gave the crown to your honour. The prince makes no inquiry, and at once imprisons your honour. How can we expect justice from such a stupid king as that? Unless he adopt a better standard of justice we will go on with our destruction."

The king heard, cursed the day on which he believed in the word of a goldsmith, beat his head, tore his hair, wept and wailed for his crime, asked a thousand pardons, and swore to rule in a just way from that day. The serpent-king and tiger-king also promised to observe their oath as long as justice prevailed, and took their leave. The goldsmith fled for his life. He was caught by the soldiers of the king, and was pardoned by the generous Gangazara, whose voice now reigned supreme. All returned to their homes.

The king again pressed Gangazara to accept the hand of his daughter. He agreed to do so, not then, but some time afterwards. He wished to go and see his elder brother first, and then to return and marry the princess. The king agreed; and Gangazara left the city that very day on his way home.

It so happened that unwittingly be took a wrong road, and had to pass near a sea-coast. His elder, brother was also on his way up to Benares by that very same route. They met and recognised each other, even at a distance. They flew into each other's arms. Both remained still for a time almost unconscious with joy. The pleasure of Gangazara was so great that he died of joy.

The elder brother was a devout worshipper of Ganesa. That was a Friday, a day very sacred to that god. The elder brother took the corpse to the nearest Ganesa temple and called upon him. The god came, and asked him what he wanted. "My poor brother is dead and gone; and this is his corpse. Kindly keep it in your charge till I finish worshipping you. If I leave it anywhere else the devils may snatch it, away when I am absent worshipping you; after finishing the rites I shall burn him." Thus said the elder brother, and, giving the corpse to the god Ganesa, he went to prepare himself for that deity's ceremonials. Ganesa made over the corpse to his Ganas, asking them to watch over it carefully. But instead of that they devoured it.

The elder brother, after finishing the puja, demanded his brother's corpse of the god. The god called his Ganas, who came to the front blinking, and fearing the anger of their master. The god was greatly enraged. The elder brother was very angry. When the corpse was not forthcoming he cuttingly remarked, "Is this, after all, the return for my deep belief in you? You are unable even to return my brother's corpse." Ganesa was much ashamed at the remark. So he, by his divine power, gave him a living Gangazara instead of the dead corpse. Thus was the second son of the Soothsayer restored to life.

The brothers had a long talk about each other's adventures. They both went to Ujjaini, where Ganganra married the princess, and succeeded to the throne of that kingdom. He reigned for a long time, conferring several benefits upon his brother. And so the horoscope was fully fulfilled.

Harisarman

There was a certain Brahman in a certain village, named Harisarman. He was poor and foolish and in evil case for want of employment, and he had very many children, that he might reap the fruit of his misdeeds in a former life.

He wandered about begging with his family, and at last he reached a certain city, and entered the service of a rich householder called Sthuladatta. His sons became keepers of Sthuladatta's cows and other property, and his wife a servant to him, and he himself lived near his house, performing the duty of an attendant. One day there was a feast on account of the marriage of the daughter of Sthuladatta, largely attended by many friends of the bridegroom, and merry-makers. Harisarman hoped that he would be able to fill himself up to the throat with ghee and flesh and other dainties, and get the same for his family, in the house of his patron. While he was anxiously expecting to be fed, no one thought of him.

Then he was distressed at getting nothing to eat, and he said to his wife at night, "It is owing to my poverty and stupidity that I am treated with such disrespect here; so I will pretend by means of an artifice to possess a knowledge of magic, so that I may become an object of respect to this Sthuladatta; so, when you get an opportunity, tell him that I possess magical knowledge." He said this to her, and after turning the matter over in his mind, while people were asleep he took away from the house of Sthuladatta a horse on which his master's son-in-law rode. He placed it in concealment at some distance, and in the morning the friends of the bridegroom could not find the horse, though they searched in every direction.

Then, while Sthuladatta was distressed at the evil omen, and searching, for the thieves who had carried off the horse, the wife of Harisarman came and said to him, "My husband is a wise man, skilled in astrology and magical sciences; he can get the horse back for you; why do you not ask him?" When Sthuladatta heard that, he called Harisarman, who said, "Yesterday I was forgotten, but today, now the horse is stolen, I am called to mind," and Sthuladatta then propitiated the Brahman with these words—" I forgot you, forgive me "—and asked him to tell him who had taken away their horse. Then Harisarman drew all kinds of pretended diagrams, and said: "The horse has been placed by thieves on the boundary line south from this place. It is concealed there, and before it is carried off to a distance, as it will be at close of day, go quickly and bring it." When they heard that, many men ran and brought the horse quickly, praising the discernment of Harisarman. Then Harisarman was honoured by all men as a sage, and dwelt there in happiness, honoured by Sthuladatta.

Now, as days went on, much treasure, both of gold and jewels, had been stolen by a thief from the palace of the king. As the thief was not known, the king quickly summoned Harisarman on account of his reputation for knowledge of magic. And he, when summoned, tried to gain time, and said, "I will tell you tomorrow," and then he was placed in a chamber by the king, and carefully guarded. And he was sad because he had pretended to have knowledge. Now in that palace there was a maid named Jihva (which means Tongue), who, with the assistance of her brother, had stolen that treasure from the interior of the palace. She, being alarmed at Harisarman's knowledge, went at night and applied her ear to the door of that chamber in order to find out what he was about. And Harisarman, who was alone inside, was at that very moment blaming his own tongue, that had made a vain assumption of knowledge. He said: "O Tongue, what is this that you have done through your greediness? Wicked one, you will soon receive punishment in full." When Jihva heard this, she thought, in her terror, that she had been discovered by this wise man, and she managed to get in where he was, and falling at his feet, she said to the supposed wizard:

> *"Brahman, here I am, that Jihva whom you have discovered to be the thief of the treasure, and after I took it I buried it in the earth in a garden behind the palace, under a pomegranate tree. So spare me, and receive the small quantity of gold which is in my possession."*

> When Harisarman heard that, he said to her proudly:

> *"Depart, I know all this; I know the past, present and future; but I will not denounce you, being a miserable creature that has implored my protection. But whatever gold is in your possession you must give back to me." When he said this to the maid, she consented, and departed quickly. But Harisarman reflected in his*

astonishment: "Fate brings about, as if in sport, things impossible, for when calamity was so near, who would have thought chance would have brought us success? While I was blaming my jihva, the thief Jihva suddenly flung herself at my feet. Secret crimes manifest themselves by means of fear." Thus thinking, he passed the night happily in the chamber. And in the morning he brought the king, by some skilful parade of pretended knowledge into the garden, and led him up to the treasure, which was buried under the pomegranate free, and said that the thief had escaped with a part of it. Then the king was pleased, and gave him the revenue of many villages.

But the minister, named Devajnanin, whispered in the king's ear: "How can a man possess such knowledge unattainable by men, without having studied the books of magic; you may be certain that this is a specimen of the way he makes a dishonest livelihood, by having a secret intelligence with thieves. It will be much better to test him by some new artifice."

Then the king of his own accord brought a covered pitcher into which he had thrown a frog, and said to Harisarman, "Brahman, if you can guess what there is in this pitcher, I will do you great honour today." When the Brahman Harisarman heard that, he thought that his last hour had come, and he called to mind the pet name of "Froggie" which his father had given him in his childhood in sport, and, impelled by luck, he called to himself by his pet name, lamenting his hard fate, and suddenly called out: "This is a fine pitcher for you, Froggie; it will soon become the swift destroyer of your helpless self."

The people there, when they heard him say that, raised a shout of applause, because his speech chimed in so well with the object presented to him, and murmured, "Ah! a great sage, be knows even about the frog!" Then the king, thinking that this was all due to knowledge of divination, was highly delighted, and gave Harisarman the revenue of more villages, with gold, an umbrella, and state carriages of all kinds. So Harisarman prospered in the world.

The Charmed Ring

Merchant started his son in life with three hundred rupees, and bade him go to another country and try his luck in trade. The son took the money and departed. He had not gone far before he came across some herdsmen quarrelling over a dog, that some of them wished to kill. "Please do not kill the dog," pleaded the young and tender-hearted fellow; "I will give you one hundred rupees for it." Then and there, of course, the bargain was concluded, and the foolish fellow took the dog, and continued his journey. He next met with some people fighting about a cat. Some of them wanted to kill it, but others not. "Oh! please do not kill it," said he; "I will give you one hundred rupees for it." Of course they at once gave him the cat and took the money. He went on till he reached a village, where some folk were quarrelling over a snake that had just been caught. Some of them wished to kill it, but others did not. "Please do not kill the snake," said he; "I will give you one hundred rupees." Of course the people agreed, and were highly delighted.

What a fool the fellow was! What would he do now that all his money was gone? What could he do except return to his father? Accordingly he went home.

"You fool! You scamp!" exclaimed his father when he had heard how his son had wasted all the money that had been given to him. "Go and live in the stables and repent of your folly. You shall never again enter my house."

So the young man went and lived in the stables His bed was the grass spread for the cattle, and his companions were the dog, the cat, and the snake, which he had purchased so dearly. These creatures got very fond of him, and would follow him about during the day, and sleep by him at night; the cat used to sleep at his feet, the dog at his head, and the snake over his body, with its head hanging on one side and its tail on the other.

One day the snake in course of conversation said to its master, "I am the son of Raja Indrasha. One day, when I had come out of the ground to drink the air, some people seized me, and would have slain me had you not most opportunely arrived to my rescue. I do not know how I shall ever be able to repay you for your great kindness to me. Would that you knew my father! How glad he would be to see his son's preserver!"

"Where does he live? I should like to see him, if possible," said the young man.

"Well said!" continued the snake. "Do you see yonder mountain? At the bottom of that mountain there is a sacred spring. If you will come with me and dive into that spring, we shall both reach my father's country. Oh! how glad he will be to see you! He will wish to reward you, too. But how can be do that? However, you may be pleased to accept something at his hand. If he asks you what you would like, you would, perhaps, do well to reply, 'The ring on your right hand, and the famous pot and spoon which you possess.' With these in your possession, you would never need anything, for the ring is such that a man has only to speak to it, and immediately a beautiful furnished mansion will be provided for him, while the pot and the spoon will supply him with all manner of the rarest and most delicious foods."

Attended by his three companions the man walked to the well and prepared to jump in, according to the snake's directions. "O master!" exclaimed the cat and dog, when they saw what he was going to do. "What shall we do? Where shall we go?"

"Wait for me here," he replied. "I am not going far. I shall not be long away." On saying this, he dived into the water and was lost to sight.

"Now what shall we do?" said the dog to the cat.

"We must remain here," replied the cat, "as our master ordered. Do not be anxious about food. I will go to the people's houses and get plenty of food for both of us." And so the cat did, and they both lived very comfortably till their master came again and joined them.

The young man and the snake reached their destination in safety; and information of their arrival was sent to the Raja. His highness commanded his son and the stranger to appear before him. But the snake refused, saying that it could not go to its father till it was released from this stranger, who had saved it from a most terrible death, and whose slave it therefore was. Then the Raja went and embraced his son, and saluting the stranger welcomed him to his dominions. The young man stayed there a few days, during which he received the Raja's right-hand ring, and the pot and spoon, in recognition of His Highness's gratitude to him for having delivered his son. He then returned. On reaching the top of the spring he found his friends, the dog and the cat, waiting for him. They told one another all they had experienced since they had last seen each other, and were all very glad. Afterwards they walked together to the river side, where it was decided to try the powers of the charmed ring and pot and spoon.

The merchant's son spoke to the ring, and immediately a beautiful house and a lovely princess with golden hair appeared. He spoke to the pot and spoon, also, and the most delicious dishes of food were provided for them. So he married the princess, and they lived very happily for several years, until one morning the princess, while arranging her toilet, put the loose hairs into a hollow bit of reed and threw them into the river that flowed along under the window. The reed floated on the water for many miles, and was at last picked up by the prince of that country, who curiously opened it and saw the golden hair.

On finding it the prince rushed off to the palace, locked himself up in his room, and would not leave it. He had fallen desperately in love with the woman whose hair be had picked up, and refused to eat, or drink, or sleep, or move, till she was brought to him. The king, his father, was in great distress about the matter, and did not know what to do. He feared lest his son should die and leave him without an heir: At last he determined to seek the counsel of his aunt, who was an ogress. The old woman consented to help him, and bade him not to be anxious, as she felt certain that she would succeed in getting the beautiful woman for his son's wife.

She assumed the shape of a bee and went along buzzing, and buzzing, and buzzing. Her keen sense of smell soon brought her to the beautiful princess, to whom she appeared as an old hag, holding in one hand a stick by way of support. She introduced herself to the beautiful princess and said, "I am your aunt, whom you have never seen before, because I left the country just after your birth." She also embraced and kissed the princess by way of adding force to her words.

The beautiful princess was thoroughly deceived. She returned the ogress's embrace, and invited her to come and stay in the house as long as she could, and treated her with such honour and attention, that the ogress thought to herself, "I shall soon accomplish my errand." When she had been in the house three days, she began to talk of the charmed ring, and advised her to keep it instead of her husband, because the latter was constantly out shooting and on other such-like expeditions, and might lose it. Accordingly the beautiful princess asked her husband for the ring, and he readily gave it to her.

The ogress waited another day before she asked to see the precious thing. Doubting nothing, the beautiful princess complied, when the ogress seized the ring, and reassuming the form of a bee flew away with it to the palace, where the prince was lying nearly on the point of death. "Rise up. Be glad. Mourn no more," she said to him.

"The woman for whom you yearn will appear at your summons. See, here is the charm, whereby you may bring her before you." The prince was almost mad with joy when he heard these words, and was so desirous of seeing the beautiful princess, that he immediately spoke to the ring, and the house with its fair occupant descended in the midst of the palace garden. He at once entered the building, and telling the beautiful princess of his intense love, entreated her to be his wife. Seeing no escape from the difficulty, she consented on the condition that he would wait one month for her.

Meanwhile the merchant's son had returned from hunting and was terribly distressed not to find his house and wife. There was the place only, just as he knew it before he had tried the charmed ring, which Raja Indrasha had given him. He sat down and determined to put an end to himself. Presently the cat and dog came up. They had gone away and hidden themselves, when they saw the house and everything disappear.

"O master!?' they said, "stay your hand. Your trial is great, but it can be remedied. Give us one month, and we will go and try to recover your wife and house."

"Go," said he, "and may the great God aid your efforts. Bring back my wife, and I shall live."

So the cat and dog started off at a run, and did not stop till they reached the place whither their mistress and the house had been taken. "We may have some difficulty here," said the cat. "Look, the king has taken our master's wife and house for himself. You stay here. I will go to the house and try to see her." So the dog sat down, and the cat climbed up to the window of the room, wherein the beautiful princess was sitting, and entered. The princess recognised the cat, and informed it of all that had happened to her since she had left them.

"But is there no way of escape from the hands of these people?" she asked.

"Yes," replied the cat, "if you can tell me where the charmed ring is."

"The ring is in the stomach of the ogress," she said.

"All right," said the cat, "I will recover it. If we once get it, everything is ours." Then the cat descended the wall of the house, and went and laid down by a rat's hole and pretended she was dead. Now at that time a great wedding chanced to be going on among the rat community of that place, and all the rats of the neighbourhood were assembled in that one particular mine by which the cat had lain down. The eldest son of the king of the rats was about to be married. The cat got to know of this, and at once conceived the idea of seizing the bridegroom and making him render the necessary help. Consequently, when the procession poured forth from the hole squealing and jumping in honour of the occasion, it immediately spotted the bridegroom and pounced down on him. "Oh! let me go, let me go," cried the terrified rat. "Oh! let him go," squealed all the company. "It is his wedding day."

"No, no," replied the cat. "Not unless you do something for me. Listen. The ogress, who lives in that house with the prince and his wife, has swallowed a ring, which I very much want.

If you will procure it for me, I will allow the rat to depart unharmed. If you do not, then your prince dies under my feet."

"Very well, we agree," said they all. "Nay, if we do not get the ring for you, devour us all."

This was rather a bold offer. However, they accomplished the thing. At midnight, when the ogress was sound asleep, one of the rats went to her bedside, climbed up on her face, and, inserted its tail into her throat; whereupon the ogress coughed violently, and the ring came out and rolled on to the floor. The rat immediately seized the precious thing and ran off with it to its king, who was very glad, and went at once to the cat and released its son.

As soon as the cat received the ring, she started back with the dog to go and tell their master the good tidings. All seemed safe now. They had only to give the ring to him, and he would speak to it, and the house and beautiful princess would again be with them, and everything would go on as happily as before. "How glad master will be!" they thought, and ran as fast as their legs could carry them. Now, on the way they had to cross a stream. The dog swam,, and the cat sat on its back. Now the dog was jealous of the cat, so he asked for the ring, and threatened to throw the cat into the water if it did not give it up; whereupon the cat gave up the ring. Sorry moment, for the dog at once dropped it, and a fish swallowed it.

"Oh! what shall I do? what shall I do?" said the dog. "What is done is done," replied the cat. "We must try to recover it, and if we do not succeed we had better drown ourselves in this stream. I have a plan. You go and kill a small lamb, and bring it here to me."

"All right," said the dog, and at once ran off. He soon came back with a dead lamb, and gave it to the cat. The cat got inside the lamb and lay down, telling the dog to go away a little distance and keep quiet. Not long after this a nadhar, a bird whose look can break the bones of a fish, came and hovered over the lamb, and eventually pounced down on it to carry it away. On this the cat came out and jumped on to the bird, and threatened to kill it if it did not recover the lost ring. This was most readily promised by the nadhar, who immediately flew off to the king of the fishes, and ordered it to make inquiries and to restore the ring. The king of the fishes did so, and the ring was found and carried back to the cat.

"Come along now; I have got the ring," said the cat to the dog. "No, I will not," said the dog, unless you let me have the ring. I can carry it as well as you. Let me have it or I will kill you." So the cat was obliged to give up the ring. The careless dog very soon dropped it again. This time it was picked up and carried off by a kite.

"See, see, there it goes—away to that big tree," the cat exclaimed.

"Oh! oh! what have I done?" cried the dog.

"You foolish thing, I knew it would be so," said the cat. "But stop your barking, or you will frighten away the bird to some place where we shall not be able to trace it."

The cat waited till it was quite dark, and then climbed the tree, killed the kite, and recovered the ring. "Come along," it said to the dog when it reached the ground. "We must make haste now. We have been delayed. Our master will die from grief and suspense. Come on."

The dog, now thoroughly ashamed of itself, begged the cat's pardon for all the trouble it had given. It was afraid to ask for the ring the third time, so they both reached their sorrowing master in safety and gave him the precious charm. In a moment his sorrow was turned into joy. He spoke to the ring, and his beautiful wife and house reappeared, and he and everybody were as happy as ever they could be.

The Talkative Tortoise

The future Buddha was once born in a minister's family, when Brahma-datta was reigning in Benares; and when he grew up, he became the king's adviser in things temporal and spiritual.

Now this king was very talkative; while he was speaking, others had no opportunity for a word. And the future Buddha, wanting to cure this talkativeness of his, was constantly seeking for some means of doing so.

At that time there was living, in a pond in the Himalaya mountains, a tortoise. Two young hamsas, or wild ducks, who came to feed there, made friends with him. And one day, when they had become very intimate with him, they said to the tortoise:

"Friend tortoise! the place where we live, at the Golden Cave on Mount Beautiful in the Himalaya country, is a delightful spot. Will you come there with us?"

"But how can I get there?"

"We can take you, if you can only hold your tongue, and will say nothing to anybody."

"Oh! that I can do. Take me with you."

"That's right," said they. And making the tortoise bite hold of a stick, they themselves took the two ends in their teeth, and flew up into the air.

Seeing him thus carried by the hamsas, some villagers called out, "Two wild ducks are carrying a tortoise along on a stick!" Whereupon the tortoise wanted to say, "If my friends choose to carry me, what is that to you, you wretched slaves!" So just as the swift flight of the wild ducks had brought him over the king's palace in the city of Benares, he let go of the stick he was biting, and falling in the open courtyard, split in two! And there arose a universal cry, "A tortoise has fallen in the open courtyard, and has split in two!"

The king, taking the future Buddha, went to the place, surrounded by his courtiers; and looking at the tortoise, he asked the Bodisat, "Teacher! how comes he to be fallen here?"

The future Buddha thought to himself, "Long expecting, wishing to admonish the king, have I sought for some means of doing so. This tortoise must have made friends with the wild ducks; and they must have made him bite hold of the stick, and have flown up into the air to take him to the hills. But he, being unable to hold his tongue. when he hears any one else talk, must have wanted to say something; and let go the stick; and so must have fallen down from the sky, and thus lost his life."

And saying, "Truly, O king! those who are called chatter-boxes—people whose words have no end—come to grief like this," he uttered these Verses:

"Verily the tortoise killed himself
Whilst uttering his voice;
Though he was holding tight the stick,
By a word himself he slew.
"Behold him then,
O excellent by strength!
And speak wise words, not out of season.
You see how, by his talking overmuch,
The tortoise fell into this wretched plight!"

The king saw that he was himself referred to, and said "O Teacher! are you speaking of us?"

And the Bodisat spake openly, and said, "O great king! be it thou, or be it any other, whoever talks beyond measure meets with some mishap like this."

And the king henceforth refrained himself, and became a man of few words.

A Lac of Rupees for a Bit of Advice

Poor blind Brahman and his wife were dependent on their son for their subsistence. Every day the young fellow used to go out and get what he could by begging. This continued for some time, till at last he became quite tired of such a wretched life, and determined to go and try his luck in another country. He informed his wife of his intention, and ordered her to manage somehow or other for the old people during the few months that he would be absent. He begged her to be industrious, lest his parents should be angry and curse him.

One morning he started with some food in a bundle, and walked on day after day, till he reached the chief city of the neighbouring country. Here he went and sat down by a merchant's shop and asked alms. The merchant inquired whence he had come, why he had come, and what was his caste; to which he replied that he was a Brahman, and was wandering hither and thither begging a livelihood for himself and wife and parents. Moved with pity for the man, the merchant advised him to visit the kind and generous king of that country, and offered to accompany him to the court. Now, at that time it happened that the king was seeking for a Brahman to look after a golden temple which he had just had built. His Majesty was very glad, therefore, when he saw the Brahman and heard that he was good and honest. He at once deputed him to the charge of this temple, and ordered fifty kharwars of rice and one hundred rupees to be paid to him every year as wages.

Two months after this, the Brahman's wife, not having heard any news of her husband, left the house and went in quest of him. By a happy fate she arrived at the very place that he had reached, where she heard that every morning at the golden temple a golden rupee was given in the king's name to any beggar who chose to go for it. Accordingly, on the following morning she went to the place and met her husband.

"Why have you come here?" he asked. "Why have you left my parents? Care you not whether they curse me and I die? Go back immediately, and await my return."

"No, no," said the woman. "I cannot go back to starve and see your old father and mother die. There is not a grain of rice left in the house."

"O Bhagawant!" exclaimed the Brahman. "Here, take this," he continued, scribbling a few lines on some paper, and then handing it to her, "and give it to the king. You will see that he will give you a lac of rupees for it." Thus saying he dismissed her, and the woman left.

On this scrap of paper were written three pieces of advice-First, If a person is travelling and reaches any strange place at night, let him be careful where he puts up, and not close his eyes in sleep, lest he close them in death. Secondly, If a man has a married sister, and visits her in great pomp, she will receive him for the sake of what she can obtain from him; but if he comes to her in poverty, she will frown on him and disown him. Thirdly, If a man has to do any work, he must do it himself, and do it with might and without fear.

On reaching her home the Brahmani told her parents of her meeting with her husband, and what a valuable piece of paper he had given her; but not liking to go before the king herself, she sent one of her relations. The king read the paper, and ordering the man to be flogged, dismissed him.

The next morning the Brahmani took the paper, and while she was going along the road to the darbar reading it, the king's son met her, and asked what she was reading, whereupon she replied that she held in her hands a paper containing certain bits of advice, for which she wanted a lac of rupees. The prince asked her to show it to him, and when he had read it gave her a parwana for the amount, and rode on. The poor Brahmani was very thankful. That day she laid in a great store of provisions, sufficient to last them all for a long time.

In the evening the prince related to his father the meeting with the woman, and the purchase of the piece of paper. He thought his father would applaud the act. But it was not so. The king was more angry than before, and banished his son from the country. So the prince bade adieu to his mother and relations and friends, and rode off on his horse, whither he did not know. At nightfall he arrived at some place, where a man met him, and invited him to lodge at his house. The prince accepted the invitation, and was treated like a prince. Matting was spread for him to squat on, 'and the best provisions set before him.

"Ah!" thought he, as he lay down to rest, "here is a case for the first piece of advice that the Brahmani gave me. I will not sleep tonight."

It was well that he thus resolved, for in the middle of the night the man rose up, and taking a sword in his hand, rushed to the prince with the intention of killing him. But he rose up and spoke.

"Do not slay me," he said. "What profit would you get from my death? If you killed me you would be sorry afterwards, like that man who killed his dog."

"What man? What dog?" he asked.

"I will tell you," said the prince, "if you will give me that sword."

So he gave him the sword, and the prince began his story:

"Once upon a time there lived a wealthy merchant who had a pet dog. He was suddenly reduced to poverty, and had to part with his dog. He got a loan of five thousand rupees from a brother merchant, leaving the dog as a pledge, and with the money began business again. Not long after this the other merchant's shop was broken into by thieves and completely sacked. There 'was hardly ten rupees' worth left in the place. The faithful dog, however, knew what was going on, and went and followed the thieves, and saw where they deposited the things, and then returned.

In the morning there was great weeping and lamentation in the merchant's house when it was known what had happened. The merchant himself nearly went mad. Meanwhile the dog kept on running to the door, and pulling at his master's shirt and paijamas, as though wishing him to go outside. At last a friend suggested that, perhaps, the dog knew something of the whereabouts of the things, and advised the merchant to follow its leadings.

The merchant consented, and went after the dog right up to the very place where the thieves had hidden the goods. Here the animal scraped and barked, and showed in various ways that the things were underneath. So the merchant and his friends dug about the place, and soon came upon all the stolen property. Nothing was missing. There was everything just as the thieves had taken them.

"The merchant was very glad. On returning to his house, he at once sent the dog back to its old master with a letter rolled under the collar, wherein he had written about the sagacity of the beast, and begged his friend to forget the loan and to accept another five thousand rupees as a present. When this merchant saw his dog coming back again, he thought, 'Alas! my friend is wanting the money. How can I pay him? I have not had sufficient time to recover myself from my recent losses. I will slay the dog ere be reaches the threshold, and say that another must have slain it. Thus there will be an end of my debt. No dog, no loan.' Accordingly he ran out and killed the poor dog, when the letter fell out of its collar. The merchant picked it up and read it. How great was his grief and disappointment when he knew the facts of the case! "Beware," continued the prince, 'lest you do that which afterwards you would give your life not to have done."

By the time the prince had concluded this story it was nearly morning, and he went away, after rewarding the man.

The prince then visited the country belonging to his brother-in-law. He disguised himself as a jogi, and sitting down by a tree near the palace, pretended to be absorbed in worship. News of the man and of his wonderful piety reached the ears of the king. He felt interested in him, as his wife was very ill; and he had sought for hakims to cure her, but in vain. He thought that, perhaps, this holy man could do something for her. So he sent to him. But the jogi refused to tread the halls of a king, saying that his dwelling was the open air, and that if his Majesty wished to see him he must come himself and bring his wife to the place. Then the king took his wife and brought her to the jogi. The holy man bade her prostrate herself before him, and when she had remained in this position for about three hours, he told her to rise and go, for she was cured.

In the evening there was great consternation in the palace, because the queen had lost her pearl rosary, and nobody knew anything about it. At length some one went to the jogi, and found it on the ground by the place where the queen had prostrated herself. When the king heard this he was very angry, and ordered the jogi to be executed. This stern order, however, was not carried out, as the prince bribed the men and escaped from the country. But he knew that the second bit of advice was true.

Clad in his own clothes, the prince was walking along one day when he saw a potter crying and laughing alternately with his wife and children. "O fool," said he, "what is the matter? If you laugh, why do you weep? If you weep, why do you laugh?"

"Do not bother me," said the potter. "What does it matter to you?"

"Pardon me," said the prince, "but I should like to know the reason."

"The reason is this, then," said the potter. "The king of this country has a daughter whom he is obliged to marry every day, because all her husbands die the first night of their stay with her. Nearly all the young men of the place have thus perished, and our son will be called on soon. We laugh at the absurdity of the thing—a potter's son marrying a princess, and we cry at the terrible consequence of the marriage. What can we do?"

"Truly a matter for laughing and weeping. But weep no more," said the prince. "I will exchange places with your son, and will be married to the princess instead of him. Only give me suitable garments, and prepare me for the occasion."

So the potter gave him beautiful raiment and ornaments, and the prince went to the palace. At night he was conducted to the apartment of the princess. "Dread hour!" thought he; "am I to die like the scores of young men before me?" He clenched his sword with firm grip, and lay down on his bed, intending to keep awake all the night and see what would happen. In the middle of the night he saw two Shahmars come out from the nostrils of the princess. They stole over towards him, intending to kill him, like the others who had been before him: but he was ready for them. He laid hold of his sword, and when the snakes reached his bed he struck at them and killed them. In the morning the king came as usual to inquire, and was surprised to hear his daughter and the prince talking. gaily together. "Surely," said he, "this man must be her husband, as he only can live with her."

"Where do you come from? Who are you?" asked the king, entering the room.

"O king! "replied the prince, "I am the son of a king who rules over such-and-such a country."

When he heard this the king was very glad, and bade the prince to abide in his palace, and appointed him his successor to the throne. The prince remained at the palace for more than a year, and then asked permission to visit his own country, which was granted. The king gave him elephants, horses, jewels, and abundance of money for the expenses of the way and as presents for his father, and the prince started.

On the way he had to pass through the country belonging to his brother-in-law, whom we have already mentioned. Report of his arrival reached the ears of the king, who came with rope-tied hands and haltered neck to do him homage. He most humbly begged him to stay at his palace, and to accept what little hospitality could be provided. While the prince was staying at the palace be saw his sister, who greeted him with smiles and kisses. On leaving he told her how she and her husband had treated him at his first visit, and how he escaped; and then gave them two elephants; two beautiful horses, fifteen soldiers, and ten lacs rupees' worth of jewels.

Afterwards he went to his own home, and informed his mother and father of his arrival. Alas! his parents bad both become blind from weeping about the loss of their son. "Let him come in," said the king, "and put his hands upon our eyes, and we shall see again." So the prince entered, and was most affectionately greeted by his old parents; and he laid his hands on their eyes, and they saw again.

Then the prince told his father all that had happened to him, and how he had been saved several times by attending to the advice that he had purchased from the Brahmani. Whereupon the king expressed his sorrow for having sent him away, and all was joy and peace again.

A Gold giving Serpent

Now in a certain place there lived a Brahman named Haridatta. He was a farmer, but poor was the return his labour brought him. One day, at the end of the hot hours, the Brahman, overcome by the heat, lay down under the shadow of a tree to have a doze. Suddenly he saw a great hooded snake creeping out of an ant-hill near at hand. So he thought to himself, "Sure this is the guardian deity of the field, and I have not ever worshipped it. That's why my farming is in vain. I will at once go and pay my respects to it."

When he had made up his mind, he got some milk, poured it into a bowl, and went to the ant-hill, and said aloud:

"O Guardian of this Field! all this while I did not know that you dwelt here. That is why I have not yet paid my respects to you; pray forgive me." And he laid the milk down and went to his house. Next morning he came and looked, and he saw a gold denar in the bowl, and from that time onward every day the same thing occurred: he gave milk to the serpent and found a gold denar.

One day the Brahman had to go to the village, and so be ordered his son to take the milk to the ant-hill. The son brought the milk, put it down, and went back home. Next day he went again and found a denar, so he thought to himself: "This, ant-hill is surely full of golden denars; I'll kill the serpent, and take them all for myself." So next day, while he was giving the milk to the serpent, the Brahman's son struck it on the head with a cudgel. But the serpent escaped death by the will of fate, and in a rage bit the Brahman's son with its sharp fangs, and he fell down dead at once. His people raised him a funeral pyre not far from the field and burnt him to ashes.

Two days afterwards his father came back, and when he learnt his son's fate he grieved and mourned. But after a time, be took the bowl of milk, went to the ant-hill, and praised the serpent with a loud voice. After a long, long time the serpent appeared, but only with its head out of the opening of the ant-hill, and spoke to the Brahman: "'Tis greed that brings you here, and makes you even forget the loss of your son. From this time forward friendship between us is impossible. Your son struck me in youthful ignorance, and I have bitten him to death. How can I forget the blow with the cudgel? And how can you forget the pain and grief at the loss of your son?" So speaking, it gave the Brahman a costly pearl and disappeared. But before it went away it said: "Come back no more." The Brahman took the pearl, and went back home, cursing the folly of his son.

The Son of Seven Queens

Once upon a time there lived a king who had seven Queens, but no children. This was a great grief to him, especially when he remembered that on his death there would be no heir to inherit the kingdom.

Now it happened one day that a poor old fakir came to the King, and said, "Your prayers are heard, your desire shall be accomplished, and one of your seven Queens shall bear a son."

The King's delight at this promise knew no bounds, and he gave orders for appropriate festivities to be prepared against the coming event throughout the length and breadth of the land.

Meanwhile the seven Queens lived luxuriously in a splendid palace, attended by hundreds of female slaves, and fed to their hearts', content on sweetmeats and confectionery.

Now the King was very fond of hunting, and one day, before he started, the seven Queens sent him a message saying, "May it please our dearest lord not to hunt towards the north today, for we have dreamt bad dreams, and fear lest evil should befall you."

The King, to allay their anxiety, promised regard for their wishes, and set out towards the south; but as luck would have it, although he hunted diligently, he found no game. Nor had he more success to the east or west, so that, being a keen sportsman, and determined not to go home empty-handed, he forgot all about his promise, and turned to the north. Here also he was at first unsuccessful, but just as he had made up his mind to give up for that day, a white hind with golden horns and silver hoofs flashed past him into a thicket. So quickly did it pass that he scarcely saw it; nevertheless a burning desire to capture. and possess the beautiful strange creature filled his breast. He instantly ordered his attendants to form a ring round the thicket, and so encircle the hind; then, gradually narrowing the circle, he pressed forward till he could distinctly see the white hind panting in the midst.

Nearer and nearer he advanced, till, just as he thought to lay hold of the beautiful strange creature, it gave one mighty bound, leapt clean over the King's head, and fled towards the mountains. Forgetful of all else, the King, setting spurs to his horse, followed at full speed. On, on he galloped, leaving his retinue far behind, keeping the white hind in view, never drawing bridle, until, finding himself in a narrow ravine with no outlet, he reined in his steed. Before him stood a miserable hovel; into which, being tired after his long, unsuccessful chase, he entered to ask for a drink of water.

An old woman, seated in the hut at a spinning-wheel, answered his request by calling to her daughter, and immediately from an inner room came a maiden so lovely and charming, so white-skinned and golden-haired, that the King was transfixed by astonishment at seeing so beautiful a sight in the wretched hovel.

She held the vessel of water to the King's lips, and as he drank he looked into her eyes, and then it became clear to him that the girl was no other than the white hind with the golden horns and silver feet he had chased so far.

Her beauty bewitched him, so he fell on his knees, begging her to return with him as his bride; but she only laughed, saying seven Queens were quite enough even for a King to manage. However, when he would take no refusal, but implored her to have pity on him, promising her everything she could desire, she replied "Give me the eyes of your seven Queens, and then perhaps I may believe you mean what you say."

The King was so carried away by the glamour of the white hind's magical beauty, that he went home at once, had the eyes of his seven Queens taken out, and, after throwing the poor blind creatures into a noisome dungeon whence they could not escape, set off once more for the hovel in the ravine; bearing with him his horrible offering. But the white hind only. laughed cruelly when she saw the fourteen eyes, and threading them as a necklace, flung it round her mother's neck, saying, "Wear that, little mother, as a keepsake, whilst I am away in the King's palace."

Then she went back with, the bewitched monarch, as his bride, and he gave her the seven Queens' rich clothes and jewels to wear, the seven Queens' palace to live in, and the seven Queens' slaves to wait upon her; so that she really had everything even a witch could desire.

Now, very soon after the seven wretched hapless Queens had their eyes torn out, and were cast into prison, a baby was born to the youngest of the Queens. It was a handsome boy, but the other Queens were very jealous that the youngest amongst them should be so fortunate. But though at first they disliked the handsome little boy, he soon proved so useful to them, that ere long they all looked on him as their son. Almost as soon as he could walk about he began scraping at the mud wall of their dungeon, and in an incredibly short space of time had made a hole big enough for him to crawl through. Through this he disappeared, returning in an hour or so laden with sweetmeats, which he divided equally amongst the seven blind Queens.

As he grew older he enlarged the hole, and slipped out two or three times every day to play with the little nobles in, the town. No one knew who the tiny boy was, but everybody liked him, and he was so full of funny tricks and antics, so merry and bright, that he was sure to be rewarded by some girdle-cakes, a handful of parched grain, or some sweetmeats. All these things he brought home to his seven mothers, as he loved to call the seven blind Queens, who by his help lived on in their dungeon when all the world thought they had starved to death ages before.

At last, when he was quite a big lad, he one day took his bow and arrow, and went out to seek for game. Coming by chance past the palace where the white hind lived in wicked splendour and magnificence, he saw some pigeons fluttering round the white marble turrets, and, taking good aim, shot one dead. It came tumbling past the very window where the white Queen was sitting; she rose to see what was the matter, and looked out. At the first glance of the handsome young lad standing there bow in hand, she knew by witchcraft that it was the King's son.

She nearly died of envy and spite, determining to destroy the lad without delay; therefore, sending a servant to bring him to her presence, she asked him if he would sell her the pigeon he had just shot.

"No," replied the sturdy lad, "the pigeon is for my seven blind mothers, who live in the noisome dungeon, and who would die if I did not bring them food."

"Poor souls!" cried the cunning white witch; "would you not like to bring them their eyes again? Give me the pigeon, my dear, and I faithfully promise to show you where to find them."

Hearing this, the lad was delighted beyond measure, and gave up the pigeon at once. Whereupon the white Queen told him to seek her mother without delay, and ask for the eyes which she wore as a necklace.

"She will not fail to give them," said the cruel Queen, "if you show her this token on which I have written what I want done."

So saying, she gave the lad a piece of broken potsherd, with these words inscribed on it—" Kill the bearer at once, and sprinkle his blood like water!"

Now, as the son of seven Queens could not read, he took the fatal message cheerfully, and set off to find the white Queen's mother.

Whilst he was journeying he passed through a town, where every one of the inhabitants looked so sad, that he could not help asking what was the matter. They told him it was because the King's only daughter refused to marry; so,when her father died there would be no heir to the throne. They greatly feared she must be out of her mind, for though every good-looking young man in the kingdom had been shown to her, she declared she would only marry one who was the son of seven mothers, and who ever heard of such a thing? The King, in despair, had ordered every man who entered the city gates to be led before the Princess; so, much to the lad's impatience, for he was in an immense hurry to find his mothers' eyes, he was dragged into the presence-chamber.

No sooner did the Princess catch sight of him than she blushed, and, turning to the King, said, "Dear father, this is my choice!"

Never were such rejoicings as these few words produced.

The inhabitants nearly went wild with joy, but the son of seven Queens said he would not marry the Princess unless they first let him recover his mothers' eyes. When the beautiful bride heard his story, she asked to see the potsherd, for she was very learned and clever. Seeing the treacherous words, she said nothing, but taking another similar-shaped bit of potsherd, she wrote on it these words—" Take care of this lad, giving him all he desires," and returned it to the son of seven Queens, who, none the wiser, set off on his quest.

Ere long he arrived at the hovel in the ravine where the white witch's mother, a hideous old creature, grumbled dreadfully on reading the message, especially when the lad asked for the necklace of eyes. Nevertheless she took it off, and gave it him, saying, "there are only thirteen of 'em now, for I lost one last week."

The lad, however, was only too glad to get any at all, so he hurried home as fast as he could to his seven mothers, and gave two eyes apiece to the six elder Queens; but to the youngest he gave one, saying, "Dearest little mother!—I will be your other eye always!"

After this be set off to marry the Princess, as he had promised, but when passing by the white Queen's palace he saw some pigeons on the roof. Drawing his bow, he shot one, and it came fluttering past the window. The white hind looked out, and lo! there was the King's son alive and well.

She cried with hatred and disgust, but sending for the lad, asked him how he had returned so soon, and when she heard how he had brought home the thirteen eyes, and given them to the seven blind Queens, she could hardly restrain her rage. Nevertheless she pretended to be charmed with his success, and told him that if he would give her this pigeon also, she would reward him with the Jogi's wonderful cow, whose milk flows all day long, and makes a pond as big as a kingdom. The lad, nothing loth, gave her the pigeon; whereupon, as before, she bade him go ask her mother for the cow, and gave him a potsherd whereon was written—"Kill this lad without fail, and sprinkle his blood like water!"

But on the way the son of seven Queens looked in on the Princess, just to tell her how he came to be delayed, and she, after reading the message on the potsherd, gave him another in its stead; so that when the lad reached the old hag's hut and asked her for the Jogi's cow, she could not refuse, but told the boy how to find it; and bidding him of all things not to be afraid of the eighteen thousand demons who kept watch and ward over the treasure, told him to be off before she became too angry at her daughter's foolishness in thus giving away so many good things.

Then the lad did as he had been told bravely. He journeyed on and on till he came to a milk-white pond, guarded by the eighteen thousand demons. They were really frightful to behold, but, plucking up courage, he whistled a tune as he walked through them, looking neither to the right nor the left. By-and-by he came upon the Jogi's cow, tall, white, and beautiful, while the Jogi himself, who was king of all the demons, sat milking her day and night, and the milk streamed, from her udder, filling the milk-white tank.

The Jogi, seeing the lad, called out fiercely, "What do you want here?"

Then the lad answered, according to the old hag's bidding,

"I want your skin, for King Indra is making a new kettledrum, and says your skin is nice and tough."

Upon this the Jogi began to shiver and shake (for no Jinn or Jogi dares disobey King Indra's command), and, falling at the lad's feet, cried, "If you will spare me I will give you anything I possess, even my beautiful white cow!"

To this the son of seven Queens, after a little pretended hesitation, agreed, saying that after all it would not be difficult to find a nice tough skin like the Jogi's elsewhere; so, driving the wonderful cow before him, he set off homewards. The seven Queens were delighted to possess so marvellous an animal, and though they toiled from morning till night making curds and whey, besides selling milk to the confectioners, they could not use half the cow gave, and became richer and richer day by day.

Seeing them so comfortably off, the son of seven Queens started with a light heart to marry the Princess; but when passing the white hind's palace he could not resist sending a bolt at some pigeons which were cooing on the parapet. One fell dead just beneath the window where the white Queen was sitting. Looking out, she saw the lad hale and hearty standing before her, and grew whiter than ever with rage and spite.

She sent for him to ask how he had returned so soon, and when she heard how kindly her mother had received him, the very nearly had a fit; however, she dissembled her feelings as well as she could, and, smiling sweetly, said she was glad to have been able to fulfil her promise, and that if he would give her this third pigeon, she would do yet more for him than she, had done before, by giving him the million-fold rice, which ripens in one night.

The lad was of course delighted at the very idea, and, giving up the pigeon, set off on his quest, armed as before with a potsherd, on which was written, "Do not fail this time. Kill the lad, and sprinkle his blood like water!"

But when he looked in on his Princess, just to prevent her becoming anxious about him, she asked to see the potsherd as usual, and substituted another, on which was written, "Yet again give this lad all he requires, for his blood shall be as your blood!"

Now when the old hag saw this, and heard how the lad wanted the million-fold rice which ripens in a single night, she fell into the most furious rage, but being terribly afraid of her daughter, she controlled herself, and bade the boy go and find the field guarded by eighteen millions of demons, warning him on no account to look back after having plucked the tallest spike of rice, which grew in the centre.

So the son of seven Queens set off, and soon came to the field where, guarded by eighteen millions of demons, the million-fold rice grew. He walked on bravely, looking neither to the right or left, till he reached the centre and plucked the tallest ear, but as he turned homewards a thousand sweet voices rose behind him, crying in tenderest accents, "Pluck me too! oh, please pluck me too!" He looked back, and lo! there was nothing left of him but a little heap of ashes!

Now as time passed by and the lad did not return, the old hag grew uneasy, remembering the message "his blood shall be as your blood;" so she set off to see what had happened.

Soon she came to the heap of ashes, and knowing by her arts what it was, she took a little water, and kneading the ashes into a paste, formed it into the likeness of a man; then, putting a drop of blood from her little finger into its mouth, she blew on it, and instantly the son of seven Queens started up as well as ever.

"Don't you disobey orders again!" grumbled the old hag, "or next time I'll leave you alone. Now be off, before I repent of my kindness!"

So the son of seven Queens returned joyfully to his seven mothers, who, by the aid of the million-fold rice, soon became the richest people in the kingdom. Then they celebrated their son's marriage to the clever Princess with all imaginable pomp; but the bride was so clever, she would not rest until she had made known her husband to his father, and punished the wicked white witch. So she made her husband build a palace exactly like the one in which the seven Queens had lived, and in which the white witch now dwelt in splendour. Then, when all was prepared, she bade her husband give a grand feast to the King. Now the King had heard much of the mysterious son of seven Queens, and his marvellous wealth, so he gladly accepted the invitation; but what was his astonishment when on entering the palace he found it was a facsimile of his own in every particular!

And when his host, richly attired, led him straight to the private hall, where on royal thrones sat the seven Queens, dressed as he had last seen them, he was speechless with surprise, until the Princess, coming forward, threw herself at his feet, and told him the whole story. Then the King awoke from his enchantment, and his anger rose against the wicked white hind who had bewitched him so long, until he could not contain himself. So she was put to death, and her grave ploughed over, and after that the seven Queens returned to their own splendid palace, and everybody lived happily.

A Lession for Kings

Once upon a time, when Brahma-datta was reigning in Benares, the future Buddha returned to life as his son and heir. And when the day came for choosing a name, they called him Prince Brahma-datta. He grew up in due course; and when he was sixteen years old, went to Takkasila, and became accomplished in all arts. And after his father died he ascended the throne, and ruled the kingdom with righteousness and equity. He gave judgments without partiality, hatred, ignorance, or fear. Since he thus reigned with justice, with justice also his ministers administered the law. Law-suits being thus decided with justice, there were none who brought false cases. And as these ceased, the noise and tumult of litigation ceased in the king's court. Though the judges sat all day in the court, they had to leave without any one coming for justice. It came to this, that the Hall of Justice would have to be closed!

Then the future Buddha thought, "It cannot be from my reigning with righteousness that none come for judgment; the bustle has ceased, and the Hall of Justice will have to be closed. I must, therefore, now examine into my own faults; and if I find that anything is wrong in me, put that away, and practise only virtue."

Thenceforth he sought for some one to tell him his faults, but among those around him he found no one who would tell him of any fault, but heard only his own praise.

Then he thought, "It is from fear of me that these men speak only good things, and not evil things," and he sought among those people who lived outside 'the palace. And finding no fault-finder there, he sought among those who lived outside the city, in the suburbs, at the four gates. And there too finding no one to find fault, and hearing only his own praise, he determined to search the country places.

So he made over the kingdom to his ministers, and mounted his chariot; and taking only his charioteer, left the city in disguise. And searching the country through, up to the very boundary, he found no fault-finder, and heard only of his own virtue; and so he turned back from the outermost boundary, and returned by the high road towards the city.

Now at that time the king of Kosala, Mallika by name, was also ruling his kingdom with righteousness; and when seeking for some fault in himself, he also found no faultfinder in the palace, but only heard of his own virtue! So seeking in country places, he too came to that very spot. And these two came face to face in a low cart-track 'with precipitous sides, where there was no space for a chariot to get out of the way!

Then the charioteer of Mallika the king said to the charioteer of the king of Benares, "Take thy chariot out of the way!" But he said, "Take thy chariot out of the way, O charioteer! In this chariot sitteth the lord over the kingdom of Benares, the great king Brahma-datta."

Yet the other replied, "In this chariot, O charioteer, sitteth the lord over the kingdom of Kosala, the great king Mallika. Take thy carriage out of the way, and make room for the chariot of our king!"

Then the charioteer of the king of Benares thought, "They say then that he too is a king! What is now to be done?" After some consideration, be said to himself, "I know a way. I'll find out how old he is, and then I'll let 'the chariot of the younger be got out of the way, and so make room for the elder."

And when he had arrived at that conclusion, he asked that charioteer what the age of the king of Kosala was. But on inquiry he found that the ages of both were equal. Then he inquired about the extent of his kingdom, and about his army, and his wealth, and his renown, and about the country he lived in, and his caste and tribe and family. And he found that both were lords of a kingdom three hundred leagues in extent; and that in respect of army and wealth and renown, and the countries in which they lived, and their caste and their tribe and their family, they were just on a par!

Then he thought, "I will make way for the most righteous." And he asked, "What kind of righteousness has this king of yours."

Then the charioteer of the king of Kosala, proclaiming his king's wickedness as goodness, uttered the First Stanza:

"The strong he overthrows by strength,

The mild by mildness, does Mallika;

The good he conquers by goodness,

And the wicked by wickedness too.

Such is the nature of this king!

Move out of the way, O charioteer "

But the charioteer of the king of Benares asked him, "Well, have you told all the virtues of your king?"

"Yes," said the other.

"If these are his virtues, where are then his faults?" replied he.

The other said, "Well, for the nonce they shall be faults, if you like! But pray, then, what is the kind of goodness your king has?"

And then the charioteer of the king of Benares called unto him to hearken, and uttered the Second Stanza:

"Anger he conquers by calmness,

And by goodness the wicked;

The stingy he conquers by gifts,

And by truth the speaker of lies.

Such is the nature of this king!

'Move out of the way, O charioteer!"

And when he had thus spoken, both Mallika the king and his charioteer alighted from their chariot. And they took out the horses, and removed their chariot, and made way for the king of Benares!

Pride Goeth before a Fall

In a certain village there lived ten cloth merchants, who always went about together. Once upon a time they had travelled far afield, and were returning home with a great deal of money which they had obtained by selling their wares. Now there happened to be a dense forest near their village, and this they reached early one morning. In it there lived three notorious robbers, of whose existence the traders had never heard, and while they were still in the middle of it the robbers stood before them, with swords and cudgels in their hands, and ordered them to lay down all they had. The traders had no weapons with them, and so, though they were many more in number, they had to submit them-selves to the robbers, who took away everything from them, even the very clothes they wore, and gave to each only a small loin-cloth a span in breadth and a cubit in length.

The idea that they had conquered ten men and plundered all their property, now took possession of the robbers' minds. They seated themselves like three monarches before the men they had plundered, and ordered them to dance to them before returning home. The merchants now mourned their fate. They had lost all they had, except their loincloth, and still the robbers were not satisfied, but ordered them to dance.

There was, among the ten merchants, one who was very clever. He pondered over. calamity that had come upon him and his friends, the dance they would have to perform, and the magnificent manner in which the three robbers had seated themselves on the grass. At the same time he observed that these last had placed their weapons on the ground, in the assurance of having thoroughly cowed the traders, who were now commencing to dance. So he took the lead in the dance, and, as a song is always sung by the leader on such occasions, to which the rest keep time with hands and feet, he thus began to sing:

'We are enty men,

They are erith men:

If each erith man,

Surround eno men

Eno man remains.

Ta, tai, tom, tadingana."

The robbers were all uneducated, and thought that the leader was merely singing a song as usual. So it was in one sense; for the leader commenced from a distance, and had sung the song over twice before he and his companions commenced to approach the robbers. They had understood his meaning, because they had been trained in trade.

When two traders discuss the price of an article in the presence of a purchaser, they use a riddling sort of language.

"What is the price of this cloth?" one trader will ask another.

"Enty rupees," another will reply, meaning "ten rupees."

Thus, there is no possibility of the purchaser knowing what is meant unless he be acquainted with trade language. By the rules of this secret language erith means "three" enty means "ten," and eno means "one." So the leader by his song meant to hint to his fellow-traders that they were ten men, the robbers only three, that if three pounced upon each of the robbers, nine of them could hold them down, while the remaining one bound the robbers' hands and feet.

The three thieves, glorying in their victory, and little understanding the meaning of the song and the intentions of the dancers, were proudly seated chewing betel and tobacco. Meanwhile the song was sung a third time. Ta tai tom had left the lips of the singer; and, before tadingana was out of them, the traders separated into parties of three, and each party pounced upon a thief. The remaining one—the leader himself—tore up into long narrow strips a large piece of cloth, six cubits long, and tied the hands and feet of the robbers. These were entirely humbled now, and rolled on the ground like three bags of rice!

The ten traders now took back all their property, and armed themselves with the swords and cudgels of their enemies; and when they reached their village, they often amused their friends and relatives by relating their adventure.

Bibliography

Adams, Kenneth Alan : *Family and Fantasy: Dread of the Female and the Narcissistic Ethos in American Culture*, Brandeis, 1980.

Bhalla, Alok : *Politics of Atrocity and Lust: the Vampire Tale as a Nightmare History of England in the Nineteenth Century*, Sterling Publishers, New Delhi, 1990.

Brandon, Clare Therese : *Charles Nodier and Deviant Romanticism*, Fordham University, 1980.

Burton, Richard F. : *Vikram and the Vampire, or Tales of Hindu Devilry*, Tynron, Thornhill, 1989.

Carter, Angela : *Come Unto These Yellow Sands*, Bloodaxe, Newcastle upon Tyne, 1985.

Carter, Margaret L. : *Dracula: The Vampire and the Critics*, UMI Research Press, Ann Arbor, 1988.

Carter, Margaret L. : *Shadow of a Shade: A Survey of Vampirism in Literature*, Gordon Press, New York, 1975.

Carter, Margaret L. : *The Vampire in Literature: A Critical Bibliography*, UMI Research Press, MI, 1989.

Charnas, Suzy McKee : *The Vampire Tapestry*, Tor Books, New York, 1986.

Coats, Daryl R. : *The Devil is Loose in London Somewhere: Five Supernatural Figures in the Works of Charles Dickens*, University of Mississippi, 1986.

Cox, Greg : *The Transylvanian Library: A Consumer's Guide to Vampire Fiction*, Borgo Press, CA, 1993.

Dalby, Richard : *Bram Stocker: A Bibliography of First Editions*, Dracula Press, London, 1983.

Dalby, Richard : *Dracula's Brood: Rare Vampire Stories by Friends and Contemporaries of Bram Stoker*, Crucible, Wellingborough, 1987.

Desmarais, James Joseph : *An Historical and Descriptive Study of the Cinematic Vampire from 1922 through 1974.* California State University at Fullerton, California, 1975.

Dillard, Jewelle : *Bloodthirst*, Pocket Books, New York, 1987.

Docherty, Brian : *American Horror Fiction: from Brockden Brown to Stephen King*, Macmillan, Basingstoke, 1990.

Gomez, Jewelle : *The Gilda Stories*, Firebrand Books, New York, 1991.

Greenberg, Martin H. : *A Taste for Blood*, Dorset Press, New York, 1992.

Haining, Peter : *The Dracula Centenary Book*, Souvenir Press, London, 1987.

Haining, Peter : *The Dracula Scrapbook: Articles, Essays, Letters, Newspaper Cuttings, Anecdotes, Illustrations, Photographs and Memorabilia About the Vampire Legend*, New English Library, London, 1976.

Herter, Lori : *Obsession*, Berkley Romance, New York, 1991.

Kipling, Rudyard : *The Vampire, and Other Poems*, Dodge Publishing Co., New York, 1988.

Leatherdale, Clive : *The Origins of Dracula: the Background to Bram Stoker's Gothic Masterpiece*, Kimber, London, 1987.

Liebman, Arthur : *Tales of Horror and the Supernatural: the Occult in Literature*, Rosen Press, New York, 1975.

Ludlam, Harry : *A Biography of Dracula: the Life Story of Bram Stoker*, Fireside Press, London, 1978.

Lumley, Brian : *Necroscope*, T. Doherty, New York, 1988.

MacAndrew, Elizabeth : *The Gothic Tradition in Fiction*, Columbia University Press, New York, 1979.

McNally, Raymond T. : *A Clutch of Vampires*, Warner Paperback Library, New York, 1975.

Menville, Douglas : *The Spectre Bridegroom and Other Horrors*, Arno Press, New York, 1976.

Moore, Steven : *The Vampire in Verse: an Anthology*, Dracula Press, New York, 1985.

Nesvadba, Josef : *Vampires Ltd.: Stories of Science and Fantasy*, Artia Pocket Books, Artia, 1964.

Parry, Michel : *The Rivals of Dracula: a Century of Vampire Fiction*, Corgi, London, 1977.

Polidori, John William : *The Vampyre, 1819*, Woodstock Books, Oxford, England, 1990.

Ramsland, Katherine M. : *Prism of the Night: A Biography of Anne Rice*, Plume, New York, 1992.

Rice, Anne : *Interview with the Vampire*, Ballantine Books, New York, 1976.

Romer, Richard Ira. : *The Cinematic Treatment of Protagonists in Murnau's Nosferatu, Browning's Dracula and Whale's Frankenstein,* Columbia University, Columbia, 1984.

Romkey, Michael : *I, Vampire*, Ballantine Books, New York, 1990.

Roth, Phyllis A. : *Bram Stoker*, Twayne Publishers, Boston, 1982.

Ryan, Alan : *The Penguin Book of Vampire Stories*, Penguin Books, London, 1988.

Senf, Carol Ann : *Daughters of Lillith: an Analysis of the Vampire Motif in Nineteenth Century Literature,* State University of New York, New York, 1979.

Shepard, Leslie : *The Dracula Book of Great Vampire Stories*, Citadel Press, New Jersey, 1977.

Simmons, Dan : *Carrion Comfort*, IL: Dark Harvest, Arlington Heights, 1989.

Stableford, John : *Empire of Fear*, Carro & Graf, New York, 1991.

Stewart, Desmond : *The Vampire of Mons*, Harper & Row, New York, 1976.

Stoker, Bram : *Dracula : Introduction by Anthony Boucher*, Easton Press, Norwalk, CT., 1965.

Stoker, Bram : *Shades of Dracula: Bram Stoker's Uncollected Stories*, W. Kimber, London, 1982.

Stoker, Bram : *The Essential Dracula: The Definitive Annotated Edition of Bram Stoker's Classic Novel*, Plume, New York, 1993.

Stoker, Bram : *The Lair of the White Worm*, Jarrold, London, 1966.

Stott, Rebecca : *The Kiss of Death: a Demystification of the Late Nineteenth Century Femme Fatale in the Selected works of Bram Stoker, Rider Haggard, Joseph Conrad and Thomas Hardy,* University of York, New York, 1989.

Sutherland, Rebecca Jean : *Dancing with the Devil: the Vampire Motif in Selected 19th Century Literature,* Northeast Missouri State University, Northeast Missouri, 1989.

Thornburg, Thomas R. : *The Questor and the Castle: the Gothic Novel as Myth, with Special Reference to Bram Stoker's Dracula,* Ball State University, 1970.

Warren, John Frank : *An Investigation of Children's Beliefs in Transcendent Figures,* Duke University, 1980.

Weinberg, Robert : *Weird Vampire Tales*, Gramercy Books, New York, 1992.

William, Polidori John : *Varney the Vampire: Or the Feast of Blood*, Dover Publications, New York, 1972.

Wilson, Colin : *The Space Vampires*, Random House, New York,. 1976.

Yarbo, Chelsea Quinn : *Blood Games*, St. Martin's Press, New York, 1979.

Youngson, Jeanne : *The Count Dracula Book of Classic Vampire Tales*, Adams Press, Chicago, 1981.

Youngson, Jeanne : *The Count Dracula Fan Club Book of Vampire Stories*, Adams Press, Chicago, 1980.

Index

T

U

V

W

Y

□□□